Edexcel GCSE
History B
Schools History Project

The changing nature of warfare (Option 1C) and The impact of war on Britain c1914–c1950 (Option 3C)

John Child   Steve Waugh
Series editor: Angela Leonard

A PEARSON COMPANY

Published by Pearson Education Limited, a company incorporated in England and Wales, having its registered office at Edinburgh Gate, Harlow, Essex, CM20 2JE. Registered company number: 872828

www.pearsonschoolsandfecolleges.co.uk

Edexcel is a registered trade mark of Edexcel Limited

Text © Pearson Education Limited 2009
First published 2009

13 12 11 10
10 9 8 7 6 5 4 3 2

British Library Cataloguing in Publication Data
A catalogue record for this book is available from the British Library

ISBN 978 184690 442 4

Produced and edited by Florence Production Ltd, Stoodleigh, Devon
Typeset and Illustrated by HL Studios, Long Hanborough, Oxford
Original illustrations © Pearson Education Limited 2009
Cover design by Pearson Education Limited
Picture research by Ginny Stroud-Lewis
Cover photo © Corbis/Bettmann
Printed in China (SWTC/02)

Websites
There are links to relevant websites in this book. In order to ensure that the links are up to date, that the links work, and that the sites are not inadvertently linked to sites that could be considered offensive, we have made the links available on the Heinemann website at www.heinemann.co.uk/hotlinks. When you access the site, the express code is 4424P.

Disclaimer
This material has been published on behalf of Edexcel and offers high-quality support for the delivery of Edexcel qualifications.

This does not mean that the material is essential to achieve any Edexcel qualification, nor does it mean that it is the only suitable material available to support any Edexcel qualification. Edexcel material will not be used verbatim in setting any Edexcel examination or assessment. Any resource lists produced by Edexcel shall include this and other appropriate resources.

Copies of official specifications for all Edexcel qualifications may be found on the Edexcel website: www.edexcel.com

Acknowledgements

The author and publisher would like to thank the following individuals and organisations for permission to reproduce material:

Photographs:

pp2 Getty Images / Hulton Archive, Corbis / Stefano Bianchetti, Getty Images / Wesley Boxce; pp3 Topfoto / The British Library / HIP; pp4 AKG, Topfoto / The British Library / HIP; pp5 Topfoto / The British Library / HIP; pp6 Getty; pp7 Topfoto / The British Library / HIP; pp9 Corbis / Stapleton Collection; pp10 Corbis / Bettmann; pp11AKG; pp12 AKG; pp13 AKG; pp14 Corbis / Jonathan Blair; pp17 Topfoto / Print Collector / HIP; pp19 Bridgeman Art Library / British Library, London, UK / © British Library Board. All Rights Reserved, Corbis / Historical Picture Archive; pp20 Corbis / Historical Picture Archive; pp21 Corbis / Christel Gerstenberg; pp22 Bridgeman Art Library / National Army Museum, London, Bridgeman Art Library / The Stapleton Collection; pp26 Bridgeman Art Library / © Central Saint Martins College of Art and Design, London; pp27 Corbis / Gianni Dagli Orti; pp28 AKG; pp29 Corbis / Gianni Dagli Orti; pp30 Bridgeman Art Library / The Stapleton Collection; pp31 Topfoto / World History Archive; pp32 Bridgeman Art Library / National Army Museum, London, AKG; pp33 Corbis / Bettmann; pp34 Corbis / Historical Picture Archive; pp35 AKG; pp36 Alamy / AKG-images; pp37 AKG, Bridgeman Art Library / Archives Charmet; pp38 Getty Images / Hulton Archive; pp39 Getty Images / Hulton Archive; pp40 Corbis / Hulton-Deutsch Collection; pp42 Corbis / David Spurdens; pp43 Corbis / Nagasaki Atomic Bomb Meseum / epa; pp44 Corbis / Hulton-Deutsch Collection, Corbis / Reuters; pp46 Corbis; pp47 Corbis; [48?]; pp50 Corbis / Reuters; pp52 Topfoto / The British Library / HIP, Bridgeman Art Library / Private Collection; pp54 Alamy / The Print Collector; pp57 Bridgeman Art Library / The Stapleton Collection, Alamy / Trinity Mirror / Mirrorpix; pp60 Getty Images / Hulton Archive, AKG; pp61 Corbis / Stapleton Collection; pp62 Topfoto; pp63 Corbis / Bettmann; pp64 Bridgeman Art Library / Bibliotheque des Arts Decoratifs, Paris, France / Archives Charmet; pp65 AKG; pp67 Alamy / Mary Evans Picture Library; pp68 AKG; pp69 Topfoto / The British Library / HIP; pp70 Topfoto / Ullstein Bild; pp71 Topfoto / The British Library / HIP; pp72 Bridgeman Art Library / Bibliotheque de L'Arsenal, Paris, France / Archives Charmet; pp73 AKG; pp74 Bridgeman Art Library / Musee de la Tapisserie, Bayeux, France / With special authorisation of the city of Bayeux Giraudon; pp75 Bridgeman Art Library / Musee de la Tapisserie, Bayeux, France / With special authorisation of the city of Bayeux Giraudon, Bridgeman Art Library / Musee de la Tapisserie, Bayeux, France; pp76 Topfoto / Print Collector / HIP; pp77 Corbis / Christel Gerstenberg; pp78 Bridgeman Art Library / Bibliotheque des Arts Decoratifs, Paris, France / Archives Charmet; pp79 Alamy / North Wind Picture Archives; pp82 AKG, Bridgeman Art Library / Private Collection, Mary Evans Picture Library; pp83 Bridgeman Art Library / Private Collection; pp86 AKG; pp87 Getty Images / Hulton Archive; pp88 Bridgeman Art Library / Private Collection; pp90 Mary Evans Picture Library; pp91 Brooklyn Eagle; pp92 Mary Evans Picture Library, Bridgeman Art Library / Boston Public Library, Boston, Massachusetts, USA; pp96 Alamy / Lordprice Collection, Topfoto / Topham PicturePoint, Getty Images / Hulton Archive; pp97 Bridgeman Art Library / Private Collection / Barbara Singer; pp99 Mary Evans Picture Library; pp100 Imperial War Museum; pp101 Getty Images / Hulton Archive; pp102 Art Archive; pp103 Imperial War Museum, Topfoto; pp104 Topfoto; pp105 Topfoto; pp106 Getty Images / Hulton Archive; pp107 Getty Images / Popperfoto; pp108 Corbis / Bettmann; pp109 British Cartoon Archive / Strube / Daily Express, November 1940; pp110 Getty Images / Hulton Archive; pp111 Getty Images / Hulton Archive; pp112 Getty Images / Hulton Archive; pp114 Mary Evans Picture Library; pp115 Getty Images; pp117 Topfoto / AP; pp, 118 Art Archive; pp120 Mary Evans Picture Library; pp122 Getty Images; pp123 Topfoto / Public Record Office / HIP; pp124 Topfoto / Topham PicturePoint; pp127 Getty Images / Popperfoto; pp128 AKG, Corbis / Hulton-Deutsch Collection, Topfoto, Advertising Archives; pp130 Mary Evans Picture Library; pp131 Topfoto / Topham PicturePoint; pp133 Getty Images; pp136 Corbis / Hulton-Deutsch Collection; pp139 Advertising Archives; pp141 British Cartoon Archive / George Whitelaw / Daily Herald December 1942; pp144 Corbis / Hulton-Deutsch Collection; pp145 Corbis / David Pollack; pp147 Topfoto / Topham PicturePoint; pp148 Topfoto, Ronald Grant Archive, Mary Evans Picture Library; pp151 Vin Mag Archive; pp152 Ronald Grant Archive, Aquarius Collection / Rank, Alamy / World Historical Archive; pp157 Corbis / Charles & Josette Lenars; pp160 iStockPhoto / Efendi Kocakafa, iStockPhoto / ZoneCreative, iStockPhoto / Chris Schmidt, iStockPhoto / Alex Slobodkin; pp162 iStockPhoto / Stockphoto4u

Written sources:

pp29 Source C, Geoffrey Parker ed. (2005) *The Cambridge History of Warfare*, Cambridge: Cambridge University Press; pp29 *Cassell's World History of Warfare* by Herwig, Archer, Travers and Ferris (2003); pp48 *The Autobiography of the British Soldier – From Agincourt to Basra*, Lewis-Stempel, John (Headline Review, 2007); pp101 Source G Copyright Siegfried Sassoon by kind permission of the estate of George Sassoon; pp109, Source G quoted in *Britain in the Age of Total War*, Chandler, M (Heinemann 2002), Source H quoted in *Britain in the Age of Total War*, Chandler, M (Heinemann 2002); pp119, Source D quoted in *Modern World*, Walsh B (John Murray, 1996); pp123 Source C and D quoted in *Bombers and Mash*, Minns R (Past Times 1999); pp124, Source A quoted in *Second World War Era*, Kelly N and Whitlock M (Heinemann, 1993); pp132 Source G quoted in *Votes for Women*, Chandler M, (Heinemann 2001); pp132 Source E, *British History 1914-45*, Taylor A J P (Oxford University Press, 1965); pp135 Source D quoted in *The Changing Role of Women*, Bellamy L and Morse K (John Murray, 1996); pp137 Source A, *Britain in the Age of Total War*, Chandler M (Heinemann, 2002); pp138 Source C, *Bombers and Mash*, Minns R (Past Times 1999); pp139 Source A *The Second World War*, DeMarco. N (Hodder, 1997); pp142 Source B, *Britain and Great War*, Hetherton G (John Murray 1996); pp157 Source A, *The Changing Role of Women* Bellamy L, Morse K and Shepherd C (John Murray, 1996).

Written sources have been freely adapted to make them more accessible for students.

Contents

Reasons for military conflict c1450 to the present day

The impact of war on Britain

The civilian experience of war

Government organisation for war

The impact of war on society

Factors influencing change

Welcome to this Edexcel GCSE History B: Schools History Project Resource

Option 1C: The changing nature of warfare and 3C: The impact of war on Britain c1914–c1950

These resources have been written to fully support Edexcel's new GCSE History B: Schools History Project redeveloped specification. This specification has a focus on change and development through studies of societies in depth and of key themes over time. Written by experienced examiners and packed with exam tips and activities, the book includes lots of engaging features to enthuse students and provide the range of support needed to make teaching and learning a success for all ability levels.

How to use this book

Edexcel GCSE History B: Schools History Project Warfare and its impact is divided into the two units that match the specification. Unit 1 begins with the Core Content which all students have to cover, followed by the two Extension Studies, of which students need to answer questions on one. Unit 3 contains guidance, instruction and practice questions on the source requirements for the exam. Throughout the book key words are highlighted in bold and their definitions can be found in the glossary on pages 166–169.

Features of this book

- **Learning outcomes** structure learning at the start of each topic.

- **Key words** are highlighted and defined for easy reference.

- A topic **Summary** captures the main learning points.

- **Activities** provide stimulating tasks for the classroom and homework.

A dedicated suite of revision resources for complete exam success. We've broken down the six stages of revision to ensure that you are prepared every step of the way.

How to get into the perfect 'zone' for your revision.

Tips and advice on how to effectively plan your revision.

A checklist of things you should know, revision activities and practice exam questions at the end of each unit and at the end of both Extension Studies in Unit 1.

Last-minute advice for just before the exam.

An overview of what you will have to do in the exam, plus a chance to see what a real exam paper will look like.

What do you do after your exam? This section contains information on how to get your results and answers to frequently asked questions on what to do next.

ResultsPlus

These features are based on how students have performed in past exams. They are combined with expert advice and guidance from examiners to show you how to achieve better results.

There are three different types of ResultsPlus features throughout this book:

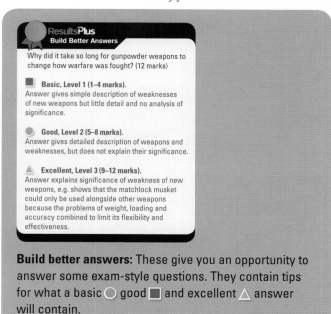

Build better answers: These give you an opportunity to answer some exam-style questions. They contain tips for what a basic ○ good ◻ and excellent △ answer will contain.

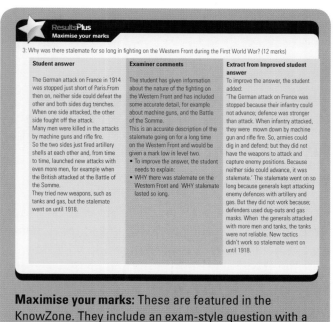

Maximise your marks: These are featured in the KnowZone. They include an exam-style question with a student answer, examiner comments and an improved answer so that you can see how to build a better response.

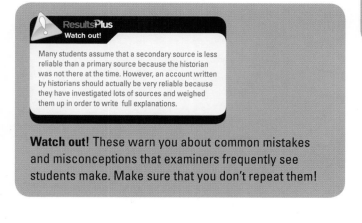

Watch out! These warn you about common mistakes and misconceptions that examiners frequently see students make. Make sure that you don't repeat them!

The changing nature of warfare

Introduction

This part of your course looks at developments in warfare from 1350 to the present day.

You will be asked to think about:

- what changed in aspects of warfare such as weaponry, tactics, recruitment, and the provisioning and movement of armies
- what made those things change and why they changed at that particular time; in particular, how society and technology changed warfare.

In this section of your study, you will learn about:

- warfare from 1350 to 1700, the time of British archers at Agincourt and the Battle of Naseby in the English Civil War
- warfare from 1700 to 1900, the time of the British victories at the Battle of Waterloo and in the Crimean War
- warfare from 1900 to the present day, including case studies on the First World War and the First Gulf War of 1991.

1350–1700

1700–1900

1900 to the present day

Activities

1 Draw your own version of the timeline below. Include all the information given from 1350 to the present day. But draw it larger.
2 During the rest of this course, as you read in more detail about changes during this time, add the key events to your timeline.
3 Study the three illustrations on this page. What changes can you see?

1415	1645	1815	1854	1914	1991
The Battle of Agincourt	The Battle of Naseby	The Battle of Waterloo	The Crimean War	The First World War	The Gulf War

1.1 The age of the archer 1350–1450

Learning outcomes

By the end of this topic you should be able to:

● describe the soldiers, weapons and fighting typical between 1350 and 1450

● explain the changes taking place in warfare during this period

● explain the longbow's impact on warfare.

Activities

1 Using the text and Source A, write down what you know about the types of soldiers and weapons which made up a typical army in 1350.

English armies in medieval times were produced by the feudal system. This was a system whereby kings and wealthy landowners gave some of their land to others in exchange for their loyalty and practical services – for example, military service:

● a king gave large areas of land to barons;
● barons promised knights for the king's army;
● barons gave some land to their tenants;
● these tenants served as knights for the barons;
● smaller landowners served as foot soldiers.

Therefore, the feudal system created an army for the king during wars (see page 68 for more detail).

Mounted Knights

Mounted knights were the rich and privileged of medieval society. A knight would go to war well-armed, with good protective clothing, and several horses and servants.

Mounted knights were the tanks of medieval battles:

● they charged the enemy, perhaps with lances, but more often just riding men down or slashing with a sword or axe;
● if necessary, knights would dismount and fight on foot with swords and daggers.

For protection, knights had shields and wore metal helmets, breast- and backplates, arm and leg guards and **gauntlets** (see page 68 for more detail).

Infantry

The infantry were the foot soldiers and the biggest part of the medieval army. They were mainly poor men, who provided their own weapons – so they were poorly armed and protected:

● most wore only leather or padded tunics for protection;
● some had metal helmets;
● some had chain mail;
● few had plate armour – it was too heavy;
● most used daggers, swords, axes and clubs.

Some infantry were archers (see page 6). Others were pike men. Pikes were three- to six-metre poles with sharp metal tips used in close formation to fend off infantry or cavalry charges.

Source A: Battle scene from about 1450. This source tells us about the different types of soldiers, weapons and protective clothing used in medieval battles. How many different weapons can you see?

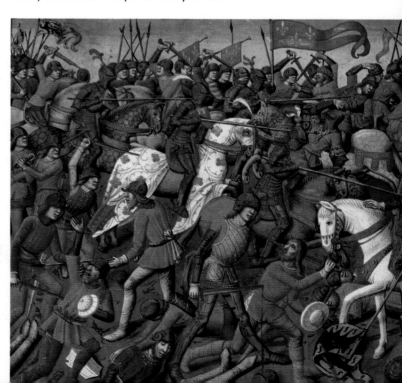

Continuity

The period from 1350 to 1450 were years of almost constant warfare across Europe. The biggest conflict was a series of wars, from 1337 to 1453, between the French and English called the **Hundred Years' War**. The major battles were fought at Crécy, Poitiers and Agincourt.

But, despite all this fighting, from 1350 to 1450 much of the medieval style of warfare continued unchanged. On this page some examples of **continuity** are described.

Armies remained small
- When Prince Edward invaded France in 1356, he had an English army of only 6,000.
- In the last conflict of the 100 Years' War, the Battle of Castillon in 1453, the English army consisted, again, of 6,000 men.

Tactics changed little
There was little change in battlefield tactics:

- archers and cavalry dominated attacks;
- pikes and shields were the main defence;
- but infantry were still the deciding force. The English at the Battle of Crécy in 1346 had 16,000 men, of whom 12,000 were infantry;
- the **feigned retreat**, successful in the Battle of Hastings 300 years before, was still often used.

Source B: A medieval painting shows peasants capturing a knight. They kill the horse, but save the knight for ransom.

Source C: A medieval painting showing soldiers pillaging the baggage train of their defeated enemy. They would also steal booty – money or weapons – from battlefield bodies.

Armies still fought limited warfare
As before, few wars were waged to conquer other countries. Kings fought wars to:

- pillage riches from foreign lands. In 1346, for example, King Edward III spent months pillaging France before the Battle of Crécy
- capture enemies for **ransom**. In 1356, at the Battle of Poitiers, the English captured the French King and demanded a sum twice the annual tax revenue of France for his return.

So warfare often consisted of raids, sorties and skirmishes, rather than battles. Since kings led armies, battles meant personal danger. They avoided battle if possible. In 1415, Henry V only fought the Battle of Agincourt because he had to (see page 70 for details of limited warfare).

Sieges remained common
Britain at this time had many castles and fortified towns. When threatened, people and armies sought safety there. So most wars at this time involved **sieges** of towns and castles.

Attackers would either have to starve people out (a slow process) or attack the walls (a dangerous one). Source D and pages 72 and 76–77 have more details.

Change – Recruitment

But some things were changing in warfare between 1350 and 1450. One was **recruitment**.

There were problems with feudal armies:

- Feudal duty was limited to about 45 days' service – enough to fight off an invasion, but not to fight overseas or in a prolonged siege.
- Feudal armies were small. English kings could only call upon about 6,000 feudal knights.
- Many knights said their feudal duty was to defend England and refused to go overseas.
- Young noblemen took part in jousting tournaments, and all young **freemen** were encouraged to practise archery. But there was no proper training as a group. So battle tactics had to be very simple.
- Feudal knights were independent, wealthy, men who resented military discipline. Some, especially in France, saw war as an exercise in **chivalry** where doing what was *honourable* was more important than doing what would win.
- Finally, feudal armies provided their own weapons. So the quality of arms and protection in the infantry was very varied

Source D: This picture tells the story of a siege in 1364. On the right, an army weakens the defences with arrows and by undermining the walls. Then, in the centre, they attack. Finally, on the left, they negotiate a surrender.

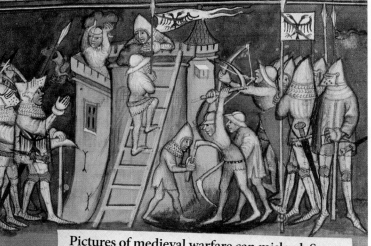

Pictures of medieval warfare can mislead. Some 19th century paintings give a romantic view of soldiers, all in armour. This is wrong. Few foot soldiers used armour.

So kings began to use **mercenaries** instead:

- Their first step was to take money in exchange for military service. This was called **scutage**. This was not new, but it became more common. It gave kings money for mercenaries.
- Then, as English society became more centralised, kings took more taxes. This gave them more money to spend on mercenaries.
- In 1415, for example, Henry V's army for his Agincourt Campaign were commanders and their soldiers hired by contract, or **indenture**.
- France stayed feudal, so the French army which Henry fought in this campaign were knights serving their feudal duties.

Paid soldiers were not new. But feudal armies were becoming mercenary armies paid for each campaign. But they were not *permanent* armies.

Source E: Knights jousting in about 1400.

Activities

2 On separate slips of paper, write definitions for booty, pillage and ransom. Pass them to someone sitting near you. See if they can correctly identify each one.

3 What was limited warfare?

4 List the drawbacks of feudal armies

5 What did rulers do to get round these problems?

Change – the longbow

The other major change in warfare between 1350 and 1450 was the development of the longbow.

Archers in armies were not new. But, until this time, English soldiers had used a small bow, about 50cm long and effective only up to 100 metres.

From about 1300, longbows of about two metres in length appeared in English armies. By 1346, of the 12,000 English infantry who defeated the French at the Battle of Crécy, two-thirds were longbow archers.

What made the longbow so special?
- It could fire 400 metres; it terrified the enemy.
- The archer could fire 15 arrows per minute. This compared to three for the French crossbow.
- The arrows could pierce plate armour.
- Knights could be pinned to their mounts by arrows which went through armour, **chain mail**, flesh and bone and into the saddle!

Source F: A modern picture of 15th century archers.

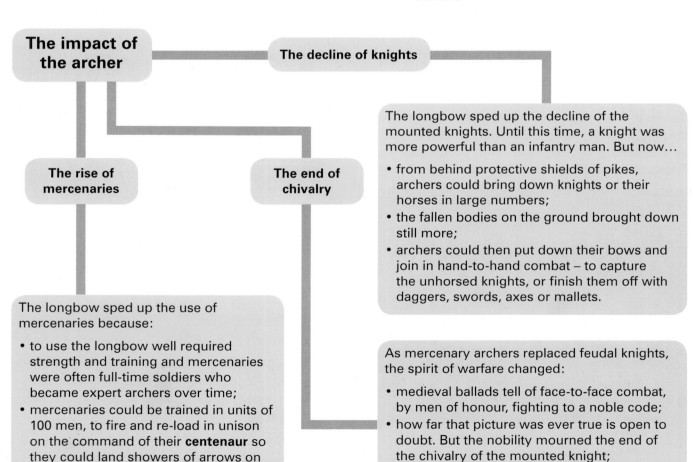

The impact of the archer

The decline of knights

The rise of mercenaries

The end of chivalry

The longbow sped up the decline of the mounted knights. Until this time, a knight was more powerful than an infantry man. But now…

- from behind protective shields of pikes, archers could bring down knights or their horses in large numbers;
- the fallen bodies on the ground brought down still more;
- archers could then put down their bows and join in hand-to-hand combat – to capture the unhorsed knights, or finish them off with daggers, swords, axes or mallets.

The longbow sped up the use of mercenaries because:

- to use the longbow well required strength and training and mercenaries were often full-time soldiers who became expert archers over time;
- mercenaries could be trained in units of 100 men, to fire and re-load in unison on the command of their **centenaur** so they could land showers of arrows on small areas – this concentration of fire had a deadly effect.

As mercenary archers replaced feudal knights, the spirit of warfare changed:

- medieval ballads tell of face-to-face combat, by men of honour, fighting to a noble code;
- how far that picture was ever true is open to doubt. But the nobility mourned the end of the chivalry of the mounted knight;
- they saw little honour in death from an arrow, shot from afar, by a faceless archer.

Warfare and society

We have seen that the way society is organised can shape how wars are fought. The feudal system, for example, produced small armies dominated by noble knights. But sometimes changes in warfare shape society.

Firstly, the decline of feudal knights boosted the power of the king. Kings no longer relied upon their nobles for military strength. Employing their own armies, using taxes, made kings much more powerful.

Secondly, the age of the longbow boosted the wealth of the English yeomanry. The yeomen were farmers who owned small farms. They provided many of the archers for English armies. After battles like Crécy, Poitiers, or Agincourt, many yeomen came home with 100,000 **ducats** from pay, booty and ransom. This was a fortune in medieval terms. Yeomen became very wealthy farmers.

Summary

- 1350-1450 was a period of gradual change in warfare
- The longbow and mercenaries were important developments which caused changes in warfare and in society.

Source G: A 19th century picture of a battle in 1473. It correctly shows archers being used, together with knights and pike men. Showing them in armour is a mistake.

Activities

5 Take a vote in class about what made the longbow so important on the battlefield:
   a) power of fire
   b) accuracy of fire
   c) concentration of fire.
   Debate the outcome of the vote.

6 Make lists of things that:
   a) changed between 1350 and 1450
   b) remained unchanged over the same period.
   Do your lists suggest that 1350–1450 was a time of change or continuity?

Challenge

7 Do you think that the longbow counts as:
   a) a *development* (something that evolves from something else) or
   b) a *change* (something different from what went before) in the history of warfare?

ResultsPlus
Build Better Answers

Explain why the longbow had an important effect upon warfare 1350–1450. (9 marks)

■ **Basic, Level 1 (1–3 marks).**
Answer is accurate, but gives little detail.

● **Good, Level 2 (4–6 marks).**
Answer gives details about the longbow, but leaves its impact on warfare unexplained.

▲ **Excellent, Level 3 (7–9 marks).**
Answer gives details of the use of the longbow, explaining its impact and how this changed battles and armies.

Boom!

The period 1350 to 1450 was one of slow development. This changed after 1450. **Gunpowder** was the reason. Very slowly, since about 1350, cannon had been developed. In 1453, the Battle of Castillon ended the 100 Years' War – it was won by cannon. Warfare would never be the same again.

1.2 The Agincourt campaign 1415

> **Learning outcomes**
>
> By the end of this topic you should be able to:
> - describe the Agincourt Campaign and the role of Henry V
> - recognise features of warfare that were typical from 1350 to 1450.

The Agincourt campaign of 1415 was part of the Hundred Years' War. These were several wars between England and France stretching from 1337 to 1453. When Henry V became King of England in 1413, he thought he could conquer land in northern France for England.

The siege of Harfleur

Henry invaded France in August 1415, with an army of about 6,000–8,000. He needed a base, so he besieged the port of Harfleur in Normandy. The town was defended by about 400 soldiers. After five weeks, the town surrendered. Any townspeople who swore allegiance to Henry were allowed to remain; the rest were ordered to depart.

> - **How typical was the siege of Harfleur?**
> - In some ways, this was a typical medieval siege – it followed the typical pattern of encirclement, battery, attack, negotiation and ransom. First, Henry surrounded the town, cutting off supplies. A French convoy carrying food and ammunition for the town was captured. Then Henry pounded the walls with catapults and prepared his men to attack. Seeing their position was hopeless, the town's commanders asked for a deal. They gave up the town in exchange for ransom.
> - But, in another way, the siege was unusual. As well as medieval catapults, Henry also pounded the walls with twelve cannon. This was one of the earliest uses of cannon by the English army.

After the siege, Henry left a small garrison in the town and took the rest of his army to winter in the town of Calais, at that time an English stronghold.

But the French had gathered a large army, led by Charles d'Albret, which shadowed Henry's movements, trying to force him into a battle.

They eventually trapped the English in a narrow stretch of ploughed land between two woods. The French army was between Henry and Calais.

On 25 October, Henry was forced to fight but would have preferred not to. His small army had just marched 250 miles in bad weather, whilst suffering from dysentery. Defeat would also mean the end of the campaign, with the risk of Henry being captured or even killed.

> - Henry V's army had only 6,000 men and 5,000 were archers;
> - The French had 20–30,000, many of whom were powerful mounted knights.

The Battle of Agincourt

The land between the armies was heavy clay – difficult ground for cavalry. French knights made it worse, by exercising horses there.

Henry placed his army where the gap in the woods was narrow, about 750 metres. He had angled stakes dug into the ground to slow cavalry attack.

He then sent archers to hide in the trees and fire into the French lines. This was called **'galling'**; the French regarded it as un-chivalrous.

It provoked an angry response. A small group of 450 French cavalry made a charge at the English lines. The infantry moved up behind them.

The longbows now showed their value:
- when the cavalry was about 200 metres away, English archers fired in volleys;
- wounded French horses fell or panicked, careering into others;
- the charge failed and cavalry retreating in the narrow space slowed down the infantry;
- arrows rained down on the French infantry, slogging through mud, some in heavy armour;
- the bodies of fallen men slowed their advance still more.

When hand-to-hand fighting began, the narrow battlefront made the extra French troops useless.

The French monk of St. Denis wrote: *'The first wave of about 5,000 men was so tightly packed that the third rank could not use their swords.'*

Henry then attacked. His archers put aside their bows and attacked from the flanks with swords. His foot soldiers pressed forward too. The French, crowded together and stumbling on bodies, retreated.

Heralds were sent to ask the French if they were conceding. The answer came back that they were. The battle had lasted only about 3 hours.

What was the outcome of the battle?
The English suffered no more than 500 deaths.

The French deaths numbered between 2,000 and 11,000, according to sources at the time, and 1500 nobles were captured for ransom.

The decisive factors seem to have been:
- decisions made by French and English commanders;
- the indiscipline of the French knights;
- the impact of the English longbow archers.

The Battle of Agincourt was important because it saved the English army and earned ransom. It also showed the strength of the English longbow.

But successful sieges, at Harfleur and other towns, were important too. These gave Henry V military and political control of the surrounding countryside.

Source A: A 19th century painting of Agincourt. Look at the soldiers, their weapons and clothes. Also look at the battlefield. How accurate do you think it is?

Activities

1 Use the text and Source A to make a list of the types of soldiers and weapons used at Agincourt.

2 Pages 3 to 7 describe warfare 1350–1450. In what ways were the siege of Harfleur and the Battle of Agincourt typical of warfare at that time?

Challenge

3 Leadership was the most important factor in fighting battles 1350–1450. Judging by the Battle of Agincourt, how far do you agree with this statement?

Summary

The Agincourt campaign illustrates a number of typical features of warfare from 1350 to 1450.

1.3 The age of gunpowder 1450–1700

Learning outcomes

By the end of this topic you should be able to:

- describe the gunpowder weapons that dominated warfare 1450–1700
- explain the impact that gunpowder weapons had on warfare.

Cannon

The formula for gunpowder arrived in Europe from China during the 13th century. Soon after, it was being used in warfare. The first known use of a gunpowder cannon in Europe is recorded in Metz (now in northern France) in 1324.

- **The Bad News…**

  Early cannon were not very effective:

  - they were so inaccurate they could only be used against large targets, like town walls;
  - they had a range of only about 100 metres, which made them vulnerable to capture;
  - they often went wrong – in 1460, King James II of Scotland was killed by a cannon, which blew up when firing.

  For 100 years, rather than replacing traditional medieval **artillery**, cannon were used with it.

Source A: A contemporary drawing showing cannon being used – by attackers and defenders – at the siege of Dublin in 1577. Notice the damage caused to the walls. Notice too that, even this late, gunpowder weapons are being used alongside much older weapons.

- **The Good News…**

  Weapon manufacturers used improved technology to make cannon more effective. By about 1450:

  - **trunnions** made it easier to change cannons' range of fire;
  - **quadrants** were used to improve aim;
  - then specialist cannon were developed – like **mortars** or **howitzers**, which lobbed cannonballs on a high trajectory over walls;
  - there were massive long-distance cannon, like 'Mad Margaret', which had a barrel five metres long and half a metre wide;
  - from about 1500, field guns were developed. These were smaller cannon, called light artillery, which were pulled around battlefields by horses. This meant cannon were not just used against stationary targets, like walls. They were now used against enemy infantry.

So, by 1450, cannon were a normal part of every army. They were expensive. To transport just 50 cannon took hundreds of wagons and oxen. But they were so effective that they were essential. The French town of Harfleur resisted Henry V's siege for five weeks in 1415; but in a second siege, in 1449, 16 cannon reduced its walls to rubble in only two weeks.

FASCINATING FACT

One huge cannon, used to attack Constantinople in 1453 was nearly 10 metres long and fired stone balls weighing half a ton. To transport it by road, 50 carpenters were used to strengthen bridges; it was then put on 30 wagons and pulled by 60 oxen.

Firearms – the matchlock

In about 1450, the first effective firearms also appeared. These were the matchlock musket and the smaller matchlock **arquebus**.

- The Good News…
  Matchlock muskets could:
  - kill at 400 metres, further than longbows;
  - pierce armour at 200 metres;
  - and, unlike archers, musketeers did not tire during battle.

- The Bad News…
  Matchlock muskets:
  - were very inaccurate;
  - frequently misfired – they were useless in rain;
  - were heavy – over 10 kilos – as heavy as 10 bags of sugar. The gunner had to balance it on a stick;
  - caused smoke, which made aiming difficult;
  - took two minutes to re-load. Re-loading under fire took courage – it was easy to lower the musket and lose the shot out of the barrel before firing, or to overcharge the weapon and knock yourself out with the recoil.

Source B: A musketeer pictured in the Drill Book for the Dutch army, issued in 1607.

> **FASCINATING FACT**
>
> The matchlock had a slow-burning match-cord, held in a lever, or cock. When the trigger was pulled, the cord set off gunpowder in a flash pan which then fired the gun.
>
> Some modern phrases come from musketeers. A misfire was 'just a flash in the pan', or 'going off at half cock'.

Firearms – the flintlock

For 200 years, these problems meant that muskets were used alongside other weapons, like bows. But technology came to the rescue.

By 1700, flintlock muskets had been invented. These did not use match-cords. They used flints to make a spark to set off the gunpowder.

- More Good News…
  Flintlock muskets:
  - could be pre-loaded. So a soldier could carry several loaded muskets into battle and fire them rapidly, without having to re-load;
  - could be used by **cavalry**. Horsemen could not re-load matchlocks. But **dragoons** (mounted soldiers) could tuck several loaded flintlocks in their belts and ride, firing, into battle.

So, despite their limitations, from about 1450 onwards cannon and firearms were used more and more. By about 1600, they dominated battlefields. Warfare would never be the same again.

As Robert Barret reported in 1598, '*Then was then, and now is now. Wars are much altered since the fiery weapons.*'

Activities

1 On a time line, plot the development of gunpowder weapons from 1200 to 1600.
2 What were the limitations of early gunpowder weapons?
3 What were their advantages?

Changes in infantry

- Musketeers gradually replaced archers in the infantry.
- Pike men disappeared too. This was because musketeers could attach long knives, or **bayonets**, to the end of their muskets.
- This turned muskets into thrusting weapons, so pike men were not needed.

The decline of cavalry

- Muskets and field cannon easily cut down cavalry charges.
- The mounted knight was already in decline by 1450.
- After 1450 there was still cavalry, but it was weaker.

New town defences

At first towns used defensive cannon from their own walls. But these walls were tall and thin. They were easy to hit and the vibration of their own cannon made them crack and fall.

So then, defenders strengthened walls with earth banks.

But gradually town walls were re-designed. The new design for fortifications involved short, thick walls with arrow-shaped **bastions** (towers). These were harder to hit and allowed defending cannon to fire out at many angles.

After about 1500 they became the norm for fortifications.

Source D: Arrow-shaped bastions on a 16th-century fort.

Military impact of gunpowder weapons

Infantry lines

Throughout medieval times, infantry had attacked and defended by forming solid blocks of men, or 'squares'. But, from about 1600, generals realised that lines of muskets were better:

- they used up to 10 lines of men;
- each line would fire, then retreat and re-load, whilst the next rank came forward to fire;
- this way they achieved a constant **volley of fire**.

The need to re-load quickly under fire led to more infantry discipline and training.

Standardised weapons

Until this time, soldiers could replace their weapons by stealing from bodies on the battlefield. Mixing swords or spears was unimportant; but once cannon and muskets became the weapons of war, it was vital the whole army had standard issue.

New siege tactics

Attacking cannon could no longer knock town walls over as easily.

So sieges became longer. And attackers had to defend themselves against the defenders' cannon.

Therefore, attackers dug trenches around the towns they besieged. Troops sheltered from attack there, set up cannon in these trenches and bombarded the enemy for months on end. After weakening the town defences, they sent in infantry attacks.

In these trenches, dug around besieged towns, we can clearly see a precedent for the trenches of the Crimean War and the First World War.

The social impact

Gunpowder weapons increased the importance of the iron industry. This was because, gradually, the security of countries depended on their ability to produce muskets and cannon.

Gunpowder weapons also raised the cost of war. This was partly the cost of weapons and partly because it was necessary to have well-drilled, permanent, professional soldiers.

Gunpowder weapons divided society (see Sources E and F). This is a common effect of new, deadly weapons – just like nuclear weapons in modern times. Few understood how metal balls or bullets could be shot instantly from the barrel of a gun to a distant target. To some, it was marvellous magic. To others, it was the work of the devil. Some captured cannoneers were so hated that they were blasted out of their own cannon.

Activities

4 Make a list of the military changes caused by the gunpowder weapons. Which change was the most significant?

5 Why were the social reactions to gunpowder weapons so varied?

Source E: For military leaders, gunpowder was a miracle weapon. In 1570, this painting, called 'Gunpowder Production', was commissioned by a wealthy nobleman.

Summary

Using gunpowder created new weapons. These weapons were so powerful that they:

● changed warfare
● increased the need for professional soldiers.

13

ResultsPlus
Build Better Answers

Why did it take so long for gunpowder weapons to change how warfare was fought? (12 marks)

■ **Basic, Level 1 (1–4 marks).**
Answer gives simple description of weaknesses of new weapons but little detail and no analysis of significance.

● **Good, Level 2 (5–8 marks).**
Answer gives detailed description of weapons and weaknesses, but does not explain their significance.

▲ **Excellent, Level 3 (9–12 marks).**
Answer explains significance of weakness of new weapons, e.g. shows that the matchlock musket could only be used alongside other weapons because the problems of weight, loading and accuracy combined to limit its flexibility and effectiveness.

Source F: This woodcut from the 1500s shows the gunpowder being made by wicked monks and demons.

1.4 Army life 1350–1700

> **Learning outcome**
>
> By the end of this topic you should be able to:
>
> ● explain how changes in warfare 1350–1700, such as the introduction of gunpowder weapons, affected armies and the lives of soldiers.

Size of armies

The period 1350–1700 was a time of great change for armies. One obvious change was that armies became bigger. Whereas the English kings Harold at Hastings in 1066 and Henry V at Agincourt in 1415 both had armies of about 6,000–8,000 men, Oliver Cromwell's **New Model Army**, formed in 1645, was 22,000 strong.

Permanent armies

In 1350, some soldiers were fulfilling their feudal duty to support their lord and some soldiers were mercenaries – soldiers paid on a temporary basis as needed. As numbers of mercenaries increased, providing them became big business. The kings of England regularly increased the size of their armies by hiring troops from small European states.

But relying on foreign troops was risky. From about 1500, therefore, although mercenaries were still used, most countries began to develop large bodies of soldiers who were permanently employed by the state – known as standing armies.

Uniforms

Permanent armies led to uniforms, but only slowly. This was because:

- soldiers associated uniforms with servants;
- few countries were able to mass-produce tens of thousands of identical uniforms;
- wear and tear made replacing uniforms very expensive.

During the 1640s, troops led by Prince Rupert, commander of the English army, fought 62 skirmishes and 11 battles, marched hundreds of miles and often slept in the open.

No 17th-century government had the level of organisation needed to care for its troops. It was easier for soldiers to provide their own clothes, from battlefield bodies if necessary, and for a while longer, all armies looked much the same. Soldiers of the French army wore some kind of blue hatband, or sash, the Dutch orange, and so on. But this was far from foolproof. During the English Civil War, at the Battle of Marston Moor, Sir Thomas Fairfax became stranded among the enemy, and, in his own words: 'Removing the signal [a white scarf] from my hat I passed as one of their commanders.'

Source A: Musketeers in typical 1640s mixed uniforms showing packets of shot and powder and coloured sashes.

However, during the English Civil War, Parliament's New Model Army adopted coats of red and white, and by 1700 the familiar red coat became the standard uniform for the English army.

Provisions

An army of 30,000 men needed 20 tons of bread and meat equivalent to 1,500 sheep – every day. Livestock was transported on the hoof, until it was eaten. But the flour and ovens for 30,000 troops needed 250 carts and hundreds of horses and oxen to pull them. And, of course, the draft animals needed feeding too. When an army ran out of supplies, soldiers had to forage for food or steal from local people.

Disease and medical treatment

In wars before 1900, five times more men died of disease than of battlefield injuries. Epidemics of diseases such as dysentery swept through armies. And troops often slept in the open on campaign. The New Model Army was not issued with tents until 1650, for example. Exposure to the elements caused even more illness. Despite these problems, medical treatment did not get a high priority. It was normal for there to be more bandsmen to provide marching music than medical staff to treat injured or sick soldiers.

Injuries from musket fire made matters worse. Shot smashed bones and drove filthy clothing into wounds, causing infection. Treatment for wounds was to scoop out fragments with unsterile instruments or bare fingers, to cauterise the wound with hot metal, melting blood vessels to prevent blood loss, and then to cover the wound with an ointment. Some ointments were useless but harmless, made with substances such as animal fat and rhubarb; others were deadly, containing excrement or mercury.

There was some progress. Ambroise Paré (1510–1590) was an army surgeon. He found that the patients for whom he used no ointments at all recovered best. He also used ligatures to stem blood flow, invented new surgical instruments and even developed artificial limbs. He published his

Activities

1 Look at the two statements in the summary box on this page. Collect some factual information from these pages to support each of the statements.

2 Conditions in the army 1350–1700 were harsh because governments didn't really care about soldiers. On the basis of the information on these pages, how far do you agree with this statement? Explain your answer.

3 How much of the change in army life 1350–1700 would you describe as progress?

findings but general progress was very slow. Indeed, many injured soldiers never even saw a surgeon. They were often left on the battlefield until the day after the battle; many died from blood loss or exposure during this time.

Treatment of prisoners

Sometimes, the injured were put out of their misery rather than taken prisoner and treated medically. A misericorde was a dagger with a long thin blade that could be thrust between gaps in armour or helmet visors to deliver the 'mercy stroke' to a wounded soldier.

There were also many religious wars during this period and this seems to have made soldiers particularly cruel to their captives because they believed they were punishing the enemies of God.

Other acts of cruelty were based on greed. Captured soldiers were sometimes tortured to make them admit if they were wealthy enough for ransom. The captors often slit the throats of all prisoners who were too poor to provide profit.

Summary

- Large permanent armies, supplemented by mercenaries, developed in the period 1350–1700.
- These armies were difficult for governments to clothe, feed and care for.

1.5 The Battle of Naseby 1645

> **Learning outcomes**
>
> By the end of this topic you should be able to:
> - explain the events of the Battle of Naseby and Oliver Cromwell's involvement
> - recognise features of the battle that were typical of warfare at the time.

The English Civil War (1642–1646) was fought between:
- the Royalist army of King Charles I and
- forces supporting Parliament.

Sir Thomas Fairfax led Parliament's New Model Army. It was a permanent, paid and well-trained army, full of religious enthusiasm. It had a very effective cavalry, led by Oliver Cromwell.

In April 1645, campaigning resumed after a winter break. The King sent 5,000 troops to besiege Taunton, a key town in the south-west of England. But Fairfax ignored the towns and tried to engage the King in battle instead.

For weeks, the two armies shadowed each other. There were occasional skirmishes. The King consulted his leading generals and decided, without waiting for reinforcement from Taunton, to engage Fairfax in battle. On 14 June, the Parliamentary army took up position on a steep ridge crested by Mill Hill. Its flanks were protected by thick hedging on one side and rough ground on the other. The King's general, Prince Rupert, set out his army opposite.

The battle begins

Eleven Parliamentary cannon fired opening shots to soften up the Royalist infantry. But their initial **salvos** went high, and soon the infantry of the two sides were so close that cannon could not be used. Cannon were therefore not a decisive factor.

The first key action was taken by Cromwell. He sent Colonel Okey and his dragoons behind the western hedging, to harass the enemy with musket fire. Stung into action, Rupert's cavalry charged. Packed solid, thigh to thigh, they broke the Parliamentary lines; two of the Parliamentary cavalry regiments fled.

But then Rupert made a mistake. He was unable to prevent his cavalry chasing after the fleeing Parliamentary troopers and launching an unsuccessful attack on the Parliamentary baggage train. This indiscipline cost the Royalists vital cavalry forces.

Meanwhile, the Royalist infantry left its high ground and marched up the slope to the main Parliamentary army. The distance between the armies was small; there was time for only one volley of musket fire before hand-to-hand fighting began. So muskets were not decisive either.

The experienced Royalist army hacked at the Parliamentary infantry, using swords and musket butts; they smashed back the Parliamentary regiments. Skippon, the Parliamentary infantry commander, brought forward reserves. The battle was in the balance. The next stage was decisive.

Source A: A map of the Battle of Naseby.

Parliamentary Army
Commanded by:
- Sir Thomas Fairfax
- Oliver Cromwell

13,000 men, including:
- about 7,000 infantry, armed with muskets and swords and protected by pike and artillery
- about 6,000 cavalry, armed with swords and muskets

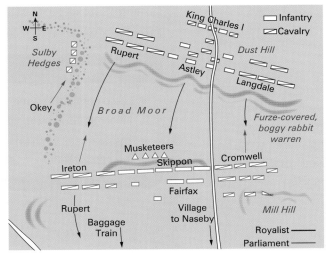

The King's Army
Commanded by:
- King Charles I
- Prince Rupert

8,000 men, including:
- about 4,000 infantry, armed with muskets and swords and protected by pike and artillery
- about 4,000 cavalry, armed with swords and muskets

Cromwell wins the cavalry contest

To support the infantry, the Royalist cavalry, led by Sir Marmaduke Langdale, charged up the slope to attack Cromwell's cavalry. Langdale was outnumbered two to one and he was forced to attack in a narrow channel, with boggy land on his left. This reduced the width of attack and allowed the defending Parliamentary forces to group solid and deep at the top of the slope. Cromwell's **Ironsides** took heavy casualties, but kept their formation and held firm. The Royalist charge faltered, stalled and fell back.

Unlike Rupert, Cromwell had good control of his cavalry and his tactics. He sent part of his cavalry to pursue the retreating Royalist horsemen; he wheeled the rest of his force to his left and attacked the Royalist infantry from the flank.

The Royal infantry advance stalled. Then, to make matters worse, Okey's dragoons attacked from the west. Assaulted on all sides, the King's infantry began to surrender or retreat back down the slope, looking for shelter. One regiment of Royalist musketeers, the Bluecoats, briefly held up the Parliamentary counter-attack, but Fairfax attacked them with his reserves. The Bluecoats were smashed by the butt-end of muskets wielded by infantry and trampled by cavalry with pistols.

Source B: A 19th-century picture of the Battle of Naseby, showing Royalist (left) and Parliamentary cavalry. Notice the features of 17th-century cavalry, by that time more lightly armoured and fighting with swords and pistols.

The bloody retreat

The Royalists were now in chaotic retreat, through woods and narrow roads. The Parliamentary army chased them for about 12 miles. They slaughtered the men they caught. One group of horsemen, fleeing through Marston Trussell, rode down a cul-de-sac: they were trapped and killed. One hundred women in the Royalist baggage train were also slaughtered as they fled. They were Welsh, but the Parliamentarians, staunchly Protestant, mistook them for Irish Catholics and killed them all.

The importance of the battle

The Battle of Naseby raised the profile of Oliver Cromwell and his Ironsides. But the Royalist cause was devastated.

- The King lost most of his infantry. About 1,000 were killed and 5,000 captured.
- He also lost 500 officers, his field artillery and his baggage train of arms, powder and food.

Naseby, in effect, ended the King's chances of winning the English Civil War.

Activities

1 In what ways was the Battle of Naseby:
   a) typical of 17th century warfare
   b) untypical of warfare at that time?

2 How important was each of the following in deciding the outcome of the Battle of Naseby:
   a) the leadership decisions of the King, Prince Rupert and Cromwell
   b) the discipline of the New Model Army compared to the Royalist cavalry?

Summary

- The Battle of Naseby illustrates several typical features of warfare at that time.
- Cromwell and the New Model Army were crucial to the Parliamentary victory.

1.6 Summary: Warfare c1350–c1700

Simple change

To help us get an overview of a long period of time, such as 1350–1700, it is sometimes useful to think about change as a simple process.

For example, if we were to think about:
- a period of no change or
- a period of rapid change

we could put them on simple graphs such as these:

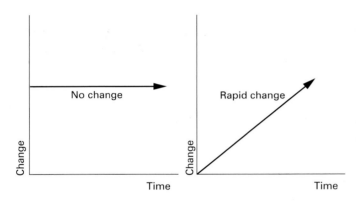

This kind of simple picture of change can help us see 'the big picture' – the overall view.

For the period 1350–1700, an overall view of change in warfare could be seen as the following:
- a period from 1350 to about 1450, when there was slow change – there were changes, but they took place gradually and had limited impact
- a period from about 1450 to 1700 when bigger changes occurred, more rapidly and with more significant effects; the biggest cause of all this change was the use of gunpowder weapons.

The year 1450 could be called a watershed because it was a time between two very different periods of change.

Activities

1 Using the graphs on this page as examples, draw your own graph showing an overall picture of change for the period 1350–1700.

Complex change

But change is more complex than simple graphs can show. They give a useful overall impression, but they hide the complexity of change.

During the period 1350–1700, several key features of warfare remained much the same. For example:
- infantry remained the biggest part of an army
- hand-to-hand weapons – swords, daggers, clubs etc. – remained much the same
- the feigned retreat remained a useful tactic
- sieges remained the most common form of war
- provisioning the army remained a hard task
- medical care for the wounded remained poor
- mistreatment of prisoners remained common.

These are examples of **continuity**.

However, some changes were taking place gradually over the whole period. For example:
- feudalism declined as a way of providing armies; rulers gradually changed to raising money from taxes and using this to pay troops
- mercenaries became a bigger part of armies
- standing armies, though small, emerged
- uniforms appeared, then slowly became the norm.

This type of change is often called development.

Alongside all this continuity and development, some changes transformed warfare – they were key changes that made things completely different afterwards. For example:
- muskets transformed the battlefield.

This type of change is a turning point.

Activities

2 Would you consider the following features of warfare 1350–1700 to be examples of continuity, development or a turning point?

   a) the decline of mounted soldiers

   b) the use of cannon after 1450

   c) disease in army camps.

Key features of battles

Because history is a combination of continuity and change, over the history of warfare battles show some features that are the same and some that are different. For any battle, we can look at key features such as:

- the size of the armies
- the composition of the armies – infantry, archers, cavalry, etc.
- the weapons used
- the tactics used
- the influence of the site of the battle
- the influence of training and discipline
- the influence of leadership decisions.

ResultsPlus
Build Better Answers

What can you learn from Sources A and B about changes in warfare 1350–1700? Explain your answer, using the sources. (4 marks)

Basic, Level 1 (1–2 marks).
Answer gives some relevant information about warfare, e.g. 'Source A shows an archer. Source B shows cannon.'

Good, Level 2 (3–4 marks).
Answer identifies changes, giving details from the sources in support. For example, warfare became more expensive. Source B shows that manufacture of cannon needed many men and a lot of materials. The bows and arrows used in Source A are much less complicated.

Source A: An illustration in a prayer book called Luttrell's Psalter, made in about 1340. It shows young men doing archery practice.

Source B: An engraving made in about 1650. It shows men casting cannon and cannon balls in a forge. There is a battle scene in the background, shown in the top right-hand corner of the engraving.

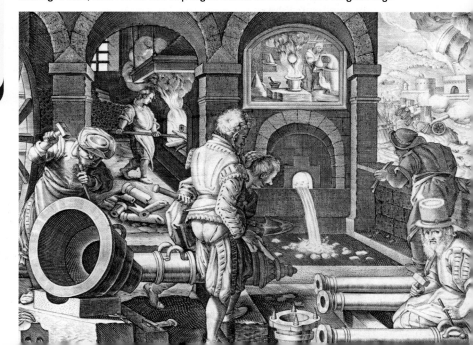

2.1 Warfare in the 18th century

20

This was a time of gradual development. For many features of warfare there was continuity

Continuity

Limited warfare continued:

- armies were still often led by rulers rather than generals;
- rulers fought wars for limited gains, happy with an agreed peace rather than total defeat for one side;
- sieges and **skirmishes** were still more common than battles.

Weapons and tactics also remained much the same.

- Infantry still made up about 75 per cent of most armies in the 18th century.
- Muskets continued unchanged. The English 'Brown Bess' flintlock musket, which came into service in 1715, remained in service for 130 years and 7.8 million were manufactured. Re-loading time fell to about 30 seconds.
- The decline in power of the cavalry continued.

Source A: An 18th-century British light artillery. Smoke from cannon and muskets made battlefields in 1750 look very different from battlefields in 1350.

What was preventing change?

- Governments were not wealthy enough to risk costly armies and weapons too often in battles.
- Transport methods were too poor to cope in bad weather. Carts and wagons became stuck in deep mud or axles broke in frozen ruts. So campaigns were still largely limited to the months of April to October.
- Communication was slow. This made it difficult to co-ordinate the movement of separate groups of troops. Horseback was still the fastest way to get news from place to place. Clocks were still rare and there was still no Europe-wide system of time zones; each region adopted its own time. Generals had to organise their armies using phrases like 'at the crack of dawn'.
- It wasn't until about 1850 that stronger, wealthier governments and improvements in industry, transport and communication changed all this.

But there were some changes.

Light Artillery

By 1700, cannon were devastating when firing at fortified walls. But they were still very heavy to move around a battlefield. A 12-pounder gun (which could fire 12 lb (5.5 kg) of shot, shell or cannonball) weighed 3,200 lb and its carriage another 5,000 lb – 8,200 lb in all – more than a fully grown elephant!

After 1700, there were two main improvements.

- Bronze was used to make lighter cannon.
- Gun carriages were also made lighter.

Light field guns, mounted on carriages and pulled by horses, became a much more effective part of 18th-century armies.

- In 1709, British field guns swept whole ranks of French off their feet, using exploding canisters at the Battle of Malplaquet.

Larger, permanent armies

But the most significant change was the growth in the size of armies. Even in peacetime armies of 50,000 became common and these were now permanent, paid armies. During wartime extra troops were recruited.

- The British Army numbered 150,000 during the War of Spanish Succession in 1709.
- Of these 80,000 were mercenaries.

And bigger armies caused other changes.

Central administration

In 1722 a new War Office was created to run the British Army from grand new buildings in Horse Guards Parade in London. It ran army administration, finance and supplies.

Standardised weapons and uniforms

This was the age of the British redcoat. The basic uniform was a brightly coloured frock coat over a waistcoat and shirt, knee-length trousers with **gaiters**, long socks and very badly fitting buckled shoes. These uniforms were impressive, but tight and restrictive.

Regiments

To make it easier to run these large armies, smaller units were formed called **regiments**, each with its own base, emblems and staff.

- The Grenadier Guards trace their history back to this time.

Source B: Drill for 18th-century soldiers. Notice the uniforms and bayonets. Neither of these were typical before 1700.

Training

Having permanent armies meant that more time could be spent, during peacetime, training for battle.

Training for the rank and file

Soldiers constantly practised marching, manoeuvring, re-loading and firing. The whole army used the same, rigid **drills**.

They learned to march onto a battlefield:

- in columns;
- at 75 steps per minute;
- and then, without pausing, wheel into firing lines.

Once in position:

- their front ranks could fire a volley;
- then retreat to the back of the line;
- to be replaced by the rank behind;
- who would then fire again.

This gave them repeated volleys every 15 seconds.

Better trained armies meant that generals could use more complex tactics on the battlefield. The army of the Duke of Wellington at Waterloo in 1815 manoeuvred much better than the armies of Henry V at Agincourt or Charles I at Naseby.

Training for officers

Training also improved, a little, for officers.

- For example, the Woolwich Engineering and Military Academy opened in 1741.

However, the impact of training schools for officers was limited, since not all officers attended. Most went straight into their regiments as cadets and learned their skills as apprentice-officers.

Activities

1 Pages 14–15 have details of armies in the period 1350–1700. Compare the information here with those pages. Make lists of:

   a) things which changed during the 18th century;

   b) things which stayed the same.

   You will continue your lists after you have read the next two pages.

Recruitment

Larger armies put a strain on recruitment, though there were few changes. Officers in European armies were young men of noble birth who bought their commissions.

Recruiting the other ranks

- Some men volunteered for **camaraderie** or adventure, some for a corporal or sergeant's pay and others for patriotic reasons. But there were too few volunteers.
- Most European countries had reserve **militia**, who were **conscripted** during wars. In England in 1757, for example, there were riots when the militia was called up.
- Criminals were sometimes offered enlistment instead of imprisonment.

Discipline

Bigger armies meant many poor recruits. The Duke of Wellington described his men as 'the scum of the earth, enlisted for drink'. So armies were ruled by harsh punishments. The thinking was 'they must fear their officers more than danger'.

Punishments

- minor punishments included reduction of rank or patrol duty;
- worse offences were punished by corporal punishment, such as whipping or branding;
- the most serious offenders had their contracts lengthened, were sent to serve overseas or hanged or shot.

Source C: A British painting, dated 1805, showing soldiers drinking with locals. Many a naive young man woke up with a hangover to find that he had signed enlistment papers.

Source D: A British soldier being flogged at Chatham barracks near London.

Accommodation and food

When armies were small, soldiers could be **billeted** in local houses and inns during peacetime. With bigger armies this was not practical, so barracks were built. Ravensdowne Barracks, constructed in 1717, was among the first to be built in England. But cost meant that barracks were basic; men slept two to a bed; there were no kitchens; and they cooked in the sleeping quarters.

And governments struggled to feed these bigger armies too:

- On campaign, soldiers were given four days' rations. Typically, this was 1 lb of bread and 1 lb of beef per day, sometimes with cheese.
- When food ran out, there was still **foraging** for food and pillage of local houses, but this was not enough. Armies had become too large.
- So every four days they had to stop, set up kitchens, bake bread and re-ration.
- The British also issued a daily rum ration. Other countries had similar arrangements, and this led to problems of alcoholism in most of the armies in Europe.

Such conditions were tolerated by paid career soldiers, but not by those who had been forced to enlist. When Britain fought in the Seven Years' War, 80,000 enemy soldiers **deserted**, despite 'two-way' sentries, half looking out for attackers, half looking in for deserters.

Medical care

As in previous centuries, the 18th century saw only slow progress in medical treatment often through the work of individuals.

Date	Event
1743	Sir John Pringle, physician general to the British Army in Flanders, pioneered the practice of agreeing with the enemy that field hospitals should be regarded as neutral safe havens for the sick. This benefited the wounded on the battlefield. Many years later this would influence the idea behind the Red Cross.
1752	Pringle published his work *Observations on the Diseases of the Army*. This set out good practice for medical treatment of soldiers. However, most standard treatments of that time were ineffective or even harmful. He recommended bloodletting, **emetics** and **purging** as well as ointments that contained mercury, which all just weakened or poisoned wounded soldiers.
1760	Dr John Hunter accompanied the British Army on an expedition to Portugal. While there he encountered the problems of bleeding patients as a treatment. He publicly condemned it as a treatment.
1761	After extensive experience treating soldiers, Hunter introduced new methods to probe gunshot wounds. However, his methods were not widely taken up. It was over a century before surgery for battlefield wounds really improved.

But all this was little real help. There were obstacles to progress. For example, there were no systems for rapid removal of casualties from the battlefield. And surgeons killed as many patients – by infecting them – as they saved. They did not know about the need for clean procedures, and routinely did no more than wipe their hands before moving from one patient's open wounds to another's.

 ResultsPlus
Build Better Answers

How much did armies change in the 17th and the 18th centuries? (12 marks)

 Basic, Level 1 (1–4 marks).
Answer is general, with some information about warfare during the 17th and 18th centuries but very little detail, e.g. armies became larger.

 Good, Level 2 (5–8 marks).
Level 2 answers are fuller, with more detailed information about matters such as the size and composition of armies, weapons, training, recruitment, discipline, accommodation, food and medicine, but without making clear where the 18th century was similar and where it was different.

 Excellent, Level 3 (9–12 marks).
Answer makes comparison noting similarities and differences, for example about the size and composition of armies or the training and care of soldiers, and comes to an overall judgement about how much change there was.

Summary

The 18th century saw a continuation of developments begun in the 17th century. Little was new, apart from the introduction of uniforms and light infantry.

2.2 Case study: A revolution in warfare

Learning outcomes

By the end of this topic you should be able to:

● understand the links between changes in society and changes in warfare.

New society, new warfare

We have seen already how changes in society caused changes in warfare. Activity 1 reminds you about examples of this.

Activities

1 Make a chart in two columns headed 'Change in society' and 'Linked change in warfare'. Find at least two examples from the period c1450–c1750 and write them on your chart.

The period 1793–1815 saw rapid change in French society because of the French Revolution (1789–1799). The French rebelled, using the slogan 'liberty, equality, fraternity'. Noble privileges were abolished and control by the king was replaced by a government elected by the people. Other monarchs in Europe went to war with France in 1792 to save the French monarchy. This became a war of survival for the new French society, and they turned to a new way of waging war.

Before...

War had been in the control of the king. The French Army was his army. He declared war; he sold officer ranks to the nobility; he employed soldiers.

After...

The new France was a society of the people. They built a new army of the people. In 1793, the **levée en masse** declared,

'Young men will go to battle; married men will forge arms; women will make uniforms; children will pick rags; old men will preach the hatred of kings and the unity of the Republic.'

This was a new way to wage war. Every French citizen was being recruited to the war effort. By 1794, they had an army of 750,000 citizens, fighting to defend their country. And in 1798, they introduced conscription. Between 1800 and 1812, this law recruited 1.3 million men.

Recruitment for officers changed too. The new French society ended the privileges of the nobility. Purchasing of commissions was ended. Instead there were examinations. Ordinary soldiers could become officers, and in the militia, soldiers were even allowed to elect officers. Before, 85 per cent of officers were nobles; by 1794, only 3 per cent were. Promotion was decided by ability. This produced a generation of outstanding generals like Napoleon Bonaparte.

This new style of army brought another change: more casualties. The new French society relied on large armies of committed, but raw recruits in brave attacks on the enemy. These tactics cost many lives. Of 2 million men who served Napoleon from 1806 to 1814, 100,000 died on the battlefield. But in a time when medical treatment had improved very little, another 300,000 died of illness or injuries in military hospitals. Of all Frenchmen born 1790–1795, 20 per cent died in wars waged by Napoleon. Society had changed warfare – and this new style of warfare would leave its scar on society.

A war economy

The new French society became a war machine. The *levée en masse* also said, 'Public buildings will be made into barracks and arms workshops, the soil of cellars will be used to extract salt-petre (for gunpowder). Horses will be taken for the cavalry and to pull artillery.' Copper for cannon was taken from church bells; iron was taken from people's gates; churches were used as foundries. In 250 state-run workshops, Paris made more muskets than the rest of Europe combined. And the war machine put out propaganda too. In 1794, France delivered 7 million pamphlets to remind troops what they were fighting for.

Unlimited warfare

So, in France during these revolutionary years there was also a revolutionary change in the nature of warfare. Warfare was no longer **limited warfare**: most of society was now involved in the war effort. The military writer Clausewitz wrote,

> 'A new force appeared. Suddenly war was the business of the people. Instead of just governments and armies, the full weight of the nation was in the balance.'

This new style of warfare has been called **total war** or 'unlimited warfare'.

18th century	1792–1815 – Revolutionary and Napoleonic Wars
Limited warfare	Unlimited warfare
King's army	National, citizens' army
Limited wars, small scale	Wide-ranging war, in Europe and world-wide colonies
Wars with limited objectives	Wars of conquest to change the rulers and the social and political way of life of conquered territories
Growing, but small, armies	Massed armies of all citizens
Growing, but limited cost	Huge armies = huge costs
Professional armies, trained, paid, disciplined	Volunteer or conscripted armies with less training
Separation of army from civilians	Involvement of civilians in the war effort
Limited casualties	Massive casualties

Activities

2   Add a new panel to the bottom of the chart you completed for Activity 1. Add two examples of changes in French society that were reflected in a change in the French approach to warfare 1789–1815.

Impact on Britain

These dramatic changes had little immediate effect on the British approach to warfare. Promotion by ability rather than status in society did not happen in the British Army until after the middle of the 19th century (see page 30), and the experience of total war, involving Britain's civilians in the war effort, did not happen until the 20th century.

Why did change in France not bring about a similar change in Britain?

What can you learn from that about the factors bringing about change?

As you study 19th- and 20th-century developments in Britain's approach to warfare, you can use this case study of France to help you look for the factors that brought about change in Britain.

Activities

3   Copy the table on this page and cut out each box, to make a set of 18th-century warfare cards and a set for 1792–1815. Show someone an 18th-century card. Can that person tell you the 1792–1815 equivalent? Then try the reverse: show the 1792–1815 card. Can they tell you the 18th-century equivalent?

Challenge

4   How far did the period 1792–1815 see a revolutionary change in warfare?

Summary

- Social change in France after 1789 was the factor bringing about revolutionary changes in the French approach to warfare 1792–1815.

- Changes in Britain's approach did not happen till much later.

2.3 The Waterloo campaign 1815

> **Learning outcomes**
>
> By the end of this topic you should be able to:
> - describe the key events of the Waterloo campaign
> - pick out features of the campaign that were typical of warfare at this time.

The background

On 15 June 1815, Napoleon took an army across the French border in a final attempt to defeat the other powers of Europe. His army was in three parts where he led the centre, Marshal Ney his left flank and Marshal Grouchy his right.

Two armies confronted him.
- The Duke of Wellington led troops from Britain, the Netherlands and German states.
- Field Marshal Blücher led a Prussian army.

The first skirmishes

On 16 June, Wellington halted Marshal Ney's troops at Quatre Bras. But on their right flank, the French forced the Prussians into retreat. The French had separated the British and Prussian armies.

Source A: A 19th-century engraving. Both sides had about 50,000 infantry at Waterloo. Infantry typically used muskets 80 metres from the enemy.

Taking up position

At the end of this manoeuvring:
- Wellington re-grouped, with 68,000 troops, near the small Belgian village of Waterloo;
- Napoleon sent Grouchy to pursue the Prussians and prepared his remaining 70,000 men to attack Wellington on 18 June.

Wellington chose his defensive position well.
- He drew up his troops on the reverse side of a ridge, to reduce the impact of enemy artillery.
- The battle area was small, about three miles across, with towns to the east and west. It was perfect for a defensive action.
- He also set up two positions in front of the ridge to break up the French assault.
  - One was at a chateau held by the the Coldstream Guards;
  - the other was a farmhouse held by the King's German Legion.

Fighting begins

Napoleon was not on top form. He was suffering with piles, making him snappy and unable to ride his horse to survey the battle. He also made two early errors.

He had discarded 30,000 troops, by sending Grouchy after Blücher and the Prussians.
- But Blücher used some men to confront Grouchy, and sent the rest to help Wellington.
- Grouchy's men were wasted; they neither tied down Blücher nor took part at Waterloo.

Napoleon made another error. He judged the battlefield too muddy for cavalry until 11.30a.m. So he tried a diversion.
- He sent an attack on the chateau, to trick Wellington into using his reserves.
- But the Coldstream Guards hung on. The French suffered heavy losses and needed reinforcements.
- What started as a diversionary attack ended up using a quarter of Napoleon's infantry. His forces were weakened before his main attack.

Source B: A modern painting. Generals survey the battle. Cavalry wait in reserve; heavy artillery pounds the enemy. Napoleon had 246 cannon at Waterloo.

The final French errors

Napoleon now made another error. It was 3.00p.m. and his troops were more or less intact. He could have withdrawn, re-joined Grouchy's 30,000 troops and fought another day. But he decided to launch Ney's force against Wellington's centre.

By about 4.00p.m. they made a breakthrough. Ney captured the farmhouse. He could set up artillery there and pound the tiring British forces.

Ney called for reserves, the Imperial Guard, for an all-out assault. Possibly annoyed by Ney's slow progress, possibly unwilling to use his reserves, Napoleon refused.

But Wellington acted decisively. He personally led troops to the heart of his line, where Ney's assault was most fierce. The line held.

At this point, Blücher's full Prussian force arrived. When Napoleon finally sent in the Imperial Guard it was too late. Napoleon's tired troops were now out-numbered. Wellington finally switched from defence to attack; the French were overrun.

About 60 per cent of French troops were killed, wounded or taken prisoner. Their battle was lost.

The French artillery attack

At 11.30a.m. Napoleon started his main offensive with a heavy artillery bombardment – normal tactics to weaken enemy defences.

- But soft ground swallowed the cannonballs and canisters, preventing injuries from ricochets and shrapnel.
- And the British position behind the slope meant many shots just sailed over their heads.

So Napoleon delayed his main assault again. By this time, an advanced group of 30,000 Prussians had arrived to help Wellington's defence.

The French infantry attack

It was 1.00p.m. when Napoleon launched his infantry attack in a wide column, 200 men across. This column had less firepower than an infantry line, but it was just as easily hit by enemy fire.

Wellington's army used infantry squares for defence. The square was not as powerful as an infantry line. But, with corners reinforced by cannon, and the first three rows of infantry firing volleys in rotation, it was hard to break down. Wellington had also hidden field artillery behind a heavy hedge. They blasted the French column. Then he sent in cavalry and 3,000 British redcoats, firing volleys of muskets. Napoleon's first assault failed; 3,000 French were captured.

Activities

1 Using the text and pictures on these pages, list the features of the Waterloo campaign that were typical of warfare between 1700 and 1815.

2 a) List ways in which the leadership of the Duke of Wellington contributed to victory at Waterloo.

b) List other factors in his victory.

c) How important was Wellington's leadership in the outcome of the Waterloo campaign?

Summary

- Several aspects of the Battle of Waterloo were typical of warfare at this time.
- Wellington's leadership was a crucial factor in success at the Battle of Waterloo.

2.4 Warfare in the 19th century

Learning outcomes

By the end of this topic you should be able to:

● explain the features of continuity before 1850 and rapid change 1850–1900

● explain the impact of technology on weapons and the battlefield by 1900.

1815–1850 – continuity

The British army looked much the same in 1850 as it had done at Waterloo.

● The core of the army remained well-drilled infantry, in highly coloured uniforms.

● Cavalry continued to be their main support.

● New technology, like the telegraph, was used from the 1830s but ignored by the army.

● The growth of artillery actually slowed.

● Numbers of men fell.

● The Duke of Wellington even remained as Commander in Chief until 1852.

What was slowing down change?

● Napoleon had gone. The threat of France was over and there seemed less need for change.

● Revolution in France had made governments suspicious of new ideas, even in warfare.

● Most army officers were from the aristocracy. They saw no reason to change the army.

● Cavalry, now weak in battle, was still admired by the upper classes. One reason was that there was no police force and cavalry were very good at controlling public protests.

Source A: The mitrailleuse was an early French machine gun that was in use by the 1860s.

1850–1900 – rapid change

This lack of progress came to an end in the mid-19th century. There were several aspects of warfare that changed. One was weaponry.

Weapon type	Improvement
Rifles	These replaced muskets as the spiral groove (or rifling) inside the barrel made the shot spin and therefore fly further and straighter. By the 1860s they could kill from almost a mile away.
	Percussion cartridges were introduced, with explosive caps at the back of the bullet. They did not need flints or sparks to fire meaning soldiers could fire reliably in damp weather
	Conical bullets were developed which could be loaded into the breech of a rifle and fired from revolving magazines containing several bullets. Soldiers could now re-load quickly, lie down and fire several shots in quick succession.
Machine guns	Gatling guns were small cannon-like weapons from the USA, but having several small revolving barrels allowed up to 150 bullets per minute to be fired.
	By the 1880s, machine guns had become smaller and lighter. Guns like the Maxim could be moved around by individual soldiers.
Cannon	Cannon could now be reliably made from steel, improving their strength.
	Cannon design benefited from the advances in rifles, including breech-loading actions and rifled barrels.
	Developments in the type of shells that cannon could fire made them increasingly more deadly. By the Boer War (1899–1902) cannons could fire percussion shells, which would explode on impact, at 10 rounds a minute.

Source B: Prussian cannon, shelling Paris in 1870. Town citizens were now in the front line.

The main cause of change

The main reason for this rapid change was industrialisation. All of Europe was in the midst of an industrial revolution by the mid-19th century.

Entrepreneurs were mass-producing many cheaper products, including weapons. They used new science and technology, like the Bessemer process to make cheap steel. The price of steel before 1850 was about about £60 per tonne. The Bessemer process could make steel at £7 per tonne. They also used more efficient factories, with standardised parts made up by conveyor-belt production.

The Royal Small Arms Factory, at Enfield in London, made rifles. In 1856, they built a new machine shop, manned by 1,000 workers, who could make 1,750 rifles per week. By 1900, they were mass-producing the famous Lee-Enfield rifle.

Activities

1 Compare pages 20 and 28. What aspects of society can slow down change?

2 List the main improvements in weapons in the 19th century

3 Explain what impact they had on the battlefield.

4 Why was industrialisation so important to these changes?

The main effects of change

These new weapons transformed battles. It was now clear that the army with the newest rifles and cannon were at a huge advantage.

• In 1898, at Omdurman, in North Africa, British troops using machine guns and rifles fought off an attack and killed 11,000 Sudanese but lost only 28 British soldiers.

A second effect was that crude frontal attacks on the enemy would became useless. Defence, using rifles, machine guns and cannon, now dominated battlefields.

Source: C From *The Cambridge History of Warfare,* edited by Geoffrey Parker.

[The British] encountered a Russian attack by the Alma river… Well aimed fire from rifles slaughtered the Russians well before the British lines came within reach of the enemy muskets.

New rifles, machine guns and cannon finally sounded the death knell of the cavalry.

Source D: From *Cassell's World History of Warfare.*

Cavalry was still seen as the premier branch of the service. But the Franco-Prussian War showed that its only real choice was idleness or suicide.

Wartime communication

The other technological change of the late-19th century was in communication.

Railways

Troops could be moved 15 times faster by rail than by marching and they arrived fresh, not tired.

The British used a railway to transport supplies in the Crimea during the war there.

And whilst railways used steam power to improve transport on land, steam ships improved the supply of overseas armies.

The telegraph

The **telegraph** also eventually changed wartime communication.

- It was impractical for soldiers to use during battles.
- But governments and general staff used it to communicate with generals on campaign.
- Newspapers took advantage of the telegraph too. By the time of the Crimean War (1854–1856) the telegraph and daily newspapers kept the public in constant contact with events on the battlefield.

Source E: Supplies being unloaded at the British Army base at Balaclava, in 1856 during the Crimean War. Notice the mixture of new and old technology – horses and sailing ships alongside the railway and steamships.

Public attitudes to warfare

Receiving daily news from the battlefield fed the appetite of the public who, all over Europe, became more enthusiastic about warfare.

- Partly this was caused by the birth of new nations; both Germany and Italy were created at this time. The new nations were keen to compete against their older rivals. They saw warfare as essential to their survival. In Germany, von Moltke said 'The most noble virtues are developed in war; courage, duty. Without war, the world would stagnate.'
- The enthusiasm for warfare was partly caused by the competition amongst European powers to win the biggest empire in colonial wars.

All this caused a revival of patriotism and nationalism. In England this new enthusiasm for war was called **jingoism**.

Army reforms

One result of this enthusiasm for war was that most countries in Europe modernised their armies:

- to make them more efficient;
- to make them reflect society of the time.

Modernising the British Army

In Britain, the new Liberal government of William Gladstone was busy modernising various aspects of society, including schools and the Church. Given the public climate, it was natural for them to turn to the army too.

From 1872 the Secretary for War, Edward Cardwell, made recruitment more attractive and improved the quality of recruits by:

- reducing the period of enlistment to 12 years (6 years active service and 6 years in reserve);
- creating a regional organisation for regiments – eg the Warwickshires, the Yorks and Lancs;
- developing 'linked battalions', in which one battalion stationed overseas whilst its linked battalion was at home, training and recruiting;
- abolishing the purchase of commissions;
- promoting on merit;
- abolishing the flogging of soldiers;
- introducing the new Martini-Henry breech-loading rifle as the main infantry rifle.

Medical Improvements

There were also medical improvements in warfare.

Florence Nightingale

During the Crimean War, Florence Nightingale saw the connection between hospital cleanliness and death rates. As a result of her work, nursing improved and hospitals became cleaner. Infectious diseases and infected wounds were reduced. Survival rates improved (see p.33 for details).

Wartime surgery

Surgery on wounded soldiers improved after 1850.

- Ether and chloroform were used as **anaesthetics**.
- Steam sterilisation made surgical instruments cleaner.
- X-rays were used in the treatment of broken limbs.

The Red Cross

A Swiss soldier, named Henry Dunant, had been outraged by the delay in treating casualties. He publicised his views.

- Public support enabled him to form an international group to help the wounded. This became the Red Cross.
- In 1864 this prompted 12 nations to draw up a treaty to agree how the wounded should be treated in wars. It was called the Geneva Convention and is still used today.

Source F: A contemporary picture of a military ambulance carrying Russian wounded, under the flag of the Red Cross in 1877.

Activities

4 a) Name two examples of improvements in communication during the 19th century.

   b) Give an example to show how each of these affected warfare.

5 How did improvements in medical care help soldiers towards the end of the 19th century?

6 How did social attitudes in Britain affect the British Army and warfare in the 19th century?

ResultsPlus
Build Better Answers

Explain why Florence Nightingale was important in improving medical care for soldiers. (9 marks)

  Basic, Level 1 (1–3 marks).
Answer offers a general comment, but with little detail, e.g. she made hospitals cleaner.

  Good, Level 2 (4–6 marks).
Answer gives details about her work but does not explain its importance.

  Excellent, Level 3 (7–9 marks).
Answer explains the importance of Nightingale's work in improving hospital design and the treatment of wounded soldiers, and in influencing the army's attitude to medical care.

Summary

- The period 1815–1850 was a time of little change.
- However, from 1850–1900 there were rapid changes in weaponry, communication and medical treatment during wars.
- The views of society and industrialisation and improvements in technology were key causes of these changes.

2.5 The Crimean War 1854–1856

Learning outcomes

By the end of this topic you should be able to:

- recognise features in the Crimean War typical of an earlier age of warfare
- recognise features of the Crimean War typical of a later age of warfare.

Source A: A cavalry charge at the Battle of Alma in 1854, looking much like Waterloo.

The Crimean War was fought between Russia and an alliance of Britain, France and Turkey. It was fought mainly on the Crimean Peninsula in the Black Sea, 4,000 miles by sea from London.

It had features of earlier warfare because:
- it was fought by small numbers of troops far from civilians;
- it was fought by troops clad in brightly coloured uniforms;
- infantry lines or cavalry charges were often used.

But it also showed features typical of later wars.
- The French used new iron-clad warships against the wooden ships of the Russians.
- British and French troops showed the benefit of new percussion rifles and rifled cannon.
- Around Sebastopol, shelling was so severe that the troops dug into siege trenches, rather like the First World War 60 years later.

Leadership

Generals sometimes disastrously used 'old' methods against 'new' weapons. Massed frontal assaults against superior firepower was very costly.
- In 1854, Russian infantry at Inkerman charged troops whose rifles had a longer range. The Russians lost 12,000 men in one attack.

These were not the only examples of poor leadership. The British commander, Lord Raglan:
- failed to reconnoitre for a suitable landing site;
- took months to establish an efficient supply line for his troops from the port of Balaclava;
- delayed his attack on Sebastopol, allowing the defenders to complete their defences.

These errors caused many people to question the way that Britain selected its army officers.

- The Turks fought on the winning side, but lost 400,000 men, killed or wounded.
- The Russians lost 500,000.
- Using newer weapons, the British and French combined lost about 150,000 men.

Source B: Russian troops dug defences like First World War trenches 60 years later.

Medical issues

The war sits on the watershed between 'old' and 'new' medical practices at war. For example, at first, diseases such as cholera and typhus and exposure caused 80 per cent of deaths in the Crimea. But then there was a change.

The Times published reports of the filthy conditions and lack of medical supplies in the military hospital at Scutari. Public outrage at this resulted in action. Florence Nightingale took a team of nurses out to the Crimea and improved the organisation and the cleanliness of the hospital. The hospital death rate fell from 40 per cent to 2 per cent. By the time the war ended, Florence Nightingale was regarded as a heroine. She launched a campaign for the improvement of nursing in military hospitals. The result of her work was the founding of the Army Medical College. She also advised on the design of hospital buildings.

Source C: This is an engraving from the time of a military hospital, sent back to Britain from the Crimea. Such information outraged public opinion and ensured changes in the ways wars were fought afterwards.

War reporting and public opinion

The Crimean War also changed war reporting.

At the start of the war, *The Times*, in London, used an officer in the British Army for war reports. Sent by horse and ship, his letters took a week to arrive.

Later, they sent a reporter, William Russell, who sent reports to London by telegraph on a daily basis. This new method of communication had a huge impact on public opinion. Russell's reports of the conditions at Scutari and the Charge of the Light Brigade shocked the public.

Transportation and supply

The war also illustrates new methods of wartime transportation.

Using steamships and railways, the British and French could transport men, weapons and supplies to the Crimea in under three weeks – despite the great distance.

They also built the first ever military railway – a 25-mile track from the Crimean coast to British trenches at Sebastopol. It could deliver 240 tons of food and supplies per day.

FASCINATING FACT

Technology allowed the French assault on the Malakoff fort at Sebastopol to be precisely timed. As soon as their shelling stopped, their infantry attacked. It was the first use of the order 'Gentlemen, synchronise your watches'.

Activities

1 List the features of the Crimean War that could be called typical of 'old' warfare.

2 List the features of the Crimean War that could be called typical of 'new' warfare.

3 The Crimean War was an overseas campaign. What problems did this cause for the British and French and how did they tackle these?

Summary

The Crimean War illustrates old features typical of 18th-century wars and new features typical of late-19th-century warfare.

2.6 Summary: Warfare c1700–c1900

Simple change

The period between 1700 and 1900 was not a time of consistent change in the history of warfare.

On a simple level:
- 1700–1790 was a time of continuity.
- 1790–1815 was a time of rapid change in France, which forced other countries, such as Britain, to change too.
- 1815–1850 was a time of stagnation – even regression.
- 1850–1900 was a time of rapid change.

Activities

1   Look back at the sections on the period 1790–1900.

a) Write a sentence or two to justify each of the four statements bullet-pointed above.
   For example:

   '1700–1790 was a period of continuity because limited warfare remained the norm, cavalry continued to decline in importance, and infantry, using the same weapons, remained the biggest part of all armies.'

b) Using the guide graphs on page 18, draw a graph showing a simple view of the course of change 1700–1900.

Complex change

Change is normally more complex than it is possible to show on a simple graph. For example:
- The period 1700–1790 was, in general terms, a time of continuity. Most things stayed the same and any changes were slow. But looking more closely, we can find examples of changes that were taking place.

Activities

2   Look back again at the sections about the periods in the four bullet points at the top of the page.

a) Now write a slightly longer paragraph on each period, qualifying the simplistic statement in the four bullet points. For example:

   '1700–1790 was, in general, a time of continuity because most things stayed the same and any changes were slow or minor. But there were some changes. Based on old heavy cannon, the French developed new, lighter, field artillery, for example. And armies generally got bigger; this encouraged countries to have better training for armies and to provide accommodation for them.'

Source A: A 19th-century painting showing the British Royal Horse Artillery using field guns during the 18th century.

Factors causing change

So the pattern of change 1700–1900 is complex. At times change was slow; at times it was rapid.
- What was it that was slowing down change?
- And what was it that was speeding up change?

Several factors were involved. Three examples are:
- attitudes in society;
- industrialisation;
- medical knowledge.

During the period 1700–1850, each of these hindered change. For example:
- Industries were still at an early stage of development. Except in Britain, the Industrial Revolution did not start much before 1850. Most production in the rest of the world was still in small workshops. This limited the changes that could take place in the development of weapons, for example.

But after 1850, each of the three factors speeded up change. For example:
- Attitudes in society changed rapidly. After 1870, British public opinion wanted a more efficient army. Gladstone's government also wanted to create more equal opportunities for all. These views caused the army reforms, led by Cardwell, that abolished the purchase of commissions and introduced promotion on merit.

Source B: An illustration printed in the *London Illustrated News* in 1867; it shows an exhibit at the Paris Exhibition of that year. The exhibit is a heavy cannon, manufactured by Krupps, the Prussian steelworks.

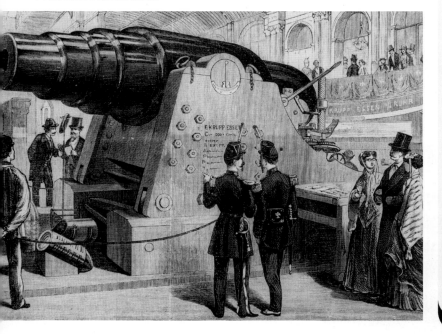

Activities

3 Choose one of the three factors causing change listed on this page. Using the two examples given, write a paragraph explaining how your factor either slowed down or speeded up change in warfare.

ResultsPlus
Build Better Answers

What can you learn from Sources A and B about changes in artillery during the period 1700–1900? Explain your answer, using the sources.
(4 marks)

■ **Basic, Level 1 (1–2 marks).**
Answer gives information from one (1 mark) or both (2 marks) of the sources, but does not address the issue of change, e.g. *'In Source A, we can see the kind of light artillery, pulled by horses, that was used on the battlefield in the 18th century. Source B shows heavy cannon used in the 19th century.'*

● **Good, Level 2 (3–4 marks).**
Answer gives information from both sources and explains what we can learn about change from this, e.g. *'Source A shows the kind of light artillery that was used on the battlefield in the 18th century. But artillery changed after that. By the middle of the 19th century, some industrialists, such as Krupps, were making much more powerful cannon. 'We can tell that from the height of the cannon (much taller than people compared to Source A) and its bore. It must have been a great deal more powerful.'*

3.1 Warfare 1900–1918

> **Learning outcomes**
>
> By the end of this topic you should be able to:
> - outline the key features of warfare 1900–1918
> - explain how far these key features were new.

The First World War 1914–1918

Britain and the other Allies went to war against the Central Powers in 1914. Britain, France and Russia were the Allies; Germany was the main Central Power. There were several key features of the war that were new to Britain.

The scale of war

The scale of the war was one new feature. With most of the world supporting one side or the other, 80 per cent of the world's population were formally at war. The armies involved were huge. Germany, for example, had an army of 877,000 by 1914.

But Britain's army was quite small in 1914. So there was an appeal for extra volunteers. This was not new – but the response was. Britain had 2.5 million volunteers by 1916. When this was not enough, conscription started. By the end of the war, in 1918, over 5 million Britons had joined the British Army. Overall, the Central Powers had mobilised 25 million men and the Allies 40 million.

Source A: Thousands of shells for the Battle of the Somme in 1916, where the British artillery bombarded German lines.

The type of war

The type of fighting that took place in the First World War was also new. The generals expected a short war that would be won by the overwhelming strength of attacking forces. They expected this because:

- Prussia had won quick victories against Austria (1866) and France (1870–1871) with the firepower of rifles, machine guns and artillery. Germany had prepared the Schlieffen Plan for a rapid six-week defeat of France.
- Britain had defeated the Boers in SouthAfrica (1900–1902) by using the overwhelming force of an army of 300,000 men.

In fact, the First World War was different.

- Defenders were more powerful than attackers. They dug into defensive positions and used rifles and machine guns to mow down attacking infantry. The German advance was halted short of Paris. But the French and British counterattack also failed. Neither side could overwhelm the other. It was stalemate. (See pages 38–39.)

Weapons

However, the weapons that dominated the First World War were not new.

- It is true that the war did see the first use of airplanes, tanks, gas attacks and submarines; and these weapons had some significance.
- But the most powerful weapons remained artillery, rifles and machine guns – weapons of the 19th century – old weapons.

What was new was:

- the scale of their use: for example, the Somme offensive lasted not hours but almost five months;
- the quantity of weapons produced and used: Britain used more shells in the 35-minute artillery bombardment at the Battle of Neuve Chapelle in 1915 than in the entire Boer War.

Total war

Another change was that every aspect of society was used to help the war effort. It was like revolutionary France had fought from 1793 to 1815. Historians have called this kind of all-out war 'total war'.

Economic power

The Allies poured all their economic power into the war effort.

- Britain produced 170 million shells during the war.
- Woolwich Arsenal in London, had 100,000 workers.

Political power

The British Government also used political power to boost the war effort.

- The Defence of the Realm Act (DORA) gave the government power to direct the war effort. It controlled railways, shipping and mines, introduced rationing and censored what papers printed about the war.

Total warfare also took its toll on society.

Loss of freedom

People were forced into jobs, rather like the *levée en masse* in France in the 1790s. British people's lives were controlled as never before.

Casualties

In all, about 10 million servicemen died in the First World War.

- About 700,000 British soldiers died which represented about 15 per cent of all British servicemen.

The scale of suffering was therefore unlike any time before.

Source B: This 1919 French illustration shows people were aware that the First World War involved far more deaths than earlier wars.

LA GUERRE EN PROGRES

La guerre a fait des progrès. C'est indéniable. Aujourd'hui elle tue mieux et plus rapidement. Si l'on compare le chiffre des pertes de la guerre 1914-1918 avec celui des pertes des huit grandes guerres des deux derniers siècles, on constate une réelle amélioration :

GUERRE DE SEPT ANS
551.000 hommes

GUERRES de la REVOLUTION
1.400.000 hommes

GUERRES DE NAPOLEON
1.700.000 hommes

GUERRE DE CRIMEE
785.000 hommes

Guerre de l'Indépendance américaine
700.000 hommes

GUERRE RUSSO-JAPONAISE
624.000 hommes

GUERRES BALKANIQUES
108.000 hommes

GUERRE 1914-1918
10.000.000 hommes

Source C: A French newspaper from 1919.

Le Petit Journal

ADMINISTRATION
61, RUE LAFAYETTE, 61   15 CENT.   SUPPLÉMENT ILLUSTRÉ   15 CENT.   ABONNEMENTS
29 me Année   Numéro 1.497
DIMANCHE 31 AOUT 1919

GUERRE 1914-1918
1.005 Milliards

Activities

1. What features of the First World War do Sources A, B and C illustrate?
2. What were the other main features of warfare at this time?
3. In what ways was the First World War typical of:
   a) earlier, 19th-century warfare
   b) a new type of warfare?

Summary

- The First World War was different from any previous British experience of warfare.
- It was bigger in scale than anything before.
- It was total war involving all people and affecting the whole of society.

3.2 Trench warfare on the Western Front

Learning outcomes

By the end of this topic you should be able to:

- outline the key features of warfare in the trenches on the Western Front
- identify similarities and differences when compared to earlier periods of warfare.

The First World War began in August 1914, when a German army of a million men attacked France.

By September, they were in sight of Paris. But in the Battle of the Marne, British and French troops halted the German advance. Troops on both sides spread north and south and dug in, to prevent the enemy outflanking them.

By the start of 1915, Allied and German trenches stretched 600 kilometres, from the Belgian coast in the north to the Swiss Alps in the south. And there they remained, hardly moving, until 1918.

This was the Western Front. It was where most British soldiers were to fight the First World War.

Fighting from the trenches

Rival trenches were normally dug anything from to 800 metres from each other. The space betwee was known as 'no-man's-land'. This area would strewn with barbed wire as added protection.

For almost four years, British generals failed to f a way of crossing no-man's-land and capturing opposition trenches.

Their only tactic was to order their men 'over th top'. This involved masses of infantry walking towards enemy fire. It soon became clear that machine guns could easily mow down attackers

However, the generals had no different tactics. T just increased the numbers of men sent over the

If troops did reach enemy trenches, fighting reverted to age-old hand-to-hand combat, thoug flame throwers and hand grenades were also us to clear trenches.

Features of the trenches

- **Front line** trenches were normally two metres deep and wide. These were the first line of defence.
- Support trenches were built further back, for off-duty soldiers and supplies.
- Reserve trenches were further back still; troops could be rested here and rushed to the front line if needed.

Trenches were dug in zigzags so that the enemy could not fire along them if they were captured.

The sides of this British trench were lined with wood.

The mud at the bottom of the trench was covered with duckboards.

Soldiers could stand on the fire step to see the enemy.

Steps enabled soldiers to go 'over the top' when they attacked.

Artillery fire was used before massed attacks, in the hope of weakening opposition defences. Some 70 per cent of all casualties in the war were caused by artillery fire. However, the trenches withstood the barrage – and the shelling ploughed up no-man's-land and made it even harder to cross.

Gas attacks were another feature of warfare in the trenches. On 22 April 1915, during the second Battle of Ypres, the Germans sent clouds of chlorine gas over the British troops; hundreds were suffocated.

Later, phosgene gas and mustard gas were used. However, wind could disperse gas or blow it off target and once gas masks were issued there was a simple defence, so gas eventually had little effect.

Life in the trenches

Life for British soldiers in the trenches had much in common with infantry through the ages. Day-to-day living conditions were harsh.
- Front-line troops lived in dug-outs, 20 metres behind front-line trenches. Fear of battle – being sent over the top – was the sharpest worry, but they complained more about everyday problems.
- Daily routines of sentry duty and weapons cleaning were tedious.
- Soldiers complained of the mud, the cold and the lack of sleep.
- Stagnant water and rats spread disease, causing diarrhoea and dysentery.

Source A: Rats were a problem in all the trenches. Here, German troops display rats caught in their trenches.

- Constant cold, damp, unsanitary conditions led to an infection called trench foot.
- Lice were a frequent irritant and caused trench fever. This involved severe headaches and sore limbs; it took a month to recover. About 25 per cent of troops in the trenches caught it.
- Another problem was shell shock – a condition caused by constant shelling. It could cause uncontrollable weeping or shaking, loss of speech or even physical paralysis. Medical treatment was patchy. Shell shock was not well understood; some sufferers were treated as cowards.

Treatment of normal wounds improved.
- Tetanus injections and sodium hypochlorite (a form of bleach) reduced infections.
- Blood transfusions were more successful.
- Even so, about 25 per cent of the wounded died.

Activities

1   In what ways were trenches on the Western Front similar to siege trenches built in the 17th century? (See page 12 for details)

2   What were the key weapons of trench warfare, and how effective were they?

3   In a small group, create a list of:
    a) the similarities
    b) the differences
    between the living conditions of infantry in the trenches compared to infantry in earlier periods of warfare.

You may need to look back through this book to remind yourself about earlier periods.

Summary

- Trench warfare was not new – although trench warfare lasting four years was.
- Artillery and machine guns were the dominant weapons of trench warfare.
- Life in the trenches for infantry had many similarities with earlier periods of warfare.

3.3 The Battle of the Somme 1916

Learning outcomes

By the end of this topic you should be able to:

- outline events at the Battle of the Somme
- evaluate Earl Haig's tactics
- explain the role of tanks, first used at the Battle of the Somme.

The first months of the war had shown the dominance of defensive machine guns and artillery. But generals persisted with massed infantry attacks. The Allies planned a new one, along the River Somme in 1916. The German positions were strong there; they had deep dug-outs as protection from artillery fire and dense barbed wire. Furthermore, the British infantry were raw volunteers from 1914 and 1915.

The British general commanding the British Expeditionary Force was Earl Haig. One of his generals, Sir Henry Rawlinson, argued for new tactics – a series of small attacks, on selected targets, by independent mobile groups of men. Haig, however, chose the more traditional strategy:

- a seven-day heavy artillery bombardment of 1.7 million shells, to destroy German defences
- a massed attack by 120,000 infantry, at walking speed, following an advancing shield shelling.

So at 7.30a.m. on 1 July, over an 18-mile front, Allied soldiers went over the top and advanced on German lines.

It was soon clear that German defences were intact. The attackers were shelled and mown down by machine-gun fire. As the advance slowed, it fell behind its artillery shield and was even more vulnerable.

By the end of the day, 20,000 British infantry were killed, 2,000 missing, 36,000 wounded and 600 captured. Half the attackers had become casualties, yet only in a handful of places had they reached the enemy lines. The attack had been a disaster.

Source A: From Henry Williamson, a junior British officer, in the first wave of infantry at the Somme.

I see men arising and walking forward; I go forward with them. Some seem to pause, with bowed heads, then sink carefully to their knees, roll over and lie still. Others roll and roll on the ground and scream. As I pass, they grip my legs in fear. I go on… up and down across pitted ground like a huge honeycomb. And my wave (of men) melts away, and the second wave comes up, and also melts away, and then the third wave merges into the ruins of the second. And after a while the fourth blunders into the writhing remnants of the others. We slow and have to run to catch up with the barrage.

The Somme offensive continued for five months. Haig made no changes to his strategy. However, he did allow some British generals, such as Rawlinson, to vary their tactics; they used smaller, carefully targeted attacks. In one assault, on 22 July, Rawlinson's men pushed three miles past the German front lines before being forced to withdraw.

Stung by such setbacks, the Germans tried attacking to regain lost ground. Eventually, when fighting died down in November, losses were about even. British casualties were about 400,000, French 200,000 and German 500,000.

Source B: An artist's impression of fighting at the Battle of the Somme in July 1916.

Tanks

The British were the first to use tanks in warfare, when they deployed 49 tanks at the Somme in September 1916. The use of the tanks had a big psychological impact. A German on the front line wrote, 'Our blood chilled. Mysterious monsters were crawling towards us over the craters. The word went along the line, "The devil is coming".'

But tanks had little real impact. Generals had no experience with tanks, so they were spread too widely and coordinated poorly with infantry.

Later, tanks became more useful. At Cambrai in 1917, 400 British tanks punched five miles through German lines. At Amiens in 1918, another 400 tanks successfully protected an infantry attack.

But they were liable to break down, had a top speed of 5 miles per hour and were vulnerable to armour-piercing bullets. Only 100 survived the Cambrai attack, and only six at Amiens. Tanks would become effective weapons – but not yet.

- Earl Haig
  General Haig's defenders say:
  - Generals from every army in the war believed that massed attacks would work.
  - Haig could not just defend. He was under pressure to regain land lost to Germany.
  - The Allies also needed to win in the west before Germany defeated Russia in the east, releasing about 1 million extra German troops.
  - The cold calculation was that these deaths were tragic for the Allies, but for Germany, as a smaller power, they would eventually be disastrous.
  - Haig had to use the weapons he had. New weapons, such as gas, airplanes and tanks, were not effective enough by 1916.

  His critics say:
  - Haig failed to learn from mistakes and explore new tactics.
  - He used new weapons badly and too little.
  - He ignored the advice of younger generals, such as Rawlinson.

Activities

1 Using the text, pictures and written sources in this topic and the previous one on trench warfare, make a list of key features of warfare on the Western Front.

2 Write a paragraph in support of each of the following phrases:
   a) The Battle of the Somme was a failure for the Allies.
   b) The Battle of the Somme was a success for the Allies.

3 How much change did tanks make to warfare between 1916 and 1918?

ResultsPlus
Build Better Answers

Why did Haig keep using massed infantry attacks at the Somme even though the British suffered so many casualties? (12 marks)

 Basic, Level 1 (1–4 marks).
Answer gives simple descriptions of tactics, but no analysis or supporting detail.

 Good, Level 2 (5–8 marks).
Answer gives more details of tactics – e.g. of the advancing shield of shells that preceded infantry – but still no analysis.

 Excellent, Level 3 (9–12 marks).
Answer links a detailed description of the slow changes in tactics to the reasons why change was so slow – e.g. the generals only had the old weapons (answer then gives details) until the new ones, like tanks, came along (answer then gives details of new weapons and when they were available).

Summary

- British tactics at the Somme were limited, but the battle badly weakened Germany.
- Tanks made a modest appearance at the Somme, but later became much more important.

3.4 The Second World War 1939-1945

Learning outcomes

By the end of this topic you should be able to:

● outline the role of technology and industry during the Second World War

● explain how societies were affected by warfare during this time.

1939–41: a war of movement

When Hitler invaded Poland in September 1939, it was feared that he would attack France next. So a British Expeditionary Force of 400,000 men was sent to defend France. When the attack came, in May 1940, British and French forces were swept aside; France fell in five weeks. Suddenly warfare was very different from how it had been in 1918.

A new attacking tactic, called **blitzkrieg**, using new technology, caused this difference.

● A *blitzkrieg* attack started with old-style shelling by artillery, but also new high-altitude bombers.

● Then several, separate groups of tanks, coordinated by radio, punched deep into enemy territory.

● These advances were followed by infantry, a traditional force but moving in small, independent attacking groups and at unprecedented speed, using lorries and parachute drops.

● Aerial cover came from Germany's new dive bombers, the terrifying Stukas.

The dominance of defence had been blown aside by the technology of aircraft, tanks, motor vehicles and radio communication.

British forces retreated to the coast where they were trapped on the beaches at Dunkirk. For ten days all kinds of British ships went to their aid; by 4 June 330,000 British troops had been rescued.

Germany planned to invade. But the Royal Navy kept control of the English Channel. And, thanks partly to the Spitfire (see picture), the Royal Air Force fought off the German Luftwaffe in the Battle of Britain. The German advance had been stopped.

Source A: The Spitfire was Britain's most successful airplane in the Battle of Britain. Each one cost about £6,000, and 20,000 had been produced by 1948.

1942–1945: total warfare returns

By 1942, Britain had been joined by the USA and the **USSR.** Each side began to use all aspects of society in their war effort. This was total war again.

In Britain, for example, to help the war effort the government changed the way society was organised.

● Compulsory conscription was reintroduced.

● To reduce reliance on imported food, rationing was enforced. There was also a 'Dig for Victory' campaign. About 1.5 million people had allotments to produce their own food.

● The government took control of food prices and wages. They did this to ensure the economy ran smoothly and to avoid public unrest.

● Key industries, such as mining, shipping and the railways, were taken under government control.

The government also ensured that industry manufactured the equipment needed by the armed forces. Britain produced 2,000 military airplanes in 1938; by 1943, it was producing 26,000 each year. This was typical of the Allied war effort. By 1944, compared to its enemies, the Allies were producing:

● twice as much steel;

● four times as many aircraft and tanks;

● seven times as many rifles and machine guns.

1944–1945: victory

With the might of the USA and USSR on her side, by 1944 Britain was fighting an outnumbered and weakened enemy.

- For example, for the D-Day landings in 1944, the Allies had air superiority of 70:1.

The Allies also had superior technology.

- The Germans had wasted some of their scientific energy on the V1 and V2 rockets, which were used to bomb Britain but had had little effect.
- British scientists developed **radar** to find and destroy enemy ships and aircraft; they also used **ciphers** to de-code secret enemy messages.
- The Allies also benefited from atomic technology. In the Far East, their main enemy was Japan. But the Allies won the race to make atomic weapons. In August 1945, the US air force dropped **atomic bombs** on Hiroshima and Nagasaki. Japan surrendered.

Source B: As an atomic bomb explodes, a mushroom cloud erupts over Nagasaki on 9 August 1945. The cloud reached 11 miles high.

This was four days after the first atomic bomb was dropped on Hiroshima. Over 200,000 Japanese were killed instantly in the explosions. Many more died later from wounds or radiation.

So far, these are the only two times that nuclear weapons have been used in warfare.

Lasting effects on society

Total war is waged against your enemy's people as well as their armies. So both sides in the Second World War blockaded enemy ports and used bombing of large towns, not just to disrupt industrial production but also to cause huge casualties and undermine public morale.

- During the Second World War, 400,000 German and 60,000 British civilians were killed in bombing raids on big cities.
- In total, over 20 million civilians were killed in Europe.
- From 1914 to 1918, civilians were 5 per cent of those who died in warfare; from 1939 to 1945, the figure was 33 per cent.

Altering things during wartime sometimes changes society permanently. For example:

- Some 100,000 West Indians volunteered for the British armed forces; there were 400 black flying crew and 6,000 ground staff in the RAF; 15,000 black seamen manned supply ships.
- Women were conscripted into the armed forces from 1941. They were also conscripted into wartime jobs in factories, on the land and in civil defence.

After 1945, there was still prejudice and discrimination against black people and women in British society. But it had been weakened by wartime experience.

The scale of casualties also affected society. In all, 55 million people died. This, and the deaths at Hiroshima and Nagasaki in particular, made society much more suspicious of war.

Activities

1. a) In what ways was warfare in the Second World War different from the First World War?
   b) In what ways was it similar?
2. In 1914, defence was more powerful than attack. By 1939, attacking forces were dominant. What caused this change?
3. What effect did technology and industrial strength have on the Second World War?
4. What impact did war have on society after 1939?

Summary

- Warfare had changed significantly between 1918 and 1939.
- Technology and industry contributed to the Allied victory in the Second World War.
- The Second World War showed how society can be affected by warfare.

3.5 Warfare 1945 to the present day

Learning outcomes

By the end of this topic you should be able to:

- explain technological improvements in modern warfare since 1945
- understand the effect of these changes upon warfare.

Technology has been the key factor in shaping the British experience of warfare since 1945. The main technological change is **nuclear warfare**.

- In 1952, Britain became the third world power (after the USA and the USSR) to develop nuclear weapons of its own.
- Britain now has about 200 nuclear warheads.

But many other nations have nuclear weapons too.

- By 2009, there were about 20 countries capable of producing nuclear weapons.

These nuclear weapons are much more powerful than the one exploded at Hiroshima.

- Cruise missiles can carry nuclear warheads hundreds of miles and hit very small targets.
- Ballistic missiles can carry nuclear warheads to hit cities thousands of miles away.
- Miniaturisation means that nuclear weapons may be very small; they could, for example, be carried unseen and exploded at will.

Source A: A British Harrier jump-jet pilot, checking the laser-guided missile fitted to his airplane.

Source B: A Corporal missile, pictured at a potential launch site in Hampshire in 1958. This missile was able to be fitted with a nuclear warhead.

Other technological changes since 1945 have produced even more equipment that has shaped modern warfare. For example:

- Helicopters have become the modern workhorses of the army. They are used to transport supplies and troops, for reconnaissance or to attack enemy troops or tanks. They provide great tactical flexibility for modern generals.
- Much of a modern army's equipment is computer-assisted or electronic. For example, missiles may be aimed and guided using satellites, lasers or gun cameras.

These changes in technology mean countries, such as Britain, have changed their approach to warfare. Major powers can no longer fight each other in total war without destroying each other. This is known as mutually assured destruction (suitably abbreviated as MAD). So, ironically, the destructive power of nuclear weapons has brought an unprecedented period of over 60 years of peace between major powers.

Modern wars

Peace between major powers has not meant the end of war. Britain has been in 80 conflicts since 1945 and British soldiers have died in combat in every year, except 1968. But modern wars take different forms, such as the examples below.

Asymmetrical wars

These are where major powers fight smaller countries. These wars have many of the features of limited warfare of the 18th century and before. For example, in the Falklands War against Argentina in 1982, Britain:

- fought with limited aims – the return of the Falkland Islands;
- used a small, paid, professional army of well-trained volunteers, with quality equipment;
- fought in a war in which their own civilians were only indirectly involved;
- returned with limited casualties – under 1,000.

Wars against terrorists

The British Army has been used to put down domestic uprisings or external terrorist attacks.

- For example, until the 1990s the IRA fought the British army in Northern Ireland. They also exploded bombs amongst civilians there and in Britain as acts of terror.
- Fighting like this is often called **guerrilla warfare**, with weaker forces fighting larger armies with a series of small attacks.

The future?

It is always difficult to predict the future. However, the history of warfare seems to suggest certain things we can be sure of.

- Warfare will always exist.
- Technology will shape whatever kind of warfare exists in the future.
- Despite the rise of technology, infantry, the core of fighting forces throughout history, will continue to have a key role.
- Civilians will always be affected by war – one reason why it is important to study it.

Society and modern wars

Social attitudes help to shape warfare. In modern society, the British public will not accept unnecessary loss of life among its soldiers. Generals have to do all they can to reduce casualties to limit the human cost of war to society.

Society also pays a financial cost for modern warfare; improved technology is costly.

- Second World War Spitfires cost about £6,000 each. In 2008, Britain ordered new Typhoon fighters at a cost of £80 million each.
- Total British military spending for 2007–2008 was just under £40 billion, about 10 per cent of total government spending – more than that spent on schools.

And civilians – including British civilians – have also paid with their lives in modern warfare. Fewer are called upon to fight, but generals and terrorists know that civilian deaths cause disruption and lower morale.

- In wars fought before 1900, civilian fatalities were 5% of deaths.
- In modern wars since 1900, civilian fatalities have been 90% of all deaths.

Some of these civilian deaths, caused by aerial or terrorist bombing, have been British.

Activities

1. What has been the impact of military technology since 1945?
2. Describe the key features of wars since 1945.
3. In groups, reflect on what you have learned from this book, and make a list of what you think will be the key features of warfare in the future.

Summary

- Technology has continued to shape warfare since 1945.
- Wars have continued since 1945, but because of nuclear weapons, they have been smaller, limited wars.

3.6 Case study: The Gulf War 1991

Learning outcomes

By the end of this topic you should be able to:
- explain modern limited warfare
- explain asymmetrical warfare
- explain the impact of technological superiority upon warfare.

British involvement in the Gulf War of 1991 is an example of limited warfare in modern times. The war had limited objectives. Iraq, led by Saddam Hussein, had invaded a neighbouring country, Kuwait. The **United Nations** condemned the attack; it authorised a Coalition of countries, led by the USA, Britain and France, to free Kuwait. Once this had been done, the Coalition left and Saddam was allowed to continue as Iraqi leader.

It is also an example of asymmetrical warfare. This is partly because the Coalition had more forces. Iraq had 250,000 troops, 2,000 tanks and 1,000 aircraft. The Coalition had 750,000 troops, 3,000 tanks and 1,800 aircraft. But mainly it is because the Coalition had better-trained and better-equipped forces.

Operation Desert Storm – air attack

The Coalition began its attack in January 1991 with a five-week aerial bombardment. This was powerful: they flew 100,000 sorties and dropped 88,000 tons of bombs. But, more important, it was technologically advanced. One effect was that the bombing was accurate.

Source A: An Iraqi aircraft hangar, hit with total accuracy by a guided bomb.

The Coalition used:
- stealth bombers dropping laser-guided bombs;
- cruise missiles fired from up to 1,500 miles away but targeted to an accuracy of ten metres;
- daisy cutters, bombs that destroyed everything within hundreds of metres of the explosion.

As a result of the bombing:
- The Iraqi air force was destroyed on the ground; only two Iraqi MiG-29s took off, and these shot each other down by mistake.
- Seventeen of Iraq's power stations were disabled; electricity supply fell to 4 per cent of pre-war levels.
- Water pumping stations and sewage plants were destroyed; raw sewage poured into the River Tigris, from which the desperate people of Baghdad were taking their water.

The bombing therefore inflicted military damage and disrupted the whole of Iraqi society. In five weeks, Iraq was reduced from one of the most advanced Arab countries to the most regressive.

FASCINATING FACT

The Coalition targeted many bombs and missiles by GPS (global positioning system). In 1990, a US officer travelled to the US embassy in Baghdad with a GPS receiver. He took one reading and flew home. This reading enabled the Coalition to use GPS to hit vital targets all over Iraq.

Operation Desert Sabre – ground attack

In February 1991 the Coalition sent in their ground troops. Again, the contest was unequal. The first contact was between rival tanks. Superior technology made all the difference. The British Challenger tank had a top speed of 45 miles per hour, was protected by Chobham armour and was armed with **depleted-uranium** shells. The Iraqi T-72 was 25 years old, had a top speed of only 37 miles per hour, armour half as strong and a gun with a shorter range. Their T-55s were even older. The Coalition tanks fired from three times the distance that the Iraqis could. One Coalition unit of tanks destroyed 50 Iraqi tanks in ten minutes.

After only three days, Saddam ordered his army to retreat. His well-trained and disciplined Republican Guard put up some resistance. But his conscripted troops were poorly trained and lacked morale; they deserted or fled in disarray. Many were killed fleeing across their own minefields. Others fled in any vehicles they could find, down the main road from Kuwait to Baghdad. Without any air cover, they were relentlessly picked off by Coalition aircraft – rather like 18th-century cavalry picking off infantry in retreat.

Casualties

About 20,000 Iraqi soldiers were killed. But since military targets in Baghdad were in the middle of a huge city, there were also about 50,000 civilian deaths. Most deaths were caused by bombing.

In contrast, there were only 350 Coalition deaths.
- About half were caused by Iraqi fire.
- Half were caused by accidents and **friendly fire**.
- Some British soldiers returned with stress-related illness or undiagnosed ailments – known as Gulf War Syndrome.

Accidental deaths and stress-related illness have probably been features of warfare for centuries. But it has only been modern **media** coverage that has brought them to light.

Decisive factors

There were two decisive factors in the war:
- financial superiority – for example, Britain spent over £3 billion on the Gulf War;
- technological superiority, especially Coalition airplanes, bombs and tanks.

But Source B suggests that one other decisive factor has also been key throughout the history of warfare.

Source B: From *The Cambridge History of Warfare*, edited by Geoffrey Parker.

Training, discipline and organisation underpins the efforts of military forces. That has been the essence of western warfare since the time of the Greeks and Romans. In Iraq, the Coalition forces had those advantages. Their opponents did not.

Source C: The wreckage of vehicles left when Coalition aircraft massacred fleeing Iraqi troops on 'the Highway of Death'.

Source D: A Coalition officer describing bomb victims.

The **overpressure** was incredible. Blood was coming from their eyes and mouths. They had no will to do anything, their legs wouldn't work, they were paralysed. Groups of soldiers ambled around, and you'd shout at them, but you wouldn't get through.

Activities

1 List the technological advantages of Coalition forces in the Gulf War.

2 There were three decisive factors in this war:
- financial superiority
- technological superiority
- superior organisation and discipline.

In a group, discuss whether:
a) one of these was the most important
b) all of them are inseparably linked.

Summary

- The Gulf War of 1991 was an example of modern limited warfare and asymmetrical warfare.
- Superior technology was a key factor in the victory.

3.7 Recruitment

Learning outcomes

By the end of this topic you should be able to:

● understand the different kinds of armies that have existed since 1350

● understand why these different kinds of armies existed.

This chapter should help you track the changes which took place in recruitment since the Middle Ages. It will also give more detail about modern recruitment.

Feudal armies

In 1350 Britain was still a feudal society. Kings granted their most powerful supporters land; in return these landowners provided service – usually as mounted knights – in the king's army. Even poorer subjects owed military service to their lord. Under the Assize of Arms of 1181 all English freemen were obliged to serve in the king's army. The body of men raised this way was called a levy.

However, feudal armies had weaknesses. These are described on page 5. English kings therefore began to turn to mercenaries.

Source A: Infantry from a mock feudal army.

Mercenary armies

After 1350, English kings increasingly allowed their subjects to pay money, called scutage, in place of serving in the army. They then used this money to pay for mercenaries – experienced soldiers, willing to fight for a fixed period of time in the king's army. The king would pay a sum of money to a mercenary leader, often called a 'captain'. In exchange, the captain would provide a number of soldiers, whom he paid a daily wage. The contract between the soldiers and the king was called an indenture.

For his Agincourt campaign in 1415, Henry V raised an army of about 8,000 men, most of whom were mercenaries. He mainly needed archers. Most of these were English countrymen, called yeomen. Kings encouraged their subjects to practise archery, so that there would be a plentiful supply of mercenaries.

Mercenaries – typical daily wage		
● Mounted knight	1 shilling	(5p)
● Mounted archer	6 pence	(2½p)
● Archer on foot	3 pence	
● Foot soldier	2 pence.	

A typical labourer's wage at this time was 4 pence per day. However, soldiers also shared the booty or ransom money from successful campaigns.

English kings would not always be able to hire English soldiers. There was a thriving market in hiring out soldiers in Europe, however, so the soldiers fighting in the English king's army could often be foreign mercenaries. This started a tradition of foreign soldiers fighting in British armies that continues to today.

Source B: *The Autobiography of the British Soldier* by John Lewis-Stempel, Headline Review, 2007.

In 1509, Henry VIII revived the English habit of warring with France. But he lacked foot soldiers, gunners, cooks and builders, since the part-time county levies would not serve abroad. So Henry recruited, via his self-styled 'captains', 25,000 volunteers. But, for more modern soldiers, musket men and pike men, Henry had to hire German mercenaries.

Standing armies

Relying on mercenaries, often foreign, was risky. English kings had always retained a very small number of soldiers as their personal guards. Gradually, these personal guards were expanded into permanent **standing armies**, manned by full-time professional soldiers.

England's first standing army was the New Model Army created in 1645 by the Parliamentarians in the English Civil War. This evolved into the British Army. Recruitment to this army in the 18th century is described on page 22. Traditionally, Britain has had a small standing army of well-trained volunteers. It could be small because, as an island, Britain relied upon the Royal Navy for protection from invasion. Britain usually employed foreign troops or paid its allies to provide additional troops in times of war.

Therefore, in 1914 the British Expeditionary Force sent to face Germany was only 100,000 strong. The Emperor of Germany called it 'contemptibly small'. The government began a recruitment campaign. By 1916, Britain had an extra 2.5 million volunteers. Men joined for a variety of reasons:

- adventure – there was a belief that the war would be short – most expected that it would be 'over by Christmas'
- jingoism – war was regarded with enthusiasm
- patriotism – a famous recruitment poster announced 'Your Country Needs You!'
- outrage against the enemy – government posters blamed Germany for the war and portrayed them as cruel
- duty – other posters declared 'Women of Britain say GO!' or featured children asking 'What did you do in the war, Daddy?'

Conscripted armies

High casualties meant that volunteers were not enough. Britain introduced conscription in 1916.

- At first only unmarried men aged 19–40 were called up; by the end of the war, it was married men, too.
- By 1918, 7 million men served in the war.

When the Second World War broke out a similar boost to recruitment was needed.

- Men aged 18–40 had to do six months of military training (known as National Service), and men aged 20 to 23 were conscripted into the army; the age group was expanded during the war.
- By the end of the war, over 3.5 million men had been enlisted.

The modern army

National Service was retained until 1960. However, as limited warfare resumed, Britain returned to its small army of highly trained volunteers. The minimum age for volunteers is 16, although soldiers cannot do active service below 18. A separate force for female soldiers was ended in the 1990s and now women serve alongside men in almost all areas. In 2008, one in six British soldiers in Afghanistan was a woman. Soldiers normally sign up for 22 years' service. Britain currently has an army of about 100,000 soldiers.

Activities

1 This is a list of the key features of feudal soldiers:

- unpaid
- little training
- part-time
- temporary.

Copy the list. Now complete your own lists for:

a) mercenary soldiers 1350–1700

b) volunteer soldiers in early standing armies 1600–1800

c) conscripted soldiers in the 20th century

d) volunteers in the modern British Army.

2 In one sentence each, explain what caused these changes:

a) feudal to mercenary armies

b) mercenary armies to standing armies

c) volunteer armies to conscription?

Summary

- Recruitment changed over time.
- Soldiers recruited to the British army included:
  - feudal armies
  - mercenaries
  - volunteers and conscripts.

3.8 Movement and provisioning

> **Learning outcome**
>
> By the end of this topic you should be able to:
>
> ● describe changes in the movement and provisioning of troops from the Middle Ages to the present day.

Movement in the Middle Ages

Feudal armies moved at the speed of a walking man. Knights travelled on horseback; horses pulled an army's carts. However, the majority of armies in 1350 were infantry, who had to march to battle. To march 15 miles in a day was good going, particularly in bad weather. Henry V's army marched 260 miles in bad weather in the two weeks before Agincourt.

The development of heavy cannon after about 1450 meant that the movement of armies became even slower. And as campaigns abroad became more common, the absence of reliable maps was another obstacle to the movement of armies.

If campaigning abroad, British armies depended upon the navy, using sailing ships, to transport them and their supplies safely to and from the theatre of war.

Source A: A British Hercules military transport aircraft, 1999.

Movement of modern armies

This situation persisted until the middle of the 19th century. Ever since that time, a series of changes in technology has radically altered the movement of armies.

● Steam ships allowed more reliable movement of troops and supplies to overseas campaigns. The picture on page 30 shows their use in the Crimean War.

● The railway caused an even greater change. It was 15 times faster than marching. It could also manage very heavy loads. In the Crimean War, the British built a 25-mile railway from the port of Balaclava to supply their trenches.

● Motor vehicles caused a huge change too. By the First World War, lorries could be used to transport troops and supplies; jeeps and motor cycles also had their uses.

● However, perhaps the greatest change was caused by air transport. By the Second World War, troops and supplies could either be transported rapidly to bases hundreds of miles away or paratroops could be dropped behind enemy lines. Since the 1950s helicopters have become the main method for moving troops over short distances.

Improved technology was the key. In the Gulf War in 1991, 40,000 British personnel were moved by air and sea to a battle site 3,000 miles from London.

Provisioning – living off the land

During feudal times, kings did not have the money to provide arms and food for their armies. Neither did they have a big enough civil service to order, store and distribute weapons and food. Feudal armies were therefore expected to provide their own weapons and protective clothing. They also 'lived off the land' – a romantic term that meant, in practice, that armies stole food from the fields and stores of the local population where they were fighting.

Baggage trains

Later, kings had more permanent armies. They also wanted to use these armies on longer campaigns, even in winter. This meant that kings had to make better arrangements for feeding their troops. The development of gunpowder weapons meant that standardised weapons were needed. Soldiers could no longer be left to provide their own weapons. Kings had to provide weapons, protective clothes and uniforms.

To provide food, weapons and other supplies for their armies, commanders at first used baggage trains. This term describes the wagons, stores and people that followed armies around between feudal and modern times. Many of these would be women; some were wives with children; others earned a living doing men's cooking, washing and sewing. Some were prostitutes; venereal disease was always rife among armies. There were also men earning a living as doctors, blacksmiths, carpenters, tailors and cobblers.

As armies became bigger, baggage trains became bigger – and more vital – too.

- An army of 30,000 men required 25,000 horses and huge quantities of gunpowder and shot.
- It also needed 20 tons of bread and the equivalent of 1,500 sheep every day.

The baggage train was vital to an army; if the baggage train was destroyed, the army was fatally weakened. You will remember the eagerness of the Royalist cavalry to attack the enemy baggage train at Naseby.

Modern provisioning

Modern technology has changed provisioning for armies. Because food and supplies can be stored centrally and then moved very quickly by land or air whenever needed, there is no need now for an army to travel with what it needs.

- During the First World War, for example, over 3 million tons of food were sent from Britain to the troops in the trenches. Some 300,000 British personnel were employed to store, distribute and cook it in field kitchens.

When on active service now, troops are given emergency rations that they carry and cook themselves as best they can.

- British troops in Afghanistan in 2009 were issued with ration packs containing pre-packed food such as corned beef, fruit dumplings in custard, chocolate – and even tikka masala – providing up to 4,000 calories.

Modern provisioning is therefore very complex. The British Army now has a separate Royal Logistic Corps to arrange its transport, catering and supplies. This has about 16,000 soldiers.

Activities

1 Draw a diagram or graph to represent changes in the ways that armies have moved around between 1350 and the present day. Annotate your diagram or graph to explain it.

2 Write a short paragraph to explain each of the following:
   a) living off the land
   b) baggage train
   c) field kitchen
   d) emergency rations
   e) Royal Logistic Corps.

Summary

- Movement in the Middle Ages mainly involved marching. In modern times, technology has speeded up movement.
- Provisioning in the Middle Ages mainly involved living off the land or baggage trains. Modern armies have specialist personnel to provide for an army's needs.

3.9 Propaganda and the media

Learning outcomes

By the end of this topic you should be able to:

● understand how much society has known about warfare from 1350 to the present

● understand how this knowledge affects the conduct of warfare.

Propaganda

During the Middle Ages, though there were many wars, people were not as informed about them as we are today. There were various reasons for this.

● Armies were small; fewer people had direct experience of fighting.

● Communication was limited. There was no radio, television or the Internet. Even the impact of written pamphlets was reduced by low levels of literacy.

● Kings did not need to inform or consult the people about their wars. They were not elected by the public; the armies they used were royal armies, not the public's armies.

There are exceptions. In the English Civil War, both the Royalist and Parliamentary forces needed the support of the people. Their military bases and food supplies would be weakened without this. So this war involved both sides putting out publicity to support their own views on the war – propaganda.

Source A: A Parliamentary English Civil War banner. It shows soldiers slaying the many-headed Royalist monster.

Source B: A First World War poster showing cruelty by Germans. It was intended to get British women to support the war.

Propaganda is part of the experience of warfare. It is biased information: it may not be lies; it could be selected facts or views. Governments put out propaganda during wars for many reasons.

● They may want to boost support for the war. In the First World War, the British public were pressurised into enlisting by government recruitment posters with slogans such as:

'Your Country Needs You!'
'Come and Do Your Bit'
'What Did You Do in the War Daddy?'

● They may want to harm their opponents, using posters such as the one above.

War reporting

There was very little independent reporting of wars before modern times. There were few newspapers before 1800, for example. But anti-war propaganda, published by opponents of the government, did exist. There were:

● novelists such as Jonathan Swift;

● pamphleteers such as Edmund Burke;

● and cartoonists such as James Gillray, all of whom attacked wars fought by the British government in the 18th century. But before 1850, there were so few means of spreading information that anti-war propaganda was weak.

The first independent war reporting to have an impact on the public was by William Russell, writing for *The Times* during the Crimean War. (See page 33.)

William Russell's war reporting outraged the public and helped to cause the reform of the army. However, it did not reduce the popularity of war. Between 1860 and 1914, British society was jingoistic, and the public supported the First World War. This meant that, on the whole, reporting of the First World War was also supportive.

Source C: *The Daily Chronicle* reporting on the Battle of the Somme in 1916.

> Some ground was gained at great loss of life to the enemy, though not without many casualties to ourselves. Fortunately the proportion of [our] lightly wounded men was wonderfully high.

Source C was written days before it was reported that only one mile was gained and 20,000 British soldiers died.

This kind of social attitude explains some aspects of the First World War that still confuse us:
- how those suffering from shell shock could be executed for cowardice;
- how generals could continue to cause massive losses, but not change tactics.

Social attitudes were still supportive of the war; generals were not held to account.

However, public support for warfare has never been so great since. It has been reduced by:
- two world wars, 1914–1918 and 1939–1945;
- the fear of nuclear war;
- greater knowledge of the horrors of war, publicised by new methods of communication such as the telegraph, radio and television, films and the Internet.

This extra publicity has brought a mixture of support and criticism of British war efforts. Some military mistakes have been reported that in earlier times would have remained unknown. Compare the source below, for example, with Source C above.

Source D: A BBC website report, September 2006.

> A coroner hearing the case of a British Royal Marine killed by friendly fire in Iraq has ruled his death was caused by serious failings by the military. Christopher Maddison, 24, from Scarborough, was killed by his own side during a river patrol in 2003. The coroner said the marine had been let down by those in command.

The influence of attitudes in society

Shifting social attitudes have changed the way wars are fought in the 20th century. Governments publicise their own version of events. During the Falklands War in 1982, the British government spokesman briefed the press daily on the progress of the war. His reports were broadcast on television.

They also make every effort to avoid casualties. Since the invasions of Afghanistan in 2001 and Iraq in 2003, the media broadcast details of every death among British soldiers. Commanders know that if there are too many deaths the campaigns will have to stop.

Yet another change caused by social attitudes is that commanders are more accountable for their actions in war. Following the Geneva Convention in 1864 (see page 31), the Hague Conventions were passed in 1899 and 1907. These set out how wars should be conducted. Since then, several war leaders have been tried and executed for atrocities during warfare.

Individual soldiers are also held to account. A British soldier was jailed for a year in 2007 for mistreating an Iraqi civilian. The British government paid the civilian £3 million compensation.

Activities

1 Why did the British public know so little about its wars before about 1850?
2 What is propaganda and what is it meant to achieve?
3 Social attitudes were very supportive of the First World War. What effects did this have on the way the war was conducted?
4 Social attitudes to war are now more mixed. What effects does this have on the way wars are now conducted?

Summary

- British people knew very little about the wars Britain fought before about 1850.
- Since then, social attitudes have changed and that has changed the way in which wars are fought.

3.10 Care of troops

> **Learning outcomes**
>
> By the end of this topic you should be able to:
> - understand how the care of troops has changed since about 1350
> - understand the causes of these changes.

Accommodation

No accommodation was provided for feudal or mercenary armies. They were formed solely for campaigns – so there was no need for barracks – and on campaign they slept in the open or found whatever cover they could.

However, once standing armies were created, they needed somewhere to live in peacetime.

Lodgings were used first; they were just rented rooms scattered around the regimental headquarters.

Barracks like the Ravensdowne Barracks were built from about 1700, but conditions were poor. This remained typical for 150 years.

A Royal Commission, reporting after the Crimean War, in 1857, found that generally:
- conditions in barracks were overcrowded;
- water for washing was limited;
- changes of clothes were rare;
- lice and parasites flourished.

Source A: Soldiers in an army barracks in 1875.

Most barracks were kept locked at night, to prevent desertions and the soldiers who unlocked in the morning sometimes vomited from the foul stench of smoke, urine and faeces which emerged each morning. The Commission's report led to improvements, though living conditions remained very basic.

And better barracks could not help with conditions on campaign, where living conditions were even more basic. Troops slept in tents, which were scant protection against the cold. They complained most when they were stationed abroad, far from home and in unfamiliar climates.

In general, then, whether soldiers were at home or on campaign, unhygienic conditions meant that infectious disease was a constant companion. The most common were typhus, typhoid, dysentery, food poisoning and skin diseases, like scabies.

Era	Pay	Problems
Early Middle Ages	None – military service was a feudal duty.	Soldiers could be more concerned with looting so that they gained something from the campaign.
Late Middle Ages	Mercenaries were paid on average the same as a labourer (about 4 pence per day).	Payment of their wages was often late or they were not paid at all.
English Civil War	The New Model Army were England's first full time, permanent soldiers. The standard pay was 2 shillings per day, a small amount but paid regularly.	Many people were opposed to a permanent army and felt it gave too much power to the state.

Since 1645 to the present day there has been a permanent army of full-time soldiers, receiving regular pay (see page 55).

Medicine

For feudal armies before and after 1350, there was no specialist medical support provided at all; the wounded treated themselves or relied upon friends.

This improved slightly when larger mercenary armies were formed. Some men and women who claimed medical expertise joined the baggage trains of armies and gave what help they could, in exchange for pay.

But it was not until standing armies were created that permanent medical staff were appointed. In the New Model Army, created in 1645, each regiment had a medical officer, with a warrant officer as his assistant. Permanently with the troops, they gave ongoing medical care, not just on the battlefield.

This system continued until 1898, when a separate, specialist Royal Army Medical Corps was created, which served the medical needs of all other troops. The RAMC is still in action today.

However, in the early days these medical staff were of limited use. From 1350 to modern times, the real problem was that nobody really understood how disease spread. This had two disastrous effects for soldiers.

- Most battlefield injuries were open wounds, caused by swords, bullets, etc. From 1350 to about 1860, surgeons wasted their time treating these with useless ointments – often moving, still smeared with one man's blood, to the next patient. Most wounds became infected and caused death from blood poisoning.
- Second, as mentioned above, the filthy living conditions of soldiers allowed germs to spread deadly infectious diseases. Until Florence Nightingale showed the value of good hygiene in the Crimea, nobody knew how to stop infections. Consequently, many more soldiers died of illness than injury on the battlefield. In the Peninsular War (1808–1814), for example, 85 per cent of British deaths were due to illness.

Real medical progress for soldiers, therefore, had to wait until after about 1860, with the use of:

- antiseptic surgery
- anaesthetics
- X-rays
- blood transfusion.

Of the 390 deaths among Coalition troops in the Iraq War, none was caused by illness.

Modern conditions

Modern society holds governments accountable for every soldier's care (see page 52–53). If soldiers on active combat do not have the pay, equipment, supplies or food they need, the media and public opinion put pressure on the government. Consequently, standards are now much higher.

In 2008, the average annual earnings of full-time employees in Britain were about £25,000. Army privates earned less than this. Army corporals, the next rank up, earned more. Higher ranks earned much more. Soldiers, except those on the lowest ranks, are paid better than they were in the past.

Conditions of service have also improved. Soldiers now have their time balanced between training at base and service on active duty. Single soldiers live in barracks in rooms for between one and four people. Married soldiers are entitled to houses at subsidised rent.

Medical care is now of a high standard. The Royal Army Medical Corps has a staff of about 3,000 men and women, and levels of training among its staff are equal to those in civilian hospitals.

Finally, during their service, modern soldiers are trained in a host of skills, ranging from combat skills to vocational skills in areas such as communications, administration and catering. Soldiers therefore leave the army well placed to earn a living in civilian life.

Activities

1 What have been the main improvements in the care of soldiers in each of the following areas:
   a) pay
   b) accommodation
   c) medicine?

2 Explain how each of the following has helped to cause improvements:
   a) permanent armies
   b) science
   c) social attitudes.

Summary

The care of troops improved slowly from 1350 to 1850, but has improved much faster since.

3.11 Summary: Warfare c1900 to the present day

The rate of change

Since 1900 the impact of warfare on society in Britain has been changing.

- From 1900–1914 and from 1918–1939, the impact of war on society grew gradually, as more newspapers, radio and newsreels made the public more aware of the realities of war.
- From 1914–1918 and from 1939–1945, the impact of war on society increased suddenly and significantly because of the effects of warfare, such as conscription and bombing.
- Since 1945, the impact of warfare has continued to grow on society. Television, films and the internet have made the public even more aware of the realities of warfare.

If we were to try to represent these changes on a simple diagram, it might look like this.

Source A: A graph showing impact of warfare on society 1900–present.

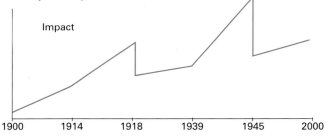

Activities

1 Now you can do a diagram. Here is a simple description of changes in recruitment since 1900:
   - from 1900 to the present day, Britain has relied upon a small army of volunteers, except
   - from 1916–1918 and 1939–1945, when there was conscription
   - and 1939 to 1960 when there was National Service.

   How would you represent these changes on a simple diagram?

Activities

2 a) Write a simple description of the rate of change in weaponry since 1900.

   b) Draw a diagram that gives a simple picture of this rate of change.

   c) What other key features of warfare since 1900 would it be possible to represent in this kind of way?

Factors affecting change

Two factors that have shaped Britain's experience of warfare since 1900 have been:
- social attitudes
- technology.

For example, the positive attitude of the British public at the time of the First World War:
- helped recruitment in 1914
- meant conscription was tolerated from 1916
- kept morale high despite hardships.

Activities

3 Write a list of ways in which social attitudes affected the British experience of warfare during the Second World War.

Technology also affected the British experience of warfare.

For example, during the First World War:
- the dominance of machine guns accounted for many British casualties on the Western Front.

Activities

4 Write a list of ways in which technology changed the British experience of war during the Second World War.

Significant factors

Some factors are more important than others because they have more impact or significance.

For example, in the First World War, the use of gas attacks was new, but it was not significant. Wind made them unreliable and gas masks were an easy solution.

Activities

5   Write a brief explanation of why tanks were not a significant factor in the First World War.

Nuclear weapons were a significant factor in shaping warfare after 1945.

Activities

6   Write a brief explanation of why nuclear weapons were a significant factor in changing the British experience of warfare from 1945.

 ResultsPlus
Build Better Answers

What can you learn from Sources B and C about changes in the movement of troops since 1900? (4 marks)

■   **Basic, Level 1 (1–2 marks).**
Answer gives information from the sources, for example noting the use of a lorry and horses in Source B, and a helicopter in C but does not address the issue of change.

●   **Good, Level 2 (3–4 marks).**
Answer identifies changes, giving details from the sources in support. For example, showing that transport had become faster and more flexible, and that troops could also be moved by air compared with the earlier era of land transport.

Source C: British troops being moved into combat by a Chinook helicopter during the Iraq War in 2003.

Source B: A British convoy moving troops and supplies during the First World War.

Introduction

For the core part of the Warfare exam you have to answer three questions.

The first question will always ask you what you can learn about an aspect of warfare from two sources. The two sources will normally be from two different periods and you will be expected to talk about change or continuity.

The second question will give you a choice between two options and you then have a choice of answering either question 3 or question 4.

As there is only a limited choice of questions in the exam you need to make sure you have good knowledge of all the topics in the specification and that you are prepared for the different types of questions that are asked.

For the exam you can be asked to show examples of change or continuity in the developments in warfare, to explain why change happened at a particular point, or to assess how important something was. Questions can focus on a single section of the core or can ask you to make comparisons across more than one section.

Self-evaluation checklist

What you should know by the end of the core content, The Changing Nature of Warfare from c1350 to the present day.

Generally, 1350 to the present day:
- what changes were taking place in warfare
- the significance of these changes
- the impact of these changes on society
- the extent of change and continuity
- what factors were causing or preventing changes in warfare
- what factors were speeding up or slowing down changes
- specifically, the effects on warfare of:
  - technology and communications
  - governments
  - individuals
  - attitudes in society.

1350 to 1700:
- types of soldiers, weapons and tactics used
- how soldiers were recruited, trained, moved and supplied
- how Henry V and the Agincourt campaign and Oliver Cromwell and the Battle of Naseby illustrate warfare at this time.

1700 to 1900:
- types of soldiers, weapons and tactics used
- how soldiers were recruited, trained, moved and supplied
- How the Duke of Wellington and the Waterloo campaign and Florence Nightingale and the Crimean War illustrate warfare at this time.

1900 to the present day:
- types of soldiers, weapons and tactics used
- how soldiers were recruited, trained, moved and supplied
- how Earl Haig, the Western Front and the Battle of the Somme and the Gulf War of 1991 illustrate warfare at this time.

Exam style questions

1: Study sources A and B [for example Source E, page 5 and Source B, page 21]. What can you learn from these sources about changes in the ways in which soldiers were trained? (4 marks)
Explain your answer, using these sources.

2: The boxes below show two weapons used in warfare. Choose ONE weapon and explain why it had an important effect on the way that battles were fought in that period. (9 marks)

The musket 1450–1700	The machine gun 1860–1918

3: Why was there stalemate for so long in fighting on the Western Front during the First World War? (12 marks)
You may use the following in your answer and any other information of your own:

- Allied and German trenches stretched from the Belgian coast to the Swiss Alps in 1915
- Gas was first used in 1915
- Tanks were used at the Somme in 1916.

ResultsPlus
Maximise your marks

3: Why was there stalemate for so long in fighting on the Western Front during the First World War? (12 marks)

Student answer	Examiner comments	Extract from Improved student answer
The German attack on France in 1914 was stopped just short of Paris. From then on, neither side could defeat the other and both sides dug trenches.	The student has given information about the nature of the fighting on the Western Front and has included some accurate detail, for example about machine guns, and the Battle of the Somme.	To improve the answer, the student added:
When one side attacked, the other side fought off the attack.	This is an accurate description of the stalemate going on for a long time on the Western Front and would be given a mark low in level two.	'The German attack on France was stopped because their infantry could not advance; defence was stronger than attack. When infantry attacked, they were mown down by machine gun and rifle fire. So, armies could dig in and defend; but they did not have the weapons to attack and capture enemy positions. Because neither side could advance, it was stalemate.' The stalemate went on so long because generals kept attacking enemy defences with artillery and gas. But they did not work because; defenders used dug-outs and gas masks. When the generals attacked with more men and tanks, the tanks were not reliable. New tactics didn't work so stalemate went on until 1918.
Many men were killed in the attacks by machine guns and rifle fire.		
So the two sides just fired artillery shells at each other and, from time to time, launched new attacks with even more men, for example when the British attacked at the Battle of the Somme.	• To improve the answer, the student needs to explain:	
They tried new weapons, such as tanks and gas, but the stalemate went on until 1918.	• WHY there was stalemate on the Western Front and WHY stalemate lasted so long.	

4.1 The changing nature of warfare from Roman Britain to c1350

Introduction

This part of your course looks at developments in warfare from Roman Britain to 1350. You will look at:

- changes in aspects of warfare like weaponry, tactics, recruitment, provisioning and movement of armies;
- what made those things change and why they changed at that particular time – especially how society and technology changed warfare.

And you will learn about:

- warfare among the Romans and Celts who lived 2,000 years ago, including a Celtic war leader called Boudicca;
- and how warfare changed in medieval times, for example at the Battle of Hastings and in the Third Crusade.

Activity

1 Draw your own version of the timeline below, but draw it larger. During the next few lessons, as you read in more detail about changes during this time, add key events to your time line.

Medieval times

Roman Britain

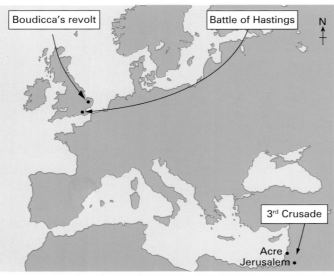

Boudicca's revolt

Battle of Hastings

N

3rd Crusade

Acre
Jerusalem

Crusades

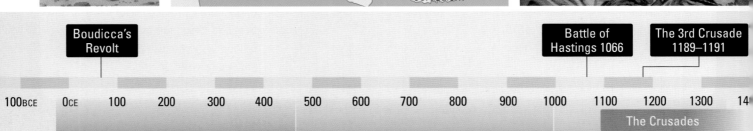

| Boudicca's Revolt | | Battle of Hastings 1066 | The 3rd Crusade 1189–1191 |

| 100BCE | 0CE | 100 | 200 | 300 | 400 | 500 | 600 | 700 | 800 | 900 | 1000 | 1100 | 1200 | 1300 | 14 |

The Crusades

Roman Empire | The Dark Ages | Medieval Times

4.2 Warfare in Roman Britain

Learning outcomes

By the end of this topic you should be able to:

● describe the key features of warfare in Roman Britain

● explain how Roman society affected the type of army at that time.

By 100CE, the Roman Empire was very large. It covered modern Italy, France and Spain, North Africa, the Middle East and the Balkans. From 43CE to about 410CE, the Romans ruled England and Wales too.

What type of warfare did the Roman army bring to Britain?

An army normally reflects the society which creates it. The Roman army is an example of this. The Roman Empire was large, wealthy and highly organised – and it created a large, well-funded and highly organised army. The people of Britain had never seen an army like it before:

● the Roman army was a well-trained, paid and permanent army of about 300,000 men;

● it had its own weapons factories, artillery ranges;

● soldiers had to have medical examinations and meet standards for age, intelligence, eyesight and height – 5 foot 10 inches;

The main unit was the **legion**:

● there were 28 legions; each had 6,000 men. This meant 150,000 fighting men;

● there were about the same number of auxiliary troops, from conquered armies and allies.

Each legion was divided into 10 cohorts – a cohort had 600 men, six **centurions** and an officer.

Each legion would have some specialist archers and 120 horsemen to act as **scouts**. It would also have its own medical staff, carpenters, vets, armourers, surveyors and priests.

The army leaves its mark

Technology was also a feature of Roman society. Ancient Rome is famous for engineering feats like **aqueducts**. This also affected the type of army the Romans brought to Britain. As well as fighters, soldiers were military engineers.

So the Roman army changed Britain by:

● building fortresses and walls (such as Hadrian's Wall) which were used for centuries after;

● building roads (such as Watling Street) which still shape modern routes;

● founding many of today's cities, such as London – some of its camps became towns, such as Chester;

● building drainage and sewage systems in towns.

Activities

1 List three characteristics of the Roman army.

2 How did the army change the physical appearance Britain?

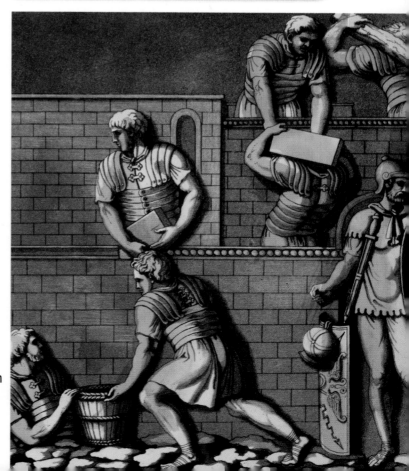

Source A: A modern drawing based on Roman carvings. It shows Roman soldiers involved in a building project.

Weapons, armour and equipment in the Roman army

Source B: A Roman carving

This is a Roman carving showing a legionary. Like most Roman soldiers he is an infantryman or foot soldier.

His main weapons were daggers and swords. You can see his dagger in the picture. Soldiers used two-foot long, double-edged swords; they were mainly used for stabbing, but could also sever limbs when swung.

Most soldiers also carried two seven-foot throwing spears with an effective throwing range of 30 metres.

Roman soldiers wore coarse tunics. As you can see, they were bare-legged. They wore leather marching sandals.

Roman society had well established metal and textile industries. So equipment in the Roman army was well developed.

To protect themselves, Roman soldiers wore light armour. Notice how it is made up of interlocking metal plates and metal helmets, with metal flaps to protect the neck and cheeks.

Also note the soldier's shield. These were usually cylindrical in shape, over a metre long and almost a metre wide. They were strong, made of wood and edged with metal. A group of soldiers could make a solid wall of shields to protect themselves from arrows or spears.

As well as his weapons and armour, a legionary had to carry tools for building and a spade for digging. A Roman army never struck camp without pitching tents and digging latrines.

Army tactics

A society as organised as the Romans produced an army with organised tactics. They used discipline, training and fitness more than weight of numbers.

The Roman writer, Flavius Vegetius, said, 'Victory comes not by numbers and courage, but by skill and training. To this, Rome owes the conquest of the world.'

Officers had manuals for tactics, such as using high ground when defending, and having the wind behind them to help arrows.

Roman generals would normally position infantry in the centre of their army, with cavalry at the sides and archers and spear throwers behind.

- First, a hail of arrows and spears would be sent to disrupt the enemy;
- then the infantry would drive forward into the enemy, forming a wedge shape or a series of wedges, protected by their shields;
- this would force the enemy back and crush them together, allowing the Roman soldiers to stab at their enemy between their shields;
- the cavalry were used to cut down retreating enemy troops.

Sometimes the army had to attack towns rather than other armies:

- legions had specialists who would use Roman engineering skills to build artillery, catapults to hurl rocks or large spears at the enemy;
- they also built towers, sheds and ladders to help soldiers attack fortified walls.

Life in the Roman army

Life in the Roman army was as organised as Roman society. Generals took training very seriously. They even used **gladiators** to train troops in the use of weapons. The Roman historian, Josephus, wrote, 'their **manoeuvres** are like bloodless battles and their battles like bloody manoeuvres.'

Roman society was wealthy enough to care for soldiers well:

- on campaign, soldiers sheltered in leather tents and rations were generous – 3 lb of bread, 2 lb of meat and two pints of wine per day;
- Roman forts had fresh water and safe ways to dispose of sewage;
- larger forts had hospitals. Army doctors used herbs as medicines and opium to kill pain. All this meant that, on average, Roman soldiers lived five years longer than other citizens.

But discipline was also taken very seriously:

- the penalty for breaking regulations during a campaign was death;
- if a group of troops misbehaved, it was decimated – one tenth of them, selected by lot, were flogged to death as a warning to the rest.

Source C: A modern picture showing a Roman army besieging a town. Note the ladders, sheds, tower and catapult, as well as the use of shields to protect soldiers under the walls.

The Roman army leaves

The Roman Empire gradually weakened and lost its control of Western Europe. The Roman army abandoned Britain in about 41CE.

There were to be no armies in Britain as large and organised as the Roman army for well over a thousand years.

Activities

3 Using the text and pictures on these pages, briefly describe the soldiers in the Roman army, their weapons, tactics and conditions of service.

4 Study Source C. When the Roman army attacked fortified towns, in what ways did it benefit from:

a) good discipline and training?

b) advanced technology and engineering?

ResultsPlus
Build Better Answers

Explain three ways in which Roman society affected the Roman army. (9 marks)

■ **Basic, Level 1 (1–3 marks).**
Answer gives very general information with little or no detail.

● **Good, Level 2 (4–6 marks).**
Answer gives details of the army but does not explain the effect of society.

▲ **Excellent, Level 3 (7–9 marks).**
Answer gives detail about the Roman Army and explains how society affected these, e.g. it describes how metal and textile industries improved Roman weapons and uniforms, or how the wealth of Roman society meant soldiers were well fed.

Summary

The origins, culture and organisation of Roman society shaped Roman warfare and the Roman army.

4.3 Warfare in the Celtic world

> **Learning outcomes**
>
> By the end of this topic you should be able to:
> - describe the key features of warfare in the Celtic world
> - explain how Celtic society affected warfare in the Celtic world.

Much of the land in Europe conquered by the Romans was occupied by people called the Celts. So the Romans fought wars against the Celts all over Europe – and in Britain, which was occupied by Celts at this time. But Celtic society – and Celtic warfare – was very different from the Romans.

The Celts did not form one united country, like the Roman Empire did. There were dozens of small independent Celtic tribes living in scattered villages, growing corn and raising cattle and pigs. This kind of society created very different wars from those of the Roman Empire.

How Celtic society affected warfare

Celtic society did not want to rule large areas of land. So Celtic warfare was mainly raiding nearby villages. They just wanted cattle, valuables or slaves – or to weaken their enemies by killing families and burning villages and crops.

Celtic society was too poor to afford large, permanent paid armies like the Romans had. So Celtic society relied on all men taking part in warfare – to defend their village or take part in a raid.

Celtic society depended upon success in warfare. If enemies captured their women or children – or even their cattle – it could destroy a village. So, successful warriors often became tribal leaders.

Celtic society relied upon their men to work the land. They could not afford to lose men in battle. So sometimes, instead of all-out-war, a small number of men were chosen to fight each other in a staged battle, which decided the outcome of the war.

Celtic weapons

The Celts were skilled in metalwork. This enabled the spear to become a key Celtic weapon. Some were long, with large spearheads for stabbing. Others were smaller, throwing spears. Most Celtic warriors also had swords up to a metre long and used for slashing, rather than stabbing. Warriors also normally had a large, decorated wooden shield, often covered in leather, with a metal boss. With no separate army, most Celtic warriors wore their normal clothes for fighting – coarse trousers, shirt and cloak, often dyed in bright colours.

Celtic society was harsh, and this made Celtic warfare brutal. Warriors did all they could to frighten the enemy. Some fought naked, with their bodies painted in dye; they had long hair dyed blond with lime, beards and droopy moustaches. Before battles, warriors beat their weapons against their shields, shouting, blowing horns and beating drums. They destroyed the enemy's sacred sites to show that they were not afraid of their gods. And they displayed the bodies of victims to intimidate their enemies. Diodorus Siculus, a Roman historian from the 1st century CE, wrote: 'They cut off the heads of enemies slain in battle and parade them on the necks of their horses.'

Source A: A modern drawing of Celtic warriors. The artist based this on Roman accounts written by Romans such as Julius Caesar, a Roman general who fought the Celts.

Celtic society had a simple class structure led by a small number of noble warriors who had better equipment. Some had leather smocks and helmets; others bronze or iron helmets, decorated with coral or even gold. A few nobles fought on horseback. Their four-cornered saddles gave them stability, enabling them to use their swords and spears better. And in some Celtic tribes, noble warriors used battle-chariots. These were two-wheeled vehicles, about four metres long. A charioteer drove while the warrior threw his spears before alighting and fighting on foot.

Source B: A Celtic helmet from the 1st century BCE found in the River Thames near Waterloo Bridge. Celtic helmets, finely decorated shields and chariots show us that not all Celtic warriors would have been equipped as simply as those in the picture opposite.

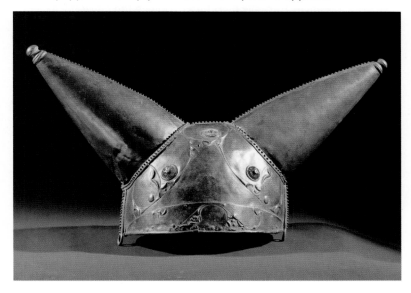

Celtic warrior bands

Some Celtic tribes became wealthy enough to pay a few full-time warriors. These formed war bands. They had warrior schools in which to practise their skills. In a society so dependent upon the success of its warriors, it is not surprising that these warrior bands were given high status in Celtic society. They sometimes even claimed to have special powers granted them by gods and held religious initiation rituals for new members.

Larger battles

Occasionally, the Celtic tribes joined together to wage larger wars. For example, as the Roman Empire became stronger and expanded across Europe, the Celts were at constant war with the Romans. In about BCE50, the Celtic leader Vercingetrix led an army of about 100,000 Celts against Julius Caesar in Gaul (modern France).

But Celtic society was not suited to large battles. It had few permanent, trained soldiers, and none of them was drilled in fighting in large groups. Indeed, since Celtic society valued the heroism of individual warriors so highly, Celts had no enthusiasm for fighting as units. Celtic society did not even have a written language, so it had no manuals to spread information about battlefield manoeuvres or tactics. And there were no clear leaders in Celtic society. So large Celtic armies formed up in tribal groups, with warriors fighting alongside those they knew. They gave no thought to creating blocks of troops using the same weapons.

Celtic armies tried to intimidate their enemies before large battles. Celtic leaders paraded before their troops, boasting of past victories. But, as befitting a simple society, Celtic tactics were also very simple – mainly just massed attacks. They often centred their attack on one point, but this cramped them for space. And Celtic warriors needed space to swing their swords. In contrast, the Romans trained for combat in compact spaces, using their short swords and daggers to stab, particularly into the armpits.

Roman victories over Celts show that a trained, disciplined and motivated army will often defeat a much larger army that lacks training and discipline.

Activities

1 Using the text and pictures on these pages, briefly describe the fighting, weapons and tactics of Celtic warfare.

2 Explain three ways in which Celtic society shaped fighting and tactics in Celtic warfare.

Summary

Celtic society shaped the fighting and tactics involved in Celtic warfare.

4.4 Boudicca's Revolt – Celts v. Romans

Learning outcomes

By the end of this topic you should be able to:

- describe the events of Boudicca's Revolt
- highlight key features typical of Roman and Celtic warfare in Boudicca's Revolt.

Historical sources

We have little contemporary information about Boudicca's Revolt. The Celts left no written accounts. Our main written sources are histories by two Romans. Tacitus was the most important Roman historian of this period. Agricola, his father-in-law, served with the Roman governor of Britain, Suetonius, and was probably an eyewitness source for Boudicca's Revolt. We also have an account by Cassius Dio, but only a summary survives. He wrote after Tacitus and used his account, but we do not know what other sources he used.

The background

Boudicca was the wife of Prasutagus, king of the Iceni, a Celtic tribe who lived in Britain, where Norfolk is today. Cassius Dio tells us she was tall, had long red hair, a piercing stare and a harsh voice. When Prasutagus died, in 60CE, he left half his wealth to the emperor Nero and half to his wife, hoping the Romans would allow her to rule as queen. In the words of Tacitus, the Roman historian:

Source A:

> The event was otherwise. The king's land was ravaged by the centurions; they pillaged his house. His wife, Boudicca, was whipped; her daughters were ravished. The relations of the king were reduced to slavery.
>
> Boudicca called a rebellion amongst the Iceni. She was joined by other Celtic tribes. The Trinovantes joined because they had been mistreated by Roman soldiers who settled in Colchester, their capital. They also resented being told to worship the ex-Roman emperor Claudius and to pay for a temple in Colchester dedicated to him.

The Revolt

The rebels' first target was the city of Colchester. The Roman inhabitants of the city appealed for reinforcements, but they were sent only 200 auxiliary troops. In the words of Tacitus:

Source B:

> Unguarded, they were surprised and overpowered by the Barbarians in one assault. The colony was laid waste with fire and sword.
>
> Petilius Cerealis marched to relieve the city with 200 men, but the British horde, flushed with success, advanced to give him battle. The legion was defeated, and the Roman infantry cut to pieces.

Soon afterwards, the rebels attacked London. At that time, it was a relatively new town, founded after the Roman conquest of Britain in 43CE. But it had grown to be a thriving commercial centre with a population of travellers, traders and Roman officials. The rebels burnt it down and killed everyone. Archaeology shows that a thick red layer of burnt debris covered coins and pottery that were dated from before 60CE and were found within the bounds of the Roman city.

Finally, the rebels attacked the city of St Albans. In the words of Tacitus:

Source C:

> The inhabitants of Verulamium [St Albans] were put to the sword. The ways of a savage people lead them always to plunder. Wherever they saw weak resistance and great booty, they were sure to attack with the fiercest rage. The number massacred in the [three] places which have been mentioned, amounted to no less than seventy thousand. To make prisoners was not in the idea of a people who despised all the laws of war. Aware that vengeance would overtake them, they were resolved to make sure to glut themselves with the blood of their enemies.

Dio's account gives more detail: the noblest women were displayed, impaled on spikes with their breasts cut off and sewn to their mouths, 'to the accompaniment of sacrifices, banquets, and wanton behaviour' in sacred places.

The Battle of Watling Street

Suetonius, the Roman governor of Britain, took an army of 10,000 and, near Watling Street, confronted the horde of 230,000 Celtic rebels. He drew them up carefully in a narrow gorge which protected his flanks; a forest behind made an attack from the rear impossible. The Britons took no such trouble. They just spread out on the open plain. Tacitus says:

Source D:

> They formed no regular line of battle. Detached groups arrived, in frantic transport, bounding with exultation, and so sure of victory, that they placed their wives in wagons at the edge of the plain, so they could see the British valour.

Boudicca drove along the ranks of the Celtic army, insulting the Romans and rousing her troops. Suetonius too addressed his men.

With Boudicca at the fore, the Celts charged. As they advanced, they were channelled by the sides of the gorge into a tightly packed mass. At approximately 40 yards, their advance was slowed by a volley of Roman spears, thrown from behind the front row of Roman shields. Very few Britons had armour. But if the Britons did use a shield, the Roman spears bent, making them impossible to pull out; the Celts had either to discard their

Source E: A modern picture of Boudicca. There are no mosaics or sculptures from the time that show us the events or what Boudicca looked like.

shields and carry on unprotected, or fight with shields weighed down by a heavy iron spear. A second volley followed, as each Roman legionary carried two throwing spears. This tactic destroyed any organised advance by the Britons.

With the Britons in disarray, Suetonius ordered his legionaries and auxiliaries to push forward in standard Roman wedges, creating a front line that took the appearance of the teeth of a handsaw. Protected by shields and with their superior discipline, the Romans were able to continue fighting as fiercely as ever, stabbing though gaps in their shield wall with swords. The Britons, in contrast, crowded together and buffeted by shields, had little space to use their slashing swords.

The Roman cavalry, spears extended, then entered the fray and attacked the Britons from the flanks. They also rode to the rear and slaughtered the oxen pulling the Celtic wagon train. As their losses mounted, the Britons lost heart and tried to retreat, but their flight was blocked by the ring of wagons. As they retreated, they were massacred by Roman cavalry. The Romans killed not only the warriors but also the women and children. Tacitus reports that 'almost 80,000 Britons fell' compared with only 400 Romans. The revolt was at an end.

Activities

1 What can you learn from Sources B and C about the reasons why the Britons were so ruthless with the Romans at Colchester and St Albans?

2 From the events of Boudicca's Revolt, what can you find that was typical of:
   a) Roman warfare
   b) Celtic warfare?

3 'In warfare, a smaller, disciplined, trained army will often defeat a larger, untrained and ill-disciplined force.' Use the events in the Battle of Watling Street to explain why this happens.

Summary

Boudicca's Revolt illustrates several key features of Roman and Celtic warfare.

4.5 Early medieval warfare: The age of the mounted knight

> **Learning outcomes**
>
> By the end of this topic you should be able to:
> - describe the key features of warfare during early medieval times
> - explain how medieval warfare reflected medieval society.

From about 700CE, the feudal system developed in Europe. This new way in which society was organised changed the way armies were formed.

Under the feudal system, a ruler granted land to his leading supporters. They became his **tenants-in-chief**, sometimes called barons. In return, they supported his rule and served as knights in his army. These knights usually divided their land among their own sub-tenants. Their tenants did not pay rent as we do today; instead they promised to give support and military service. Lists of knighthoods in 1166 stated:

Source A:

> In 1166 Robert, Baron of Stafford, held land from the king, and promised him in exchange 60 knights. Robert sub-let most of that land; in exchange, he was promised 51 knights. He kept the rest of the land and personally provided the other nine knights.

Mounted knights

So feudalism made knights an elite class of landowners – and an elite class of feudal soldiers.

These wealthy knights could provide their own horses, swords, shields and lances. At first, they wore just an iron cap, a quilted **hauberk** and a round shield; as they became wealthier, armour developed. By 1300, metal breastplates and back plates were common. After about 1400, for a while knights wore full suits of armour, though these were soon seen to be impractical. Knights also went to war with servants, tents, carts and kitchen equipment.

Medieval infantry

However, knights were the minority of feudal society and therefore the minority of most armies. The largest part of an army was the infantry. In England, Henry II extended the feudal system. In 1181 he passed a law, called the Assize of Arms. This law said that all freemen who owned a small amount of property had to provide their own arms and fight – usually as infantry – for the king.

Some foot soldiers were pike men. Their weapons were originally spears. But during medieval times, spears developed into three- to six-metre pikes. Pike men gathered in dense squares or circles around their own knights or archers and pointed their pikes towards the enemy as protection against cavalry or infantry charges. By adding an axe-head near the top of their pikes, they created **halberds**, with which they could thrust and cut.

Source B: An illustration from the 14th century showing mounted knights, archers and, in the top left, pike men.

About half the infantry were normally archers.

- Some shot crossbows, which were more accurate than normal bows and so powerful their bolts could pierce armour. But crossbows were slow to re-load, so less useful in battle than bows.
- Bows were more common in England than crossbows. At this time, they were quite short – about 50cm. A trained bowman could fire 10–15 arrows per minute with an effective range of up to 200 yards.

69

Soldiers' equipment

After about 950CE, some wore chain mail shirts and wore iron helmets. Infantry rarely used plate armour in early medieval times; it was too expensive and too heavy.

Infantrymen in feudal armies were normally poor, so many had no special protective clothing for battle at all.

Those most prepared wore a **gambeson** or a leather jacket for protection and carried a shield.

Source C: A contemporary picture of men-at-arms fighting at the Battle of Halidon Hill, in 1333.

Medieval infantrymen usually carried a small dagger, a mace or a sword for hand-to-hand combat. Some would carry an axe.

In general, medieval infantry were very poorly equipped. One reason was cost. In about 1300, a pike or halberd, mace, axe and short mail shirt together cost about half a year's average wages.

Training and discipline

Feudal societies could not have permanent armies. A knight or soldier's military service to his lord was limited – normally to about 45 days. Kings and some wealthy knights might have small numbers of permanent, paid soldiers, called men-at-arms. But their main armies were summoned to do their feudal duty for a battle or campaign and then dismissed.

This reduced the chance of training.

- A knight's fighting skills were part of the culture of noble families, so young men practised in mock fights and tournaments.
- And training was useful for archers, so, in England various laws were passed requiring young men to practise archery.

But there were no permanent barracks for feudal armies and no central training for military leaders or their troops.

So tactics had to be simple. Foot-soldiers had no drill, so commanders found it very difficult to manoeuvre their forces in battles.

A further problem was lack of discipline. Knights were independent; they were not used to military discipline. They sometimes followed personal glory rather than orders.

The only real discipline amongst knights was their code of chivalry, which taught them to treat enemies with respect. In the Battle of Brémule in 1119 only three knights were killed; but 140 were taken prisoner. This was partly chivalrous mercy.

It was also partly because the captors could claim the horses and armour as **booty** and demand a ransom to set their prisoners free again.

Limited warfare

The feudal system produced small armies. William the Conqueror's army of 8,000 at the Battle of Hastings in 1066 was considered large. King Henry II of England could only call upon 6,000 knights in the 12th century.

The **campaigning season** was limited too. Fighting was only possible from the late spring – after crops had been sown – until the autumn, after which the weather could make it impractical to move troops and fight battles.

These factors meant that this was an age of limited warfare.

The aims of most wars were limited too. Rulers often used their armies like private possessions – to force a rival to give him land or money, or to settle a dispute between royal families. Unlike later, rulers rarely destroyed their enemy's army or conquered their country.

Fighting was also limited. In feudal society, rulers had good reasons to avoid battles:

- at a time when rulers led armies, losing could mean they were killed, like King Richard III at the Battle of Bosworth in 1485;
- or they could be captured, like King John II of France at the Battle of Poitiers in 1356.

Being captured meant paying a huge ransom in exchange for freedom.

So, instead of fighting, commanders might spend most of their time manoeuvring their armies to avoid a battle or to trap their enemy in a hopeless position. This manoeuvring might involve skirmishes or raids. Occasionally an army would just **plunder** an area, either to destroy an enemy's food supplies or capture a town to seize booty.

Even if you wanted a battle, it was not easy:

- it was difficult to know where your enemy was; commanders relied on **intelligence** from scouts using imperfect means like smoke signals, church bells or pigeons;
- if the commander of a feudal army wanted to fight, he would have to hold a council of war with his leading noblemen to get their agreement.

Battlefield tactics

So, in feudal society, battles were not the most common means of waging war. But when battles were fought, these were the tactics employed:

Preparing for battle

Generals would try to draw up their armies in positions which were difficult to attack – on the top of slopes or protected at the back and sides, perhaps by woodland, marshes or rivers.

They would then try to weaken the enemy, perhaps using arrows or, commonly using cavalry.

Cavalry attack

Knights considered themselves the elite of feudal society, and they liked to take the leading role in battles. They were the tanks of medieval warfare. They would form into a tightly packed group and charge, hoping to burst through the enemy defences. A mounted knight (150 lb), his armour (60 lb) and weapons (40 lb) required a sturdy horse. At a top speed of about 15 miles per hour – probably as fast as you could run – the combined weight of the knight and horse made a colossal impact.

Source D: A 14th-century picture of knights leading a charge at the Battle of Muldorf, 1322.

Defence

The defending infantry would try to weaken the cavalry attack. They would:

- fire arrows into the attacking cavalry;
- position troops behind spiked posts;
- put troops in tight squares, protected by pikes;
- lay **caltrops** on the ground to injure the attacking horses.

The infantry charge

Befitting their place in society, the attacking infantry followed the mounted knights, to exploit gaps in the enemy defences. If necessary, knights dismounted and also fought on foot.

Once hand-to-hand combat began, fighting was like frenzied butchery. Face-to-face, men tried to smash an opponent's skull or arms with a mace or axe, or to pierce his armour joints, or slash his belly or cut the tendons in arms or legs with an axe or a sword.

Retreat

Sometimes mounted knights charged and then pretended to retreat; this sometimes tricked infantry into chasing them. Once they were away from their protective spears or pikes, the knights then turned upon the disorganised infantry. Unprotected foot soldiers were at a massive disadvantage against mounted knights.

The same was true at the end of a battle. In hand-to-hand fighting, once one side turned and fled in disorder, it usually led to slaughter. It was common for more soldiers to be killed in the final retreat than in the battle itself.

Leadership

There was usually little difference in the size of medieval armies or their weapons. Often the outcome of a battle was therefore determined by the quality of leadership or the discipline of the troops.

Source E: Infantry at the Battle of Courtrai in 1302, using halberds, swords and axes, while stumbling on the bodies of the dead.

The age of the mounted knight?

The noble, mounted knights were the most powerful force on the battlefield. They are often described as the decisive force.

But this is partly because records of battles come mainly from histories, songs, poems and novels written by the noble classes themselves, boosted by romantic images of jousting tournaments. So, even in early medieval times, the importance of the mounted knight may have been exaggerated. Infantry were always the largest part of feudal armies.

The decline of the mounted knight?

By 1350, towards the end of medieval times, the power of the mounted knight was in decline – because of tactics and technology. From about 1300, commanders changed their tactics to use longbow archers to weaken cavalry. They also used pike men with halberds to hook knights off their horses and hack them to death with their axe-heads.

By 1350, gunpowder brought muskets and cannon; horsemen were very vulnerable to these. Although cavalry remained a feature of armies for some time, they were never the powerful force they once were.

Activities

4 In what ways was warfare in medieval times 'limited warfare'?

5 Why were battles not the most common form of warfare in medieval times?

6 Why did the battlefield power of the mounted knight change during medieval times?

Siege warfare

Attacking armies could only conquer an area if they captured its castles. So invasions normally turned into a series of sieges. Siege tactics were much the same as they had been in Roman times. They normally followed a familiar pattern of :

- encirclement;
- battery;
- attack;
- negotiation.

Encirclement

Encirclement cut off the town or castle from reinforcements, supplies and, possibly, water supply. Sometimes this was enough to starve the castle or city into surrender.

Battery

Battery involved attacking or undermining the walls. Medieval artillery, such as **trebuchets** or **mangonels** could be used to hurl rocks and other missiles at the walls. Or tunnels could be built under the walls and then deliberately collapsed in the hope of bringing the wall down. **Battering rams** were used against gates.

Source F: The siege of Jerusalem in 1099, from a French manuscript dated 1462. Notice the use of swords, bows, crossbows, ladders, fire and a siege tower.

Attack!

After weakening the walls, attackers could then mount an assault. They used ladders and siege towers. It took great bravery, training and discipline. Normally, attacking armies were bigger than defending garrisons so, once inside, the result could be slaughter.

Negotiation

If they thought their plight was hopeless, defenders would sometimes agree to negotiate a surrender.

This would usually involve paying the attacking army large amounts of money either to go away or, at least, not to kill the inhabitants when they took over.

Defenders usually decided to wait behind their walls, rather than risk battle. They hoped that
- attackers ran out of food, money or patience;
- or infected water and exposure to the weather meant they fell victim to disease;

- or an army was sent to relieve the town.

Most sieges failed for these reasons. Lincoln was relieved in 1141 for example. Calais held out for 11 months in 1346 against an English siege.

Feeding the Medieval Army

The feudal system provided men for an army; but it did not provide food and supplies. Provisions were therefore suppled in various ways.

Baggage trains

An army would set out with supplies carried by a large baggage train of carts, mules and horses. But there was a lot to carry:

- each man in the army needed about 3 lbs of food per day and each horse 20 lbs of fodder – grass or hay.
- Water in streams or wells caused illness, so armies carried mead, beer or wine if possible.

Supply by sea

The best generals marched near coasts or rivers so they could get extra supplies from ships. During the Third Crusade in the 12th century, Richard I of England supplied his army by sea. An army supplied by ships could move at about 20 miles per day.

Plunder

When food ran out, soldiers were sent to forage the countryside or plunder villages. An army that needed to forage as it marched slowed to about five miles per day. Foraging left a wasteland that could cause more deaths among the population from starvation than casualties in battles.

Source G: A medieval army pillaging a house in Paris in about 1350. Notice that they are not just taking food.

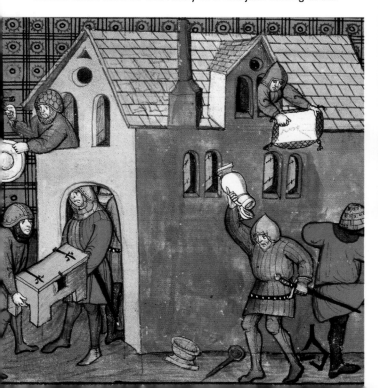

Caring for the Medieval Army

No medieval commanders had the means to provide properly for their soldiers. More died from a lack of general or medical care than were killed outright on the battlefield.

General care

Medieval knights usually went on campaign with servants to look after them. An army baggage train also usually contained hundreds of women, usually wives or family members. These women and servants would:

- cook, wash and mend clothes, dig latrines and care for the animals;
- search soldiers and their clothes for lice and fleas, which could cause deadly diseases which spread through the army.

Medical care

Medieval armies had few, if any medical staff. Any wound which pierced the intestines or the chest normally caused fatal infection. Wounded men were often left, unattended on the battlefield overnight after a battle. Many died from blood loss, infection or exposure. It was an act of mercy for the victorious side to return to the battlefield the next day and despatch the wounded.

Activities

7 How did besiegers attack a town or castle?

8 List the reasons why most sieges failed.

9 Describe how medieval armies were
   a) fed
   b) cared for.

Summary

In medieval Europe feudalism shaped society; it also shaped medieval warfare.

4.6 The Battle of Hastings 1066

Learning outcomes

By the end of this topic you should be able to:

● understand the key features of the Battle of Hastings and William I's leadership there.

● recognise typical features of warfare during early medieval times.

In early August 1066, Duke William of Normandy gathered an invasion fleet. He intended to attack England and claim the throne. But northerly winds kept him in port. It was 28 September before the he could set sail.

During those weeks the English king, Harold, suffered set-backs.

● Firstly, many of his soldiers became impatient and returned home to harvest their crops.

● Then a gale weakened his fleet.

● Finally, a Viking army of 10,000 men invaded the north of England. Harold had marched his army for six days to defeat the invaders at the Battle of Stamford Bridge.

But all this left the south coast unguarded; William landed unopposed. He ravaged local villages, taking supplies and goading Harold to fight him.

Harold's war council urged him not to rush to battle. Harold ignored their advice. He tried to surprise William by the speed of his response and set out on the 190 mile march south. But William had sent out scouts, who spotted his approach.

Source A: An extract from the Bayeux Tapestry, a Norman record of William's invasion. This part shows the Norman knights foraging for food.

The armies

Norman army	Saxon army
Army size: 8,000 in total ● 2,000 knights ● 4,000 infantry ● 2,000 archers	Army size: 7,500 in total ● 2,000 elite **housecarls** ● 5,500 **fyrd** militia with no cavalry
Arms: ● Knights were well-armed with lances, spears and swords. They also had mail shirts and metal helmets. ● Archers had short bows with a killing range of 100 yards. ● Other archers were armed with crossbows.	Arms: ● Housecarls used swords and 5 foot long battle axes. ● They were also armoured in mail shirts and metal helmets. ● The fyrd were mainly farmers who had little military training. Most would have a spear and shield and little else.

The Battle

So on the morning of 14 October, Harold drew up his forces near the road from Hastings to London, on Senlac Hill, about 10 miles inland.

It was a fine defensive position, his right flank protected by a marsh and the centre and left flank by a steep slope. The battle began at about 9.30a.m.

William's strategy was

● to weaken the enemy with arrows,

● followed by an infantry attack,

● then a cavalry charge.

But Harold's men had formed a strong **shield wall** on the hill, with his housecarls at the centre.

● Norman arrows hit shields and had little effect.

● The English fought off the infantry charge, hurling down stones and javelins.

● When the Norman cavalry charged, the Saxon shield wall was intact and bristling with spears.

Source B: This extract from the Bayeux Tapestry shows the Norman cavalry failing to breach the Saxon shield wall.

The Norman cavalry charge stalled. Many horses were killed or shied away. The Normans retreated and the Saxon infantry chased them down the hill. In the melee, William's horse fell.

Norman sources – like the Bayeux Tapestry - say that William raised his helmet, showed his face, declared that he was alive and rallied his knights. The Normans turned and set upon the English infantry. Many, including Harold's two brothers, were killed before they could scramble back to the safety of the shield wall.

The battle then resumed, as before. The Norman knights even tried to use the tactic of feigned retreats to lure the Saxons off the hill again. The battle became a matter of **attrition**, with heavy face-to-face, hand-to-hand combat at the edge of the shield wall.

For hours, the Norman assaults failed.
- But gradually, as housecarls fell, their places were taken by less powerful fyrdmen.
- Then Harold was killed, possibly shot in the eye by an arrow and ridden down by knights.
- This deflated Saxon morale and the fyrdmen fled, pursued by Norman knights.

About 5,000 English and 3,000 Normans had died.

Summary

The Battle of Hastings shows several features typical of warfare at the time.

The verdict

William's victory was a triumph for the feudal army of mounted knights, archers and infantry.

It was also a victory for leadership.

- Harold chose his ground well.
- But he would have been better to wait for reinforcements.
- William marshalled his troops well and inspired them when needed.
- William also benefited from good luck.

Activities

1 What can you learn from the Bayeux Tapestry about the armies that fought at the Battle of Hastings?
2 How far was the Battle of Hastings typical of medieval warfare?
3 How did each of these contribute to victory at the Battle of Hastings?
   a) Size of the Norman army.
   b) The discipline of the armies.
   c) Leadership.
   d) Luck.

Source C: The death of Harold.

4.7 The Third Crusade and the siege of Acre 1189-1191

The Crusades were a series of holy wars in medieval times, in which Christian armies from Europe tried to capture Christian sites in the **Holy Lands**, which had been occupied by Muslims. At first, the soldiers of the Third Crusade besieged and captured the coastal town of Acre. After this, they tried to fight their way into Jerusalem, but failed.

At the start of the siege of Acre, the crusaders attacked the city walls with siege towers. One tower was four stories high and could carry 500 men. It was covered with hides, soaked in vinegar, to ward off fire. But a mangonel on the city walls launched a flaming pot of **Greek fire**. A Muslim chronicler, Ibn al-Athir, reported:

'The fire spread. The tower was consumed. It happened too swiftly for the Christians to flee. Men, weapons, everything was burned.'

The Muslim leader, Saladin, used the normal tactics of the time to help the defenders. He
• sent them supplies by sea and
• harassed the attackers, cutting off supplies.

The crusaders' food and water started to run out. By winter, the weather worsened. Disease spread. So many were the dead that bodies were carted to Acre's moat to help fill it in. A French contemporary chronicler, Ambroise, described the problems of the besieging army:

'A crowd gathered when a horse was killed; Even the entrails were eaten…Owing to the rain, a severe disease spread among the men; their limbs went soft with dropsy (swelling), and from the violence of the disease, the teeth of some were loosened and fell out.'

Richard I of England joined the siege in June 1191, bringing an army of about 8,000. The first attempts by his men to scale the walls, using ladders, failed. But then his **sappers** undermined a key stronghold, 'The Accursed Tower'. And two huge siege engines nicknamed 'Evil Neighbour' and 'God's Own Sling' began to fracture the walls. It was a gradual process of attrition.

In July 1191, a large breach was made in the walls. The town realised its plight was hopeless. It surrendered, paying a ransom of 2,000 prisoners and 200,000 gold pieces. The siege had lasted two years and cost the besiegers 10,000 lives.

Source A: This map of Acre shows that the town had typical features of a fortified town, with water on three sides and high walls and towers protecting the other.

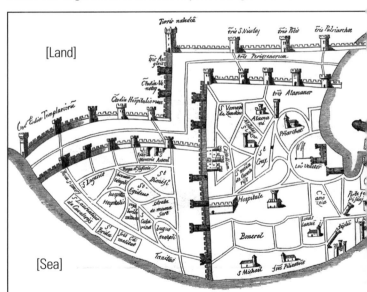

After the siege of Acre, the crusaders moved on Jerusalem, staying close to the coast, to get supplies by sea. Typically, Richard and Saladin shadowed each other's armies, looking for advantage and avoiding battle if they could. There was one battle, at Arsuf, but Richard never won control of the land around Jerusalem. Eventually, the two sides negotiated a treaty allowing Christians access to the holy city. Richard left the Holy Lands in October 1192.

The itinerary of Richard I

The memoires of Crusaders were collected in a chronicle soon afterwards, by a London clergyman called Geoffrey de Vinsauf. His book was called *The Itinerary of Richard I and others to the Holy Land*. All the extracts on this page come from *The Itinerary*. They give us extra information about siege warfare and armies in medieval times.

Attacking the walls

The King proclaimed that anyone who removed a stone from the wall would receive two pieces of gold. The young men swarmed forward. Even in the midst of the enemy's missiles they worked on bravely at tearing at the wall.

Undermining the walls and scaling ladders

Meanwhile, men reached the foundation and filled the space dug out with logs, and set them on fire; these ignited the piles of wood forming the foundations of the wall, which sunk down gradually, with a slight inclination, without falling altogether. So on the one side were the French applying ladders to the wall that was partially thrown down, and trying to cross over; whilst the Turks were also mounting ladders on the other side to defend the breach.

Source B: A medieval catapult, called a ballista.

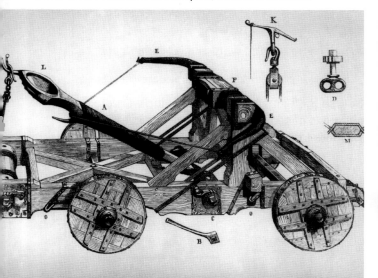

Battering ram

With great labour and expense a machine (was built) like a ceiled (covered) house. It used a mast of a ship, with its head covered with iron, which was impelled by many covered men; and, by frequent blows, they tried to cast down the city walls.

Harassing a marching army

The Turks annoyed our men, and, keeping to the side of our army, did them all the injury they could, by throwing darts (spears) and arrows. The Templars on that day lost so many horses by the attacks of the Turks that they were almost reduced to despair.

Plunder

Whoever was greedy of gain, and wished to plunder the booty, returned to the place of battle, and loaded himself to his heart's desire.

Activities

1 After reading these two pages, in a group of four pass a piece of paper round. Each time it reaches a person, he or she must write on it one typical feature of early medieval warfare illustrated by the Third Crusade. See which group can get the longest list.

2 Does the siege of Acre illustrate the strengths or the weaknesses of sieges as a form of warfare? Justify your answer.

Summary

The Third Crusade and siege of Acre show typical features of warfare at that time.

4.8 Summary: Warfare from Roman Britain to c1350

In the preceding pages, we have looked at:
- Roman Britain
- Celtic society
- medieval feudal society.

These different societies cover almost 1,500 years.

Today, we are used to things improving as time goes by. When this happens, we can picture progress in a simple diagram, like this.

Source A: Graph showing continuous, steady improvement.

However, the story of warfare from Roman times to 1350, is not a simple story of steady progress.
- Things certainly improved at the start of the Roman Empire; the Roman army which conquered Britain was improving in weapons, organisation, leadership and training.
- But during exactly the same years, there was no improvement at all in Celtic armies or wars.
- When the Romans left Britain, in 410CE, all the improvements were lost.
- After 1066, the Normans brought feudalism to Britain; armies began to improve again. But, they were still less advanced in 1350 than the Romans had been in over 1,000 years before.

What we learn from this is that change is much more complicated than we might have thought.

Activities

1 Just to illustrate how complex change is, try drawing a graph for 100BCE to 1350CE to accommodate the four bullet points above. It is possible; but it's not simple!

Another thing about modern life is that many things seem to be constantly changing, very fast. Take fashion, computers and holiday travel, for example. They are all totally different now from how they were 50 years ago.

This constant change sometimes hides how common continuity is. Throughout the long period we have been studying, some key features of warfare stayed the same. For example:
- Most armies remained small – usually no more than 10,000 men.
- Infantry remained the biggest part of armies.
- Infantry decided the outcome of most battles.
- Swords and spears, of various kinds, remained the most important weapons.
- The feigned cavalry retreat remained a useful tactic and, for infantry, they were never more vulnerable than when in retreat.

Activities

2 Look at the three case studies in this section:
  - Boudicca's Revolt
  - the Battle of Hastings
  - the Third Crusade.
  List things that were similar in each one.

Source B: A modern picture of Celtic warriors. The picture is based on written descriptions of Celtic warriors from about 50BCE

We have also discovered something else about:

- Roman society
- Celtic society
- medieval feudal society.

Each one had a very different kind of society. This meant that each society's warfare was different from that in the other societies. Differences in society caused differences in weapons, tactics, the organisation and recruitment of armies and army life.

For example:

- The Roman Empire was centralised; power and wealth were concentrated in the hands of the emperor. He could therefore afford a permanent, paid and well-equipped army. This meant that ordinary citizens did not normally fight in battles.
- Celtic society was decentralised; power and wealth were divided among thousands of Celtic villages. There was no central army; each village or tribe arranged their own forces. The quality of weapons varied. Every man was expected to fight.
- Feudal society was also decentralised. A king gave away to his supporters power over much of his land. In exchange, he received military service. Most men might expect to fight. But soldiers provided what weapons they could. Leadership was often disputed.

So at any given time changes in the organisation of society will often explain changes in the key features of warfare at that time.

Source C: A 19th-century picture showing an army of soldiers gathering in about 1250CE.

ResultsPlus
Build Better Answers

Why were armies in Britain so different by 1250CE than the Celtic ones in Britain in about 50BCE?
(16 marks)

■ **Basic, Level 1 (1–4 marks).**
Answer is general, with some information about armies in 50BCE and 1250CE, but very little detail.

● **Good, Level 2 (5–8 marks).**
Level 2 answers are fuller, with more detailed information about armies, including army size, weapons, protective clothing and organisation, but without making it clear why this occurred.

▲ **Better, Level 3 (9–12 marks).**
Answer will explain why the armies were different, linking a key feature of each society to features of their armies, and supporting the explanation with accurate information. For example, showing the significance of feudal obligations.

▲ **Excellent, Level 4 (13–16 marks).**
Answer will explain reasons for a range of changes, for example in organisation, recruitment and tactics, based on the differences in the two societies.

The changing nature of warfare from Roman Britain to c1350

Examination requirements

The extension study:

● The extension study is examined in Question 5 of the Development Study paper.

● There are two parts to the question, 5a and 5b.

● Question 5a is allocated 9 marks; Question 5b is allocated 16 marks.

● Examples of Questions 5a and 5b are on page 81.

You will be asked the same sort of questions as in the core, and you may also be asked to link this section with the core when you talk about change and continuity.

You should spend about 35 minutes of your exam on this section.

Self-evaluation checklist

What you should know by the end of Extension Study 1, The Changing Nature of Warfare from the Roman World to 1350.

Roman warfare:

● what kind of army the Roman Empire had

● how Roman society influenced the nature of its army

● how the Roman army was organised

● the weapons and tactics of the Romans

● life in the Roman army.

Celtic warfare:

● what kind of society the Celts had

● what kind of fighting took place

● who did the fighting

● the weapons and tactics of the Celts.

Boudicca's Revolt:

● the events of Boudicca's Revolt

● what type of fighting took place

● why the Romans were the victors.

Medieval warfare to c1350:

● what the feudal system was

● how the feudal system shaped armies

● the weapons and tactics of feudal armies especially mounted knights and medieval infantry

● why the use of the mounted knight declined

● the main features of siege warfare

● life in the medieval army

● the meaning of 'limited warfare'.

The Battle of Hastings:

● the events of the Battle of Hastings

● how far it was typical of medieval battles

● why the Normans won.

The Third Crusade and siege of Acre:

● the events of the crusade and siege

● how far fighting during these events were typical of battles and sieges of the time.

General issues:

● how different types of society produced different types of warfare.

Exam style questions

(a): Describe the key features of the Roman army. (9 marks)

(b): Why was the army of the Celts different from the army of the Normans?
Explain your answer. (16 marks)

You may use the following in your answer and any other information of your own.

- The Celts were a rural people divided into many tribes and villages.
- Norman society was organised under the feudal system.
- The Norman army contained many mounted soldiers.

ResultsPlus
Maximise your marks

What role did the mounted knight play in warfare in medieval times before c1350? (9 marks)

Student answer	Examiner comments	Improved student answer
The mounted knights were landowners who had to fight for the king in exchange for land.

They had good weapons. They used swords and shields and lances. They wore a hauberk and a helmet for protection. They took their own horses to war. | The student knows who the knights were and what weapons and protective clothes they wore.

This is accurate information about the mounted knight. The answer will get a mark low in level two for describing the mounted knight. To improve the answer, the student must explain the knight's role. | To improve the answer, the student added:

They were quite like the tanks of medieval warfare. The combined weight of knight and horse could make a huge impact. They were the main attack force of the army. They smashed their way into the enemy infantry. Mounted knights also chased the enemy if they retreated, because they were easy to kill.

Even though they were the main attack force, they were only part of the army. William the Conqueror only had 2,000 knights in an army of 8,000. Other soldiers had a role too. |

5.1 Reasons for military conflict c1450 to present day

Introduction

War is defined as an armed conflict between two or more nations or two sides within the same nation. There are many different types of conflict, including civil wars, religious wars, wars of conquest and wars fought for independence. Conflicts are caused by a variety of factors – economic, political, ideological and religious.

In this section of the course we will look at reasons for conflict in relation to three case studies:

- In the years 1642–1649 England experienced a civil war that was partly political – a power clash between King Charles I and Parliament – but also economic, ideological and religious.
- The American War of Independence was, on the surface, a war for the freedom of the thirteen colonies from British control. Again, however, its origins were economic – the issue of taxation – and ideological – the idea of representation.
- The reasons for the outbreak of the First World War were even more complex and included political and military rivalry between the Great Powers of Europe, fighting for freedom and the ambitions of Kaiser William II.

All three conflicts were due to the interaction of a variety of reasons that could not be resolved peacefully.

Charles I

Portrait of Charles I, whose belief in the Divine Right of Kings brought about the English Civil War.

American War

American colonists showing their opposition to British control by throwing British imported tea overboard in 1773.

First World War

The murder on an Austrian prince by a Serbian terrorist was the event that triggered the outbreak of the First World War.

1642–1649
The English Civil War

1739
The War of Jenkins' Ear

1776–1783
The American War of Independence

1914–1918
The First World War

FASCINATING FACT

One of the strangest reasons for conflict was the War of Jenkins' Ear, 1739. A Spanish ship intercepted a British merchant ship off Cuba in 1731. The British captain, Robert Jenkins, supposedly insulted the Spanish captain, who used his sword to cut off Jenkins' ear. In 1738 Jenkins reported the incident to a committee of the House of Commons and said that his ear was 'cut off in April 1731 in the West Indies by Spanish coast guards who had boarded his ship.' This report gave the British an excuse to declare war on Spain.

Activities

1 What does Source A suggest about the actions of the Royalist soldiers?

2 Why do you think the poster was produced?

3 Devise a suitable caption for this poster.

83

Source A: A poster published during the English Civil War by Parliament. It shows the actions of Royalist soldiers fighting on the side of the King, Charles I.

5.2 General motives for conflict

Political

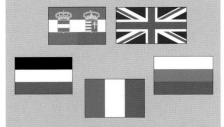

Some wars are fought for national pride or rivalry. The arms race between the Great Powers was a major motive for rivalry in the years before 1914, with countries competing for the largest and most powerful armed forces.

Ideas/conviction

War is often caused by a clash of beliefs or principle, the conviction that you are right and the other side is wrong. This often leads to a refusal to compromise. The English Civil War was partly due to the belief of Charles I in the Divine Right of Kings, a belief not shared by Parliament. Neither side would back down or compromise.

Self-defence/survival

This is when one side goes to war to defend its very existence. For example, the Austrian ultimatum to Serbia, in July 1914, in the events leading to the First World War, threatened the very existence of Serbia.

Aims of leaders

A number of conflicts have been due to the ambitions or aims of leaders. All three conflicts discussed in this chapter involved ambitious leaders: Charles I, George III and Kaiser William II of Germany.

Motives for military conflict

Miscalculations

Miscalculations occur when one side in a conflict makes decisions based on a misunderstanding of the possible actions or reactions of the other side. Charles I did not fully understand the consequences of his decision to enter the House of Commons in 1642 in order to arrest the five MPs.

Independence

Many wars are fought for freedom from the rule of another country. The American colonists eventually believed their interests would be better served if they ruled themselves.

Insoluble differences

Wars eventually break out because the two conflicting sides have differences that cannot be resolved. These insoluble differences can be the culmination of other motives for war:

- a clash of ideas/beliefs or a strong conviction that you are right that leads to a refusal to compromise, such as Charles I

- a failure to understand the views/ideas of the other side, such as George III's failure to grasp the changing attitudes among many American colonists

- a strong sense of grievance on both sides, such as the Austrian outrage in 1914 at the assassination of Archduke Franz Ferdinand and the Serbian outrage at the Austrian ultimatum which followed.

Struggles over authority

Conflicts are often due to a refusal to accept authority or control. For example, in the lead-up to the English Civil War, Parliament refused to accept the authority of Charles I.

Activities

1 Think of a war you have studied in history.

a) Was it caused by any of the motives in the spider diagram?

b) Create an ideas map to record the motives for the war, making any links between the motives.

2 Make a copy of the following grid. As you study each of the three conflicts:

- Identify any of the general motives explained on page 84.
- Add a brief summary, just a few key words, for each conflict.
- Record any further motives specific to each conflict in the two blank rows.
  These may be unique to one of the conflicts.

Motive	English Civil War	American War of Independence	First World War
Political			
Ideas/conviction			
Self-defence/survival			
Aims of leaders			
Miscalculation			
Independence			
Struggles over authority			
Insoluble differences			

ResultsPlus
Build Better Answers

Explain three reasons why the American War of Independence happened. (9 marks)

■ **Basic, Level 1 (1–3 marks).**
Will state reasons but without detail. For example, 'they wanted to rule themselves'.

● **Good, Level 2 (4–6 marks).**
Will describe events in detail or will back up one reason with information. For example, they might say 'they disagreed over taxation', and give details.

▲ **Excellent, Level 3 (7–9 marks).**
Will go on to explain another reason with details.

Summary

There are several general reasons for conflict, including political, economic, religious, ideological and the ambitions of one person.

5.3 Reasons for the English Civil War

Learning outcomes

By the end of this topic you should be able to:

● outline the reasons for the English Civil War

● explain how these reasons led to the conflict.

On 4 January 1642, Charles I forced his way into the House of Commons with over 400 armed guards to arrest five MPs. He was too late. The five MPs had made their escape along the River Thames. It proved to be a miscalculation on the part of the king because it was the event that sparked off the English Civil War. Charles's actions were due to the failure of the two sides, the king and parliament, to resolve their differences, to reach a compromise. What were these differences?

Activities

1 After you have read the 'King' and 'Parliament' panels, show the meaning of the following terms using sketches:

   a) Divine Right of Kings

   b) ship money

   c) Puritans.

2 Study Source A. What reasons does Pym mention for conflict between the king and Parliament?

Source A: Part of a speech made by John Pym, a leading MP, in April 1640.

I shall explain to you the grievances which trouble the country. Firstly Parliament was dissolved before our complaints were heard. Several gentlemen were imprisoned for speaking freely to Parliament. Secondly, there have been changes in matters of religion. The introduction of Catholic ceremonies, of altars, pictures, crucifixes, crosses and the like. Thirdly, there is an attack on our property. The taking of taxes, without any grant or law.

King

The powers of the English monarchy had increased under the Tudors especially Henry VIII and Elizabeth I.

Charles I inherited the beliefs of his father, James I, in the 'Divine Right of Kings'. He thought that monarchs received their power and right to rule from God and that they must be obeyed. Most of the 122 peers and nobles supported this ideal.

Charles was very short of money because of foreign wars and his extravagant lifestyle. He forced wealthy businessmen to give him loans and in 1635 imposed 'ship money', a tax to pay for the navy, on all areas, not just ports. He twice dismissed Parliament, in 1628 and 1639, when they tried to impose conditions on loans he needed.

Charles I upset Parliament when, in 1625, he married a Catholic, Henrietta Maria. He encouraged William Laud, the Archbishop of Canterbury, to make churches more beautiful and adopt a similar style of worship to that of the **Catholic Church**. He brought back stained windows and special clothes for priests.

Charles was determined to impose his religious ideas on Scotland and make them accept a new English Prayer Book. Most people in Scotland were Presbyterians, **Protestants** who believed that the Church should be run by people of equal rank and status, not the king. Charles twice sent an army to force these changes on the Scots.

Parliament

At the same time a growing and powerful middle class had emerged, some of which became MPs, who wanted more of a say in how the country was run.

The House of Commons did not accept the 'Divine Right of Kings' and wanted more control of policy, especially the king's spending. They were partly influenced by ideas of liberty and democracy but mainly wanted to protect their own interests.

Parliament refused to grant the king the normal right to collect customs duties throughout his reign. It also opposed forced loans and tried to limit the king's powers to raise taxes. This was known as the Petition of Right of 1628.

Since the reign of Elizabeth I, Puritans had become more powerful in the House of Commons. Puritans were strict Protestants who wanted religion to be simple and hated the Catholic Church. They strongly opposed the reforms of Archbishop Laud.

Parliament sympathised with the Presbyterians of Scotland who refused to accept the English Prayer Book. When, in 1639, Charles asked Parliament for a grant to raise money to send a second army to Scotland, Parliament refused and was dismissed by Charles.

Activities

3 Make your own ideas map to show the main reasons for the English Civil War:

a) In the central box put the title 'Reasons for the English Civil War'.

b) Prioritise your reasons by rank ordering them, with the most important directly above the central box and the rest going round clockwise from there to the least important.

c) Give reasons for your ranking.

 ResultsPlus
Build Better Answers

'Charles I was mainly to blame for the outbreak of the English Civil War'. Do you agree? (16 marks)

You may use the following to help you with your answer, and information of your own

- Charles believed in the Divine Right of Kings.
- Parliament tried to limit the king's power to raise taxes.
- Charles I married a Catholic.

 Basic, Level 1 (1–4 marks).
Will add a small amount of information to one of more of the bullet points given.

 Good, Level 2 and 3 (5–12 marks).
Answers which receive 5–8 marks will add details to the bullet points or give other detailed information. Better answers which receive 9–12 marks will show how one or more reasons led to war. For example explaining, with details to back up the points, how the divisions over Charles' belief in the Divine Right of Kings led to insoluble differences between the two sides.

 Excellent, Level 4 (13–16 marks).
The best answers will deal with three or more reasons, and show why one was more important than the others.

Summary

The English Civil War was due to a power struggle between Charles I and Parliament caused by political, economic, ideological and religious differences.

5.4 Reasons for the American War of Independence

Learning outcomes

By the end of this topic you should be able to:

- outline the reasons for the American War of Independence
- explain how these reasons led to the conflict.

In 1773 a group of Boston colonists dressed up as native American Indians and dumped thousands of pounds worth of tea into the harbour. The event, known as the Boston Tea Party, was one of the reasons for the outbreak of the American War of Independence in 1775.

Once again war broke out because of insoluble differences between two sides – the British government and the thirteen American **colonies**. These differences were due to political, economic, religious and ideological reasons as well as territorial expansion and the desire for independence.

Activities

1. In pairs, produce an amusing cartoon showing the events of the Boston Tea Party.

2. Using the following events produce a flow chart showing the causes of the American War of Independence:
   - 1773 Boston Tea Party
   - 1756–1763 Seven Years' War
   - 1776 Declaration of Independence
   - 1765 The Stamp Act
   - 1774 Intolerable Acts
   - 1763 No expansion westwards

   On your flow chart indicate how one event led to another.

3. In pairs, study Source B. Write a brief reply from the British government to Franklin.

4. This is a group activity. Imagine that the United Nations existed in the 1770s. You have been sent on a peacekeeping mission by the UN to prevent the outbreak of war. What solution would you suggest?
   a) Examine the reasons.
   b) Thought shower ideas with members of the group.

Source A: A lithograph of 1845 showing the Boston Tea Party of 1773.

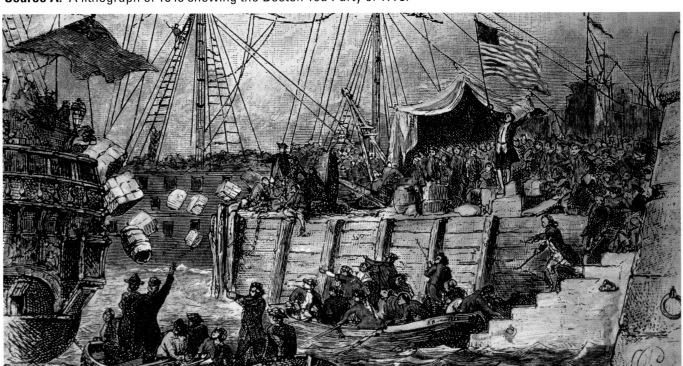

Why did war break out?

Effects of the Seven Years' War (1756–1763)

The Seven Years' War was fought between France and Britain for control of their respective colonies in Canada and India. Although Britain won, the war had important effects on its relationship with the Thirteen Colonies:

- The war removed the French from Canada. The Thirteen Colonies no longer feared a possible French invasion and they were therefore less dependent on the protection offered by the British.

- The war had proved very expensive. The British believed that the Thirteen Colonies should make a contribution to the cost of the war. In other words, the British wanted to impose greater control over the Thirteen Colonies at a time when they felt less need for this.

Who was in control?

The conflict was very much about the level of political control from Britain, the mother country, over its colonies. In the years before 1763 the British had been lax in their control of the Thirteen Colonies. Following the Seven Years' War, George III and the British government took a much greater interest in the American Colonies. However, leading colonists, influenced by ideas of the **Enlightenment** and the rights of people to overthrow corrupt governments if they threatened the rights of man, resented this greater central control. This greater level of control was first shown in 1763 when the British government banned all expansion west along the line of the Allegheny Mountains as this land was to be left to the Indians. New colonists were to be encouraged to go north to Nova Scotia or south to Florida instead. This limit on expansion caused much discontent among colonists, costing many, including George Washington, a good deal of money because these areas provided opportunities for trade and investment.

Misunderstanding of the role of colonies

At the heart of these differences were fundamental differences about the role of the Thirteen Colonies. To the British, they were largely there to provide raw materials to Britain and to be consumers of British goods. In contrast, many colonists saw themselves as carving a new society from the wilderness and did not want to be restricted by decisions made 3,000 miles away in London.

The Boston Tea Party

Even greater resentment was caused by the issue of tea. In 1773 the British government allowed the East India Company to dispose of its surplus tea in the Thirteen Colonies. This threatened the healthy trade in tea smuggling and led to the 'Boston Tea Party' (see Source A). However, the British responded with a series of laws known as the Intolerable Acts, which tightened their control over the Thirteen Colonies. One of the acts, the Boston Port Act, closed the port of Boston until the British had been compensated for the tea lost in the Boston Tea Party. This reveals the lack of understanding of George III and the British government. Moreover, they had underestimated the extent of opposition in the Thirteen Colonies to British rule.

'No taxation without representation'

Following the expense of the Seven Years' War, George III and the British government decided that the Thirteen Colonies should pay their way and make a greater financial contribution to the cost of the war. This led to the imposition of a series of taxes. For example, in 1765 Britain introduced the Stamp Act, which was a direct tax on the paper required for legal transactions and newspapers. These taxes were resented by many colonists, whose slogan became 'no taxation without representation', that is, they argued that they should not be made to contribute to an economy controlled by a government that they had no vote to elect representatives to.

Source B: Benjamin Franklin speaking against the Stamp Act.

> I never heard any objection to the right of laying duties to regulate commerce; but a right to lay internal taxes was never supposed to be in Parliament, as we are not represented there…

Declaration of Independence

The leading colonists, such as Samuel Adams, John Adams, George Washington and Thomas Jefferson, were influenced by ideas of republicanism, and as the situation deteriorated in the early 1770s they began to support the idea of an independent American republic. This culminated in the Declaration of Independence in 1776.

Source C: From the Declaration of Independence.

> We hold these truths to be self-evident, that all men are created equal… that they are endowed by their Creator with certain unalienable Rights, that among these are Life, Liberty and the pursuit of Happiness.

Summary

The American War of Independence was due to political, economic and ideological differences in the attitude of the colonists and Britain, the mother country, which led to a demand for independence.

5.5 Reasons for the First World War

Learning outcomes

By the end of this topic you should be able to:

- outline the reasons for the First World War
- explain how these reasons led to the conflict.

The **assassination** of Franz Ferdinand set off a chain of events that, within six weeks, led to the outbreak of the First World War. However, the conflict was due to international rivalry between the Great Powers of Europe – France, Britain, Germany, Russia, Italy and Austria-Hungary – which had been building up for over 30 years.

Source A: A sketch showing the assassination of Franz Ferdinand, the heir to the throne of Austria-Hungary, by Gavrilo Princip, a Serb, 28 June 1914.

Political rivalry

There was rivalry between the Great Powers, which led to the creation of two competing **alliance systems**.

The Triple Alliance (Austria-Hungary, Germany and Italy) and the Triple Entente (Britain, France and Russia) were like two rival armed gangs, each trying to get the upper hand. A dispute between one member of each alliance system could involve the other members. Indeed, in 1914 five of the six powers went to war – France, Britain and Russia against Austria and Germany.

Economic rivalry

There was increasing competition in trade and industry, especially between Germany and Britain. Britain had, for many years, been the leading industrial nation and had dominated trade in many parts of the world. German industry, however, rapidly expanded in the late 19th and early 20th centuries and challenged British supremacy. Moreover, in certain industries, especially chemicals, Germany led the way.

The arms race

There was also rivalry between the Great Powers to build up the size of their armed forces, and this was known as the arms race. In the years 1900–1914 the main European powers more than doubled their spending on their armies. Each of the Great Powers, with the exception of Britain, had trained a huge army of conscripts – young men forced by the law to become soldiers for a year or so. Ever more destructive weapons were being developed and improved, such as machine guns and huge field guns. The arms race brought war nearer because:

- It increased tension between the Great Powers. It had a rolling 'snowball' effect. When one country increased its army, another would follow suit.
- As each country increased its army or weapons it became more confident of success and more willing to test out its armed forces.

Territorial expansion

There was great rivalry between France and Germany over the two French provinces of Alsace and Lorraine. In 1871 Prussia (later Germany) had defeated France and seized these two provinces. Many in France wanted revenge on Germany and the return of the lost provinces.

Source B: This cartoon titled 'A Chain of Friendship' appeared in the American newspaper the *Brooklyn Eagle* in July 1914. The caption read: 'If Austria attacks Serbia, Russia will fall upon Austria, Germany upon Russia, and France and England upon Germany.'

British involvement

On 2 August 1914 Germany invaded Belgium as part of a plan to knock France out of the war quickly. The following day Britain declared war on Germany in order to preserve the independence of Belgium, guaranteed by the Treaty of London of 1839. The Germans had not expected this. Britain was defending the principle of Belgian neutrality as well as fighting to ensure the survival of Belgium as an independent nation.

The aims of one leader

The German Kaiser (Emperor) William II has often been blamed for causing the First World War. He certainly increased tension with other powers, especially Britain, through his determination to increase the size of the German empire and navy. Germany, with the most powerful army in the world, threatened British supremacy at sea. In 1906 Britain launched the super-battleship Dreadnought, which triggered a naval race between Germany and Britain to see who could build the most battleships. This poisoned relations between the two countries.

Activities

1 What was meant by the following:
   a) the arms race
   b) the alliance system
   c) the lost provinces
   d) Dreadnought?

In addition, there was rivalry between the Great Powers to build up their empires, especially in Africa and the Far East. A large empire could provide valuable raw materials and a market for manufactured goods.

Austro-Serbian rivalry

The immediate trigger for war, the assassination of Franz Ferdinand, was due to rivalry between Serbia and Austria-Hungary. Serbia wished to unite all Serbs within a greater Serbia. This meant the independence of many Serbs living within the Austro-Hungarian Empire. This rivalry grew worse when, in 1908, Austria seized Bosnia-Herzegovina, an area where many Serbs lived. This also infuriated Russia who regarded herself as the protector of Serbia.

Activities

2 Draw an ideas map to show the rivalries between the various countries.
   a) In the central box put 'Rivalries of the Great Powers' with lines to Russia, Austria-Hungary, Serbia, France, Britain and Germany.
   b) Draw lines to show rivalry between the powers. On the connecting lines briefly explain the reason for the rivalry.

3 Study Source B. Do you think it gives an accurate view of the rivalry between the Great Powers in 1914? Explain your answer.

Summary

The First World War broke out because of political, economic, military and territorial rivalries between the Great Powers as well as the ambitions of Kaiser William II of Germany.

5.6 Summary: Reasons for military conflict c1450 to the present day

Examine the following eight sources about the causes of the three different conflicts.

Source A: A photograph of Kaiser William II.

Source B: Reactions to the reforms of Archbishop Laud.

> This year being Laud's first as Archbishop of Canterbury, great offence was taken when he set up pictures in the windows of the palaces at Lambeth and Croydon, and at his bowing towards the altar which all the people protested against as being Catholic.

Source C: A description of the Boston Tea Party, 1773, by George Hewes, who took part in the event.

> In about three hours from the time we went on board, we had thus broken and thrown overboard every tea chest to be found in the ship, while those in the other ships were disposing of the tea in the same way, at the same time. We were surrounded by British armed ships, but no attempt was made to resist us.

Source D: Part of the resolution of the Assembly of the American colony of Virginia against the Stamp Act of 1765.

> Resolved therefore, that the General Assembly of this Colony have the only and sole exclusive right and power to lay taxes and impositions upon the inhabitants of this Colony, and that every attempt to vest such power in any person or persons whatsoever other than the General Assembly aforesaid has a manifest tendency to destroy British as well as American freedom.

Source E: Sir Edward Grey, the British Foreign Secretary, speaking in 1909.

> There is no comparison between the importance of the German navy to Germany, and the importance of our navy to us. Our navy is to us what their army is to them. To have a strong navy would increase Germany's prestige and influence, but it is not a matter of life and death to them as it is to us.

Source F: An engraving showing Charles I entering the House of Commons, 4 January 1642, to arrest the five MPs.

Source G: Minutes of a secret meeting between Kaiser William II and his commanders, 1912.

> The Kaiser predicted that if the Austrians did not face up to the Serbian menace, there would be considerable trouble from the Slav peoples within the Austro-Hungarian empire. Von Moltke, the Army Chief, said that England was seen as Germany's main enemy. He believed war was bound to happen and said 'The sooner, the better'.

Source H: Charles I asking for a loan from Parliament in 1627.

> Our treasures exhausted and our coffers empty, we summoned a Parliament, but not finding that success therein which we had just hope to expect, we are resolved to require the aid of our good and loving subjects by lending us a sufficient sum of money to be repaid them as soon as we shall be in any way able to do so.

Activities

1 Working in pairs, make a copy of the following grid.

	English Civil War	American War of Independence	The First World War
Political			
Economic			
Military			
Religious/ ethnic			
Territorial expansion			
Ambitions of one person			
Ideology			
Independence			
Self-defence			
Other reasons			

a) Examine each of the eight sources on these pages. Which reason or reasons for warfare does it suggest? Place the source letter in the appropriate box. Some sources may suggest more than one reason and be placed in more than one box.

b) Add a brief explanation of any other reasons for these conflicts.

What similarities/differences are there between the motives for each of the conflicts?

c) Make a copy of the following Venn diagram:

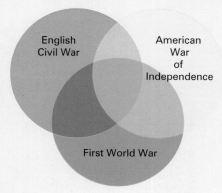

d) Using the grid you have been completing while studying the three conflicts, look for similarities between the three conflicts.

- Write in on the Venn diagram motives that are common to two of the conflicts, for example the Civil War and the American War of Independence. Give an example of the motive from each conflict.

- Which are common to all three? Give an example of the motive from each conflict.

- Were any motives unique to one conflict?

2 How similar/different were the motives for the three conflicts? Make a copy of the following grid and give examples of the motives.

	Similarities in motives	Differences in motives
English Civil War/ American War of Independence		
English Civil War/ First World War		
American War of Independence/ First World War		

3 Which conflicts:
- have the greatest similarity of motive?
- have the greatest difference?

Give a brief explanation for each decision.

4 'There was much change in the reasons for conflict between the English Civil War, the American War of Independence and the First World War.' Discuss.

KnowZone
Reasons for military conflict c1450 to the present day

Examination requirements

The Extension Study:

● The extension study is examined in Question 6 of the Development Study paper.

● There are two parts to the question, 6a and 6b.

● Question 6a is allocated 9 marks; Question 6b is allocated 16 marks.

Examples of questions 6a and 6b are given below. You will be asked the same sort of questions as in the core and you may also be asked to link this section with the core when you talk about change and continuity.

You should spend about 35 minutes of your exam on this section.

Self-evaluation checklist

What you should know by the end of Extension Study 2.

English Civil War:

● context leading up to the war

● the reasons for the conflict including:

  ● political reasons

  ● economic reasons

  ● ideological reasons.

American War of Independence:

● context leading up to the war

● the reasons for the conflict including:

● political reasons

● economic reasons

● ideological reasons.

First World War:

● context leading up to the war

● the reasons for the conflict including:

  ● political reasons

  ● economic reasons

  ● ideological reasons.

You also need to be able to compare and contrast the three case studies.

Exam style questions

(a): Explain three main reasons why Britain went to war in 1914. (9 marks)

(b): Charles I was at war against his own subjects in the Civil War and George III was at war against his subjects in the American War of Independence. How similar were the motives of the two kings for going to war? (16 marks)

You may use the following in your answer and any other information of your own.

- Charles I believed in the Divine Right of Kings.
- In 1765 representatives from nine American colonies refused to accept the Stamp Act, which had been passed by the British parliament.
- In 1773 a mob threw 342 crates of tea into Boston Harbour.

ResultsPlus
Maximise your marks

6(a): Describe the effects of the Seven Years' War on relationships between the British Government and the Thirteen Colonies. (9 marks)

Student answer	Examiner Comments	Extract from improved student answer
In the Seven Years' War the British and French fought in Canada. The British succeeded in driving the French out. After the war the British decided the Thirteen Colonies should pay more in taxes to help pay for the war, which was very expensive. In 1765, the British parliament passed the Stamp Act, but there was a lot of opposition in America to the new taxes.	This is a good answer because it contains accurate information which is relevant to the question. But, to improve to level three, it must focus more on the effects of the Seven Years' War. The answer is describing events rather than explaining how relationships were affected.	To improve the answer, the student added: This affected the relationship between the British Government and the Thirteen Colonies because the colonists challenged the right of the British to tax them, and they began to resent British control. The Seven Years' War also had the effect of making the colonists less dependent on the protection of the British, once the threat from the French was removed. This made them less likely to accept increased British control at just the same time as the British tried to increase their control. As a result of this, their relationship got worse.

The impact of war on Britain

Introduction

Britain was involved in two world wars in the first half of the 20th century: the First World War, 1914–1918, and the Second World War, 1939–1945. During both wars, because the nature of war was very different from previous conflicts, there were great changes in the experiences of civilians, especially women, and in the role of government.

For the first time, the enemy brought the war direct to Britain through air raids, including the Zeppelin raids of the First World War and the Blitz of 1940–1941. Moreover, the government made use of propaganda and censorship in order to ensure support for the war effort and hatred for the enemy. Indeed, the government took on a far more active role in the organisation of total war (see page 149), from control of the media to rationing and the evacuation of schoolchildren during the Second World War.

The two wars profoundly changed British society in the years 1914–1950 and had a particular impact on the role and status of women in Britain.

Women

WOMEN OF BRITAIN
COME INTO THE FACTORIES
ASK AT ANY EMPLOYMENT EXCHANGE FOR ADVICE AND FULL DETAILS

Careless talk

You never know who's listening!

CARELESS TALK COSTS LIVES

Blitz

1914	1915	1916	1917	1918
Outbreak of the First World War. Government introduces the Defence of the Realm Act (DORA).	Lloyd George becomes Minister of Munitions and encourages the employment of women workers.	Government introduces conscription.	Britain has food supplies for only six weeks because of U-boat sinkings. Government introduces voluntary rationing.	The Representatic the Peoples A gives the vote women over age of 30.

Activities

1 Work in pairs.

   a) Sit back to back.

   b) One of you should describe the poster on this page to the other, who should make a sketch based on your description (rather than what you can remember from looking at it in your textbook!).

   c) Compare your version of the poster with the original.

2 Why do you think this poster discouraged waste?

3 How did the artist get his message across?

FASCINATING FACT

During both the wars the government tried to discourage excessive drinking of alcohol because of its effects on the workforce and therefore on the war effort – it caused lateness and frequent absenteeism. Lloyd George was particularly concerned about the impact on munitions workers in 1915. He reduced pub opening hours and had beer watered down. Some workers composed a song 'Lloyd George's Beer', which criticised these measures. Despite government laws, not surprisingly, beer consumption actually increased during both conflicts.

1920s	1928	1939	1940	1941	1942
he young men known as pers' begin to r short skirts smoke and k in public.	Women over the age of 21 are given the vote.	Outbreak of the Second World War. Government again introduces conscription. Compulsory evacuation of schoolchildren.	Government introduces the Essential Work Order (EWO).	Conscription of women into the labour force.	The Beveridge Report.

6.1 The civilian experience of war

Learning outcomes

By the end of this section you should be able to:

- describe methods of censorship and propaganda in the two world wars
- explain the effects of air raids and bombings on Britain
- understand how to make inferences and what questions to ask about sources
- evaluate the purpose or message of a source.

Getting an overview

Activity

1 Match the following words:
- Zeppelin
- the Blitz
- censorship
- propaganda

to their meanings:
- controlling what is written or said
- German airships
- one-sided information
- German air attacks on Britain 1940–1941.

Propaganda

Propaganda is limited, often one-sided information that is spread to persuade people to support certain ideas or policies. It was used by British governments during both wars to win support for the war effort and turn people against the Germans. In the early years of the First World War propaganda was used to persuade men to volunteer for the armed forces. During the Second World War it was used to raise morale, especially after German bombing raids.

Censorship

Censorship is the control by a government of the spread of all information – such as information contained in the media, personal letters, films and newspapers – that might be useful to the enemy or that might upset the morale of the public if it became general knowledge. During the First World War soldiers' letters home from the war front were censored in case they upset the soldiers' loved ones. During the Second World War radio broadcasts, newspapers and films were all under the control of the Ministry of Information.

Air raids

During the First World War, British civilians were the target of attacks from the air for the first time, with the Germans using bomber planes and airships called Zeppelins. The threat to the public was far more serious during the Blitz of 1940–1941, when the Germans tried, unsuccessfully, to destroy civilian morale by bombing major towns and cities.

Civilian attitudes

Censorship and propaganda were effective in the early years of the First World War – thousands of young men were enthusiastic about the war and rushed to volunteer. However, attitudes changed from 1916 as the horrors of war became apparent. During the Second World War censorship and propaganda ensured that the German Blitz did not destroy civilian morale.

6.2 Propaganda and censorship during the First World War

During the First World War the British government carefully controlled what people wrote, said or heard about the war. This was in order to keep up **morale**, ensure people supported the war effort and, in the early years of the war, persuade young men to volunteer for the armed forces.

Censorship

The Defence of the Realm Act was passed in August 1914. This gave the government the powers of **censorship** throughout the war. Only news issued by GHQ (army headquarters) or government departments could be published. A newspaper could be taken to court if it used unauthorised material. Letters written by soldiers from the battle front, especially from the Western Front, were censored by officials in the armed forces.

This censorship was to ensure that the public did not find out about the worst features of the Western Front, especially the heavy casualties and often poor living conditions. In addition, the government did not want the British people exposed to the enemy (German) view of the war (that Germany was in the right as they were fighting a war of self-defence). The government believed it could not tell people the whole truth because people might begin to question whether it was worth fighting at all. Furthermore, letters or newspaper articles might divulge classified military information, and that information needed to be removed.

Source A: A photograph of dead German troops, killed by a British bombardment of July 1917.

> Dear Mam and Dad,
>
> Near Amiens
>
> 12 July 1916
>
> I am writing this letter from a trench near Amiens, in France, where the Northumberland Fusiliers are stationed. Yesterday we launched an attack against the Germans. We captured a stretch of their trenches. However, two of my close mates were killed by German machine guns. I've made some really good friends in the trenches. However, the food is awful and there are rats everywhere. However, we must not give up. It looks like we are getting ready for another attack tomorrow.
>
> Love
>
> Billy

Activities

1 Work in pairs. Imagine you are army censors.

   a) Study Source A. Would you censor or publish this? Give reasons for your answer.

   b) Make a copy of the letter written by a soldier on the Western Front. Highlight any words, phrases or sentences that need to be removed because they might upset morale or give away military information.

Propaganda

The government used **propaganda** in the early months of the war to ensure support for the war effort and to encourage young men to volunteer for the war effort. The British government therefore set about convincing the public that the Germans were evil and had to be stopped. Often stories were wildly exaggerated to make the enemy appear even worse.

By the end of 1914 it was widely believed in Britain that the German armies in Belgium were bayoneting babies and murdering many innocent civilians. The newspapers published artists' impressions of women being crucified. One of the most famous stories was that there was a German factory where human corpses were melted down and made into soap. The campaign to turn the British against the Germans was so successful that Germans living in Britain were attacked and shops with German names were looted.

Propaganda posters were also used to encourage people, especially women, to work at home and to go without in order to support the war effort. This was especially important in 1917, when German U-boat attacks seriously reduced Britain's food supplies. The public were asked to cut down, especially on food, and avoid wastage. The government also made very effective use of conscience posters, which were designed to shame young men into joining up.

Source B: An article in the *Accrington Observer*, 19 September 1914.

In the towns and villages where the German army stop they begin by requisitioning food and drink, which they consume till they are drunk. Then the scenes of fire, murder and especially pillage begin, accompanied by acts of deliberate cruelty, without respect to sex or age. They seize the opportunity to decimate the population, pillage the houses, and then set them on fire. After a preliminary attack and massacre, they shut up the men in the church, and then order the women to return to their houses and to leave their doors open all night.

Source C: A poster of December 1914. It followed a German naval raid on Scarborough.

Inferences

What can you learn from Source B about the German army in 1914?

This is an **inference** question, which means it is asking you to think:

- What is the source suggesting? What message is it trying to put across?

For example: *Source B is suggesting that German soldiers were committing atrocities against the people of Belgium.*

When answering inference questions in the exam, once you have given an inference, you should support it with evidence from the source.

For example: *Source B says the German army is murdering and pillaging.*

Activities

2 What can you learn from Source C about the German raids on Scarborough?

3 Explain, with examples, two uses of propaganda by the British government during the First World War.

Civilian attitudes to war

From 1914 to 1916 the British people were remarkably consistent in their support for the war (see Sources D, E and F). This was due to several reasons:

- Many people had genuine sympathy for Belgium after the German invasion.
- Government propaganda and censorship successfully whipped up hatred of the Germans.
- Most people were convinced that it would be a short, victorious war, over by Christmas 1914 at the latest.
- Some people had a glorified view of war and had not yet experienced its horrors.

Source D: A British soldier writing in August 1914.

> I adore war. It is like a big picnic. I have never been so well or so happy. Nobody grumbles at you for being dirty. I have only had my boots off once in the last ten days and only washed twice.

Source E: A queue of volunteers outside a British recruiting office in 1914.

Source F: A British newspaper report, 4 August 1914.

> Whitehall was full of people highly excited… Cries of 'Down with Germany' and 'Berlin by Christmas' were heard. Hundreds were buying Union Jacks. There was a deafening roar when the King appeared on the balcony of Buckingham Palace. A hostile crowd gathered outside the German Embassy and smashed windows.

The same enthusiasm was not apparent in the years 1916–1918. Indeed, more and more people became critical of the government, the generals and the general conduct of the war. For example, Siegfried Sassoon served in the army during the First World War and became increasingly angry about the way in which the generals were running the campaign (see Source G).

Source G: Siegfried Sassoon, writing in 1917.

> I believe that the war is prolonged by those who have the power to end it. I believe that this war upon which I entered as a war of liberation and defence has now become a war of conquest and aggression. I have seen and endured the sufferings of the troops and I can no longer be a party to prolonging those sufferings for ends [aims] which I believe to be evil and unjust.

This change of attitude was due to several factors:

- The Battle of the Somme (July–November 1916) did much to change the mood in Britain because of the heavy casualties – 58,000 on the first day – and the failure to advance.
- The stalemate on the Western Front meant that the war had dragged on far longer than many had anticipated.
- By 1916 the flood of volunteers was drying up. The government introduced conscription, which brought increasing opposition from those who believed that it was wrong to force men to join the armed forces.

Activities

4   Study Sources D, E and F. How far do they support the view that there was a wave of enthusiasm with the outbreak of war?

5   What can you learn from Source G about attitudes in Britain to the war by 1917?

6   Give two reasons for this change of attitude.

6.3 Propaganda and censorship during the Second World War

Censorship and propaganda played important roles in the Second World War and were controlled by the Ministry of Information.

Censorship

The government again had emergency powers that enabled it to control information and ensure that the press did not publish and the BBC did not broadcast any information that might be helpful to the enemy or might lower morale. Newspapers were carefully controlled and had to submit their articles to the censor before they were printed. One newspaper, the *Daily Worker*, was banned in 1941 because it claimed that employers were making a lot of money out of the war by exploiting their workers. The BBC was not controlled by the government, but it did censor itself.

Propaganda

Propaganda was used in Britain once again during the Second World War to boost morale, maintain public support for the war effort and also to provide people with important information and instructions. However, conscription meant it was not necessary to use it to encourage volunteers for the armed forces.

The Ministry of Information (MoI) decided against a policy of exaggerating victories or enemy activities as had happened in the First World War. Instead, the MoI tried to get across the truth about the horrors of war and avoid giving the public any false hopes of victory. However, its early efforts were seen by the public as dull and uninspiring.

Source A: An early Second World War propaganda poster.

Activities

1 Work in pairs. You have to decide which photographs should and should not be censored.
   - Make a copy of the following grid.
   - Categorise each of the photographs from the list that follows the grid.

Censored	Not Censored

   - a street in London completely destroyed by German bombing raids
   - a smiling soldier rescued from Dunkirk
   - British vehicles and tanks left on the beaches of Dunkirk
   - A German bomber plane being shot down
   - A family rescued during the Blitz
   - Churchill visiting an area of London which has been bombed.

Activities

2 Study Source A. Why do you think people at the time thought it was dull and uninspiring?

3 Work in a group for this task. Imagine you work for an advertising firm and have been appointed to advise the government on its propaganda posters. What advice would you give to improve Source A?

Government propaganda was most effective when it appealed to British humour. For example, there was a series of posters to stop people giving military information to spies.

Source B: A very popular government propaganda poster.

BETTER POT-LUCK
with Churchill today
THAN HUMBLE PIE
under Hitler tomorrow
DON'T WASTE FOOD!

Source C: Another government propaganda poster.

A MAIDEN LOVED
AN IDLE WORD
A COMRADE LOST
AND ADOLF SERVED

Posters were also used, as they had been in the First World War, to encourage people to conserve food or fuel. In addition, wartime propaganda made good use of the image of the prime minister, Winston Churchill, to inspire support for the war effort and keep up morale. This was particularly important in the months after the Dunkirk evacuation and the defeat of France, when Britain stood alone against Germany.

The BBC played an important role in keeping up morale. By the end of the war, an estimated 25 million people were listening to their programmes. They were selective in what they broadcast. For example, their propaganda broadcasts did much to transform the military disaster at Dunkirk into a morale-boosting triumph by mentioning the bravery of the rescue operation and ignoring the humiliation of defeat and retreat (see Source D).

Source D: From a broadcast by the popular playwright and broadcaster J. B. Priestley, 5 June 1940, the day after the Dunkirk evacuation ended.

Among those paddle steamers that will never return was one I knew well, for it was the pride of our ferry service to the Isle of Wight… And now never again will we board at Cowes. She has paddled and churned away – for ever. But now – look – this little steamer, like all her brave and battered sisters, is immortal. She'll go sailing proudly down the years in the epic of Dunkirk. And our great grand-children, when they learn how we began this war by snatching glory out of defeat, and then swept on to victory, may also learn how the little holiday steamers made an excursion to hell and came back glorious.

Activities

4 What can you learn from Source D about the Dunkirk evacuation? Try to make at least two inferences, supported from the source.

5 Study sources B and C. What are the messages of these two posters? How do the posters put across their message?

6 Make a copy of the following table. Complete it to show the similarities and differences between censorship and propaganda during the two wars.

	Similarities	Differences
Censorship		
Propaganda		

7 'Propaganda and censorship were more effective during the Second World War than the First World War.' Discuss.

6.4 The experience of air raids and bombing

British civilians experienced a new threat during the First and Second World Wars – direct attacks from the enemy in the form of bombing raids.

Zeppelin attacks during the First World War

From January 1915 Zeppelins began to make bombing raids on British cities. These were airships filled with hydrogen that could fly at 4,600 metres (15,000 feet) – well above British fighter planes, which could fly at a maximum height of only 13,000 feet. There were 51 Zeppelin raids between 1915 and 1916. Their main target was London, where strict **blackout** regulations, involving the switching off of lights so that German bombers could not see their targets, and other precautions were enforced.

Source A: A nurse, Ursula Somervell, kept a diary in which she described Zeppelin raids.

> We had a pretty terrifying time with Zepps again last night. We were woken at 10.30 by a terrific noise of bombs, aircraft, guns etc. all apparently around us. We rushed on dressing gowns, said a prayer and got downstairs as quickly as we could. There was a tremendous glare in the sky to the west of us, which came from a big fire in Wood Street. I believe most of the damage was done on Oxford Street. A lot of people were killed in a motorbus. It would have been terrifying to be out, as I believe there is a fearful panic in the streets. I am afraid there must have been many casualties.

Source B: A letter from Mrs Holcombe Ingelby to her son, August 1915, describing a Zeppelin raid.

> I turned out of bed and looking up above us saw two Zepps. The searchlights were on them and they looked as if they were among the stars. They were very high and like cigar-shaped constellations they kept pulling away from the searchlights, only to be caught again. It was lovely.

The British public soon became angry because of the apparent lack of defence against the Zeppelin. The first Zeppelin was not shot down until 3 September 1916, and the successful pilot was awarded the Victoria Cross.

However, the Zeppelin attacks stopped in 1917 due to improved British defences, including the use of searchlights, which meant that the Zeppelins could be easily spotted. Moreover, if a Zeppelin was hit, it burst into flames. The crew had little chance of surviving (see Source C). In all, 57 Zeppelin raids on Britain killed 564 civilians and injured a further 1,370 people.

Source C: A painting of 1917, based on eyewitness accounts, of the shooting down of a Zeppelin.

Source D: Sybil Morrison describes the shooting down of a Zeppelin, in an article in a local newspaper, 3 September 1916.

It was like a big cigar I suppose and all of the bag part had caught fire. And it seemed to come floating down slowly instead of falling down with a bang. We knew there were about 60 people in it and that they were being roasted to death. Of course, you weren't supposed to feel any pity for your enemies. Nevertheless, I was appalled to see the good, kind-hearted British people dancing about in the streets at the sight of 60 people being burned alive – clapping and cheering and singing.

Activities

3 What can you learn from Source D about the shooting down of the Zeppelin?

4 Devise two different propaganda captions for the painting Source C:
   - one for use in Germany
   - one for use in Britain.

5 Work in a group for the following task. Study Sources A–D. Put together a newspaper report on a Zeppelin raid. Include:
   a) a catchy headline
   b) a description of the damage caused
   c) different eyewitness accounts from civilians of the raid and the shooting down of a Zeppelin.

German bombing raids, 1916–1917

In May 1917 the Germans began to use aircraft known as Gotha IV bombers (see Source E) and by the end of the war there had been 57 raids. These did not cause as much damage as the ones during the Second World War would because the bombs they carried weighed only 100 kilograms and were capable of destroying only a few houses.

Nevertheless, the raids did have a dramatic effect on British civilians, as they had not experienced anything like this before. Moreover, the loss of life was high, as there were few ways that people could protect themselves since there were no shelters. For example, in June 1917, 20 Gothas carried out a bombing raid on London in which 162 civilians were killed and 432 injured. In total, 850 people were killed in Gotha raids during the First World War.

The public outcry against these raids forced the government to bring into operation better searchlights, balloons and anti-aircraft guns. As a result, 7 out of 19 Gotha bombers were shot down in the raid of 19 May 1918. The Germans could not afford such losses and called off further raids.

Source E: A photograph of a Gotha IV bomber, 1917.

Activities

6 In pairs, study Sources A–E. Make a copy of the following table.

	Value	Limitations
Diary (Source A)	First-hand account that gives immediate reactions to the attack. Evidence of panic caused.	Only one account of one reaction. May not be typical.
Letter (Source B)		
Painting (Source C)		
Newspaper report (Source D)		
Photograph (Source E)		

- One of you should give examples of the value of these different types of sources.
- The other should give limitations. An example has been done for you.
- Try to use evidence from the sources themselves not from your knowledge of the topic.

6.5 The Blitz

During the Second World War the German bombing raids were far more serious than in the First World War because advances in technology meant that more powerful bombers and more destructive bombs could be used. These attacks were known as the Blitz, which is a shortened version of the German word *blitzkrieg*, which means lightning war. The German raids, which began on 7 September 1940, targeted British towns and cities with the aim of destroying civilian morale, forcing the British into submission (see Source A) and undermining British armaments production.

Source A: Field Marshal Kesselring explained, in his memoirs written in 1957, the aims of the Blitz.

> Our main assignments now were the disturbance of production and incoming supplies. The underlying purpose was to slow down British armament production and begin a full-scale economic war. To destroy civilian morale we began 'reprisal raids' at the same time.

British towns and cities suffered heavy bombing from the autumn of 1940 to May 1941, with the targets usually military or industrial centres.

From May 1941 the attacks became less and less frequent as Hitler diverted resources to the invasion of the Soviet Union.

- The primary target was London, which was bombed every night from 7 September to 2 November 1940, especially the docks and factories of the East End. Some 12,500 people died during December 1940.
- In the south, Bristol, Southampton and Plymouth were also targeted. The naval base at Portsmouth was the target for a massive attack on 10 January 1940 where 930 civilians were killed and 3,000 injured.
- Coventry was badly hit by a series of raids in November 1940 with the Germans using incendiary bombs to increase the damage caused. People were so terrified that they fled from the city each night, sleeping with relatives or in open fields in nearby countryside (see Source B and Source C).
- In the north, Manchester was attacked in December 1940 while Liverpool suffered its worst raid – from over 500 bombers – in May 1941.
- Glasgow and the Clyde shipyard towns were hit hard in the spring of 1941.
- Belfast suffered badly in April and May 1941. At least 1,000 people were killed and 150,000 were made homeless.

Source B: A street in Coventry the morning after the raid of 14 November 1940.

Source C: From *Mrs Milburn's Diaries*. She describes Coventry about six weeks after the November 1940 raids.

> It was not long after we reached the outskirts of Coventry that we saw the evidence of the raiders' visit, and as we drew nearer the damage became greater. We went along Trinity Street and the devastated Rex Cinema, bombed twice over, and the other buildings near with all the windows blown out and boarded up. The old stone Grammar School had lost its windows, too, and was pitted and blackened and the Hospital seemed much more damaged than we expected. It was deliberate bombing of non-military objectives guaranteed, as the German brutes think, to terrify the ordinary citizen into fright and submission.

Source D: A photograph of damaged houses in a street in Walthamshaw, London, September 1944 after a V1 attack. This photograph was censored.

Activities

1 What can you learn from Source A about the aims of the Blitz?

2 Many people were more upset by the later V1 and V2 raids than the Blitz of 1940–1941. Give two reasons for this.

3 Study Source D. Why do you think it was censored?

V1 and V2 raids

There were further air attacks in 1944–1945 from V1 and V2 missiles. About 6,000 V1 bombs reached targets in Britain, causing 20,000 casualties and great damage to houses (see Source D). The V1 was a flying bomb powered by a rocket engine and was nicknamed the doodlebug because of the noise it made. It flew towards the target area and then came down wherever it ran out of fuel. People on the ground could hear the engine cut out and then a shriek as the bomb hurtled to the ground.

The V2 was a more serious threat because it was so fast, flying at supersonic speed, and it could not be shot down or seen. It was the first guided missile. About 500 V2s hit London between September 1944 and March 1945 causing over 9,000 casualties.

ResultsPlus
Build Better Answers

Study Sources B and C. Compare the usefulness of these sources for finding out about the bombing of Coventry. (10 marks)

■ **Basic, Level 1 (1–3 marks).**
Will take some information from the sources (for example 'there was a lot of damage in Coventry') or make an undeveloped comment about the nature of the source (for example that the photograph shows you what the damage looked like).

● **Good, Level 2 (4–7 marks).**
Will describe useful information in the sources in detail or explain in detail why the nature and origin of the sources make them useful.

▲ **Excellent, Level 3 (8–10 marks).**
Will explain the usefulness of what we can learn from the content of the sources when we take into account their nature and origin. For example, showing, using details from the source, that we can get an accurate picture of the damage from Source B, because this photograph was taken immediately afterwards, but it is only a single frame of the situation in one area compared with Source C which gives a wider impression.

Effects on industry

Bombing of industrial targets was generally not effective because precision was needed. Some factories were isolated, unlike housing estates, and they could easily be missed at night. Most factories were able to resume production within two to three days of being hit.

Effects on civilians

The bombing affected everyday life, especially the blackout and the use of air raid shelters. Homes, shops, businesses and even trains and cars had to 'black out' to avoid providing a target for the German bombers. People did eventually get used to operating in the blackout, although the number of car accidents doubled during this period.

The government gave out air raid shelters before and in the early months of the war. Some 2 million **Anderson shelters** were provided. These definitely saved thousands of lives by protecting people from shrapnel and flying glass. However, they offered little protection from falling masonry and many poorer people did not have gardens in which to build them. In 1941, therefore, 500,000 Morrison shelters were provided, which could be set up indoors.

Only 27 per cent of people used these private shelters. The rest used public shelters or 'self-chosen' shelters, such as the London underground (see Source E). At the beginning of the war, the government had rejected the use of the underground for shelter, but the force of public demand made them change their mind. In September 1940 they opened up 80 stations. People felt safer in these stations and enjoyed the comradeship and shared sacrifices.

Surveys suggested that only 40 per cent of Londoners regularly took shelter. This accounts for the high casualty rates. By June 1941, 43,000 civilians had been killed and 1.5 million homes lost due to German bombing raids.

On 10 September 1940 a bomb hit Buckingham Palace while the king and queen were at Windsor. Even though the damage was slight, people were impressed with the attitude of the Royal Family who insisted on staying at Buckingham Palace throughout the war.

Source E: People sleeping in an underground station in London during the Blitz.

Activities

4 Source E was used for propaganda. Write a suitable caption for the photograph.

The 'Blitz Spirit'

The Blitz provided the media, especially newspapers, with the ideal opportunity to portray the Nazis as evil murderers who must be defeated (see Source C). Moreover, at first sight, the bombing appears to have been a failure. Far from destroying morale and bombing Britain into submission, it had the opposite effect and made the British people even more determined to stand up to Hitler. People seemed cheerful in the face of great hardships and determined to get on with everyday life. The underground was full of people singing as they sheltered from the bombs.

However, high morale was not felt by everyone, everywhere. Censorship and propaganda was very effective in playing down the negative (and quite understandable) reactions of individuals or groups who were badly affected by the bombings (see Source G).

Source F: A cartoon from the *Daily Express*, November 1940.

" IS IT ALL RIGHT NOW, HENRY ? "
" YES, NOT EVEN SCRATCHED."

Source G: Extract from a local government report on the East End of London, September 1940.

The whole story of last weekend has been one of unplanned hysteria. The newspaper versions of life going on normally in the East End are greatly distorted. There was no bread, no milk, no telephones. There is no humour or laughter. There was thus every excuse for people to be distressed. There was no understanding in the huge government buildings of central London for the tiny crumbled streets of massed populations.

Source H: Extract from an official report into the effects of the bombing of Portsmouth, January 1941.

By 6.00 p.m. all traffic is moving northwards. The movement begins at 3.30 p.m. and continues to dusk. The people are making for the bridge on the main road out of Portsmouth in order to sleep in the northern suburbs, the surrounding hills, or towns and villages in the radius of twenty miles. One night it was estimated that 90,000 people left the city. Looting and wanton destruction have reached almost alarming proportions. The effect on morale is bad and there is a general feeling of desperation.

Source I: From the autobiography of T. Clarke, a special constable in the Blitz, published in 1974.

Of the Blitz spirit I shall write little. We in 'S' Division were luckier than many London police, but we had our fill of its cruelty and horror, and its sickening destructiveness, its white dusty filth, and its peculiar stink of fresh decay. Just these few words and it begins to depress me again.

Activities

5 Study Sources G, H and I. Do they support idea of the 'Blitz Spirit'? Explain your answer.

6 'Although less in number, the Zeppelin raids of the First World War were more devastating for the British people than the Blitz of 1940–1941.' Discuss.

6.6 Source analysis skills

As well as making inferences from sources (see page 100), you also have to explain why sources have been produced, in other words, the purpose of the source, or its underlying message.

> **Details**
> Posing for photographer in front of damaged Buckingham Palace.

> **Inference**
> Seem quite happy despite bomb attack.
> Brave enough to stand near where bombings took place.

Source A: A photograph used in national newspapers of the King and Queen outside Buckingham Palace the day after the raid of 10 September 1940.

> **Overall message**
> Royal Family suffering as much as normal people of London and not letting it affect their morale.

> **Purpose**
> This was to keep up morale among those in London and other cities experiencing the Blitz by showing that even the Royal Family, whose Palace has been damaged, can put on a brave face.

Source B: A photograph published in a national newspaper. It shows a family giving the 'thumbs up' sign on what is left of their bombed out Anderson shelter, in 1940.

Activity

1 Why do you think the newspapers chose to use this photograph (Source B)?

- Look at the details of the photograph.
- Make inferences from the photograph. What is it suggesting? What is its tone or attitude?
- What is the overall message of the photograph?
- Why does it have this message?
- You may also be asked how the person who produced the source gets across their message.

ResultsPlus
Build Better Answers

How does the photographer get his message across in Source B? (8 marks)

■ **Basic, Level 1 (1–2 marks).**
Answer describes or explains the message of the photo.

● **Good, Level 2 (3–5 marks).**
Answer takes some details from the picture and links this to the message the photographer is trying to give.

▲ **Excellent, Level 3 (6–8 marks).**
Answer explains the message of the photo and then shows how all the details in the photo do this.

Summary

Propaganda and censorship were used in Britain during both wars to keep up the morale of the people and ensure support for the war effort.

- An 'inference' is something you can work out from the source which it does not say directly.
- Zeppelin and Gotha raids did not cause much damage but they did seriously alarm British people.
- The Blitz of 1940–1941 caused considerable damage to several towns and cities and many civilian deaths. There were mixed reactions from Britons.
- In analysing the purpose of a source it is important to work out its underlying message, attitude or tone.

7.1 Government organisation for war

Learning outcomes

By the end of this section you should be able to:

- describe some of the effects of government action on society during the wars
- explain the part played by women in the armed services and workforce
- understand the part played by rationing and evacuation
- cross-reference sources for support, challenge and reliability.

Activities

1 Study Source A, which was used for propaganda.

   a) Why was it chosen to be used for propaganda?

   b) Write a caption for the photograph.

2 What do DORA and EPA stand for?

3 Give two examples of the powers used by the government during the two wars.

The powers of the British government were greatly extended during the course of the two world wars.

Government powers
The government had very wide-ranging powers during both conflicts. The Defence of the Realm Act (DORA), August 1914, allowed it to take over industries and control what the public knew about the war. The Emergency Powers Act (EPA) of May 1940 gave the government almost unlimited powers. From then on, civilians could be told to do anything and be sent anywhere.

Rationing
In both wars Britain suffered from food shortages, mainly due to the sinking of merchant ships by German U-boats, and had to bring in rationing. This meant that the government controlled what people could eat and drink. Although at first voluntary, rationing was soon made compulsory.

Evacuation
Evacuation was brought in just after the German invasion of Poland, in September 1939, due to the fear of air attack. About 1.5 million people, mainly children, were evacuated from towns or cities to live with families in the 'safer' countryside.

Source A: Children being evacuated by train.

Mobilisation of women
In both wars, women were used to cover the shortages of male workers as a result of conscription and war casualties. During the First World War, women's armed forces were set up for the first time, and they played an important part in both conflicts. Moreover, women were also employed in jobs previously done only by men, especially in heavy industry.

Role of Government

Conscription
Conscription is the system of forcing men and sometimes women to serve in the armed forces. It was first brought in by the government in 1916 to cover the heavy losses on the Western Front and the decline in men volunteering. It was reintroduced in May 1939, just before the outbreak of the Second World War.

7.2 Government powers

During both wars, the role and powers of the government were greatly extended.

The Defence of the Realm Act 1914

People's lives were greatly affected by the passing of the Defence of the Realm Act, which gave the government special powers. During the First World War, the government added extra powers, which included the right to take possession of any factory, workshop or piece of land and also to censor newspapers. Here are some of the things people were not allowed to do according to DORA:

- talk about military affairs in public places;
- spread rumours about military affairs;
- light bonfires or fireworks;
- buy binoculars;
- buy whisky or brandy in a railway refreshment room;
- ring church bells;
- fly a kite;
- use invisible ink when writing abroad;
- melt down gold or silver;
- trespass on railways or bridges.

As the war progressed, the government brought in many other measures. These included:

- introducing British Summer Time (putting the clocks forward an hour) to provide more daylight for work in the evening;
- controlling the consumption of alcohol, to try to reduce absenteeism from work due to drunkenness, by cutting down on pub opening hours, giving instructions for beer to be watered down and not allowing customers in pubs to buy rounds of drinks;
- appointing special constables to help maintain law and order;
- making strikes illegal in certain vital industries;
- not allowing workers in certain occupations, such as mining and farming – known as reserved occupations – to join the army because their skills were needed at home in Britain.

Activities

1   Working in pairs, choose four regulations from DORA telling people what they could not do and give reasons why they were introduced. Why did the government want to control this behaviour?

Conscription in the First World War

One of the important powers used by the government during the First World War was conscription. At first the government was reluctant to force men to join the armed forces. Instead, they encouraged them to volunteer through the use of conscience posters and peer pressure. However, the number of volunteers began to slow down during the course of 1915 due to news of the conditions at the war front and the high numbers of casualties, which were published in local newspapers. Moreover, conscription became necessary because Britain was unable to cover the heavy losses incurred, especially on the Western Front.

As early as August 1915 the government introduced the national registration of all single men. This was later extended to married men. It gave the government a list of men who could be called upon to fight if necessary. However, in January 1916 the Military Service Act made all unmarried men between the ages of 18 and 41 liable for service in the armed forces. In May 1916, the act was extended to include married men. From 1916 to 1918 a total of 3,500,000 men were conscripted into the armed forces. There were only four exceptions:

- men in reserved occupations, i.e. in important industries such as mining;
- men with ill health;
- men with family responsibilities, i.e. in situations where someone else in the family would suffer if they were conscripted;
- **conscientious objectors**.

Source A: An example of a conscience poster used by the government to encourage men to join up, 1915.

Source B: A cartoon in a pacifist newspaper, 1916.

COMPULSION BILL

"GOT HIM"

Activities

2 Study Source A. How does the poster encourage men to join up?

3 How does the cartoonist get across his message in Source B? Explain your answer, using evidence from the source.

Conscientious objectors

Some 16,100 men objected to the war because of their consciences – in other words, they refused to fight because of their moral or religious beliefs, and they had to appear before a military **tribunal** to prove that they deserved to be exempt from military service. Of these, around 9,500 helped the war effort by working behind the lines in non-fighting roles or by doing essential work connected with the armed forces.

Source C: From a Quaker, a member of a religious group who believe in non-violent behaviour.

It was right at the beginning that I learnt that the only people from whom I could expect sympathy were soldiers and not civilians. I was waiting in the guardroom when five soldiers under arrest came in. When they asked me what I was in for, I was as simple as possible. 'I am a Quaker and I refused to join the army because I think that war is murder.' 'Murder,' one of them whispered. 'It's bloody murder.' As they went away they each came up to me and shook me by the hand – 'Stick to it matey,' they said, one after the other.

Source D: From an interview in the 1960s with Percy Wall, who was sent to a prison camp because he refused to fight in the First World War.

The attitude of the soldiers at the camp varied. A very small minority told us they would like to see us shot. Others wished to know exactly what we were standing for and some of them told us they would be conscientious objectors next time. Another group seemed to think we were simply trying to get out of going to the trenches.

Source E: Conscientious objectors at a prison camp.

The remaining conscientious objectors were sent to prison camps where they were often treated with great cruelty (see Source F and Source G). For example, at a Home Office Works Centre in Dyce, near Aberdeen, conditions were so cold and harsh because tents were the only form of accommodation that many caught pneumonia and several died. At another centre, the prisoners' job was to handle the rotting corpses of animals. In total, ten died in prison, 63 died soon after release and 31 went insane because of their experiences.

Source F: A letter from the commander of the Military Detention Barracks at Wandsworth to the *Daily Express*, 1918.

> I had them placed in special rooms, nude, but with their full army kit for them to put on as soon as they wished. There were no blankets left in the rooms, which were quite bare. Several of the men held out naked for several hours but they gradually accepted the inevitable. Forty of the conscientious objectors who passed through my hands are now quite willing soldiers.

Source G: From an interview with a conscientious objector in 1928.

> Our ankles were tied together and our arms were tied tightly at the wrists to the cross and we had to remain in that position for two hours. The second evening we were placed with our faces to the barbed wire fence. I found myself drawn so closely to the fence that when I wished to turn my head I did so very carefully to avoid my face being torn. To make matters worse, it came on to rain and a bitterly cold wind blew across the top of the hill. Another man, Jack Gray, was put into a sack, thrown into a pond eight times and pulled out by a rope round his body.

Activities

4 What can you learn from Sources C and D about attitudes to conscientious objectors?

5 Why do you think the government published the photograph (Source A)?

6 Working in a group, put together arguments for and against conscientious objectors that people at the time would make. Make a copy of the scales below and add these arguments.

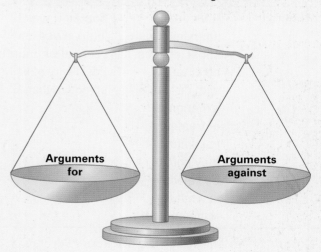

7 'It took greater courage to be a conscientious objector rather than to join up.' Discuss.

Cross-referencing sources

How far do sources D, F and G suggest that conscientious objectors were badly treated? Explain your answer using each of the sources.

In the question above, you are being asked to cross-reference the sources and come to a decision:

- think about their content – what they suggest
- identify support and challenges between the sources
- then assess the strength of the support or challenge by thinking about the nature of the sources – in other words, the type of source. (There is more guidance on nature in Section 8, page 136.)

Here is a planning grid, with examples of how to use the sources to answer the question. Make a copy of and complete the grid.

	Support	**Challenge**
Contents	D suggests some soldiers wanted to shoot him. In Source F they are made to stand naked.	Source D suggests sympathy and some support from soldiers. Source F suggests being forced to fight for their country.
Nature	Both are interviews with conscientious objectors with direct experience of treatment in camps but they could be selective in what they remembered.	Source D was interviewed many years after Source G. Possibility of being more objective than G.

Now write an answer to the question. For your conclusion you need to make a final judgement on the extent of support between the three sources for the statement. In other words you need to allocate a weight to each source. Where would you place the sources?

← No support   Little support   Some support   Strong support →

Include this in your conclusion.

Emergency Powers Act 1940

The Emergency Powers Act was introduced by the government in May 1940, after the British Army had been forced to retreat from Dunkirk and there was a real threat of invasion. This was a time of desperation, with France on the verge of defeat and with every likelihood of a German invasion. The Act gave the desperate British government almost unlimited powers over people and property. From then on, civilians could be required to do anything and be sent anywhere.

Conscription in the Second World War

Military conscription was introduced in April 1939, that is, before the war had begun, to avoid the mistakes of the First World War. This was the first time conscription had been introduced in peacetime. At first, men were only supposed to serve for six months, but most were kept on for the remainder of the war. Between May 1939 and the autumn of 1941, all men aged between 18 and 52 were conscripted. Unlike the First World War, during the Second World War there were few complaints about conscription (see sources H and I). However, there was some criticism of the government for the slow pace with which it was brought in.

Source H: From the memories of James Palmer written in 1994. He was called up in May 1939.

It was with mixed feelings that I sat down on the platform bench waiting for the train. Dad and my girlfriend Muriel had come along with me and both looked terribly upset. I felt both excitement and anxiety. I knew that I would not like being in the army, yet I felt pleased at being one of the first to go. I was looking forward to the experience. It was only for six months, so the papers said, and I would come home before Christmas.

Source I: Men volunteering to serve in the Royal Navy, 1939.

By the end of 1940, 200,000 had deferred their call-up for the armed forces because of the importance of their occupation. Over 1 million volunteered or asked for their call-up to be speeded up in the same period.

As well as few complaints, there were two further differences from the First World War:

- From the start of the Second World War all men aged 18–41 had to register for work – either to fight or work in a reserved occupation.
- In December 1941 the conscription of women was introduced. At first it applied only to unmarried women aged 20–30, but in 1942 the minimum age was lowered to 19 and in 1943 the maximum age was raised to 43.

Activities

8 How far do Sources H and I suggest that recruitment was popular in 1939?

9 What differences and similarities were there between recruitment and conscription in the First and Second World Wars?

7.3 The mobilisation of women

Women played a key role during both world wars, in the armed forces and in the workforce.

First World War

During the First World War women were recruited into the armed forces for the first time. At first, in 1916, they were used as volunteers in Voluntary Aid Detachments (VADs), where they worked behind the lines as nurses (see Source A).

Source A: A VAD volunteer describes her experiences, after the First World War.

> Looking back at my time as a VAD in hospital, I think that it was the happiest time I ever spent, for it was all so worthwhile. The men who suffered did so because of their terrible heroism, not just because they had pneumonia or had been run over in the street. And no matter how tired one was, what terrible things one had to do, it was worthwhile to work until one could work no longer.

However from 1917–1918 women were recruited as full-time members of the armed forces:

WAAC	WRNS	WRAF
The Women's Auxiliary Army Corps was set up in January 1917. It took over many of the office jobs in the army, which freed the men to fight (see Source B).	The Women's Royal Naval Service was set up in 1917. Women did not go to sea or fight. As with the army, they took over office duties.	The Women's Royal Air Force was set up in 1918. Women did not fly the planes or fight. Instead, they carried out routine office and domestic duties.

From the early stages of the war, British industry began to suffer a desperate shortage of labour. By early 1916, Britain had up to 2 million workers fewer than were necessary to keep the country going. This was due to the number of men who had volunteered for the armed forces between 1914 and 1916. Gradually, more and more women were employed to do male jobs (see Source C).

Source B: A recruitment poster for the WAAC.

- Women were soon employed in place of male clerks. By the end of the war half a million women had replaced men in office jobs.
- At first, employers and unions resisted the employment of women in manufacturing industries. Employers believed they did not have the skills, and unions believed employing women would bring down wages. However, by 1916 the shortages were so great that women had to be employed. By 1918 almost 800,000 women were working in engineering, especially in **munitions** work.

- Women were also employed in other jobs previously regarded as exclusively for men. They worked in transport as paid bus conductors and drivers, and as grave diggers, postal workers, fire fighters, chimney sweeps, blacksmiths and welders.
- There was a Women's Voluntary Police service in most major cities.
- About 260,000 women worked in the Women's Land Army where they took the place of male farm workers.

Source C: A table showing the work of women during the First World War from B. Walsh, *Modern World History*, Murray, 1996, p. 77.

Area of work	Women in 1914	Women in 1918	Women replacing men
Metals	170,000	594,000	195,000
Chemicals	40,000	104,000	35,000
Food and drink	196,000	235,000	60,000
Timber	44,000	79,000	23,000
Transport	18,000	117,000	42,000
Government	2,000	225,000	197,000

Activities

1. What do the following abbreviations stand for?
   a) VADs
   b) WAAC
   c) WRNS
   d) WRAF.
2. What can you learn from Source A about the VADs?
3. Study Source B. How does the poster get across its message?
4. Study Source C. In which area of work was there the greatest change?

Second World War

From late 1941 women, unless they were pregnant or had small children, were sent to work in industry or the **auxiliary** armed services. By 1943, 90 per cent of single women and 80 per cent of married women were doing work of national importance.

The women's armed services included the WRNS, the WAAF (Women's Auxiliary Air Force) and the ATS (Auxiliary Territorial Service). The WRNS was the most popular service followed by the WAAF – many women thought that the uniforms of these services were more exciting than the dull khaki of the ATS. By 1944 there were 450,000 women in these services, with 212,000 in the ATS. As during the First World War, the women did the routine office, driving and domestic duties and freed the men to do combat duty.

Despite not being involved in combat, women did hard and often dangerous jobs too. They worked as mechanics, welders, pilots, carpenters and even gunners on anti-aircraft guns – though they were not allowed to fire the guns. A total of 335 women were killed in the ATS and another 300 wounded.

Source D: A booklet prepared by the War Department in 1942. It was given to American soldiers coming to Britain.

British women officers often give orders to men. The men obey smartly and know it is no shame. For British women have proved themselves in the war. They have stuck to their posts near burning ammunition dumps, delivered messages on foot after their motorcycles have been blasted under them. They have pulled aviators from burning planes. There isn't a single record of any British woman in uniformed service quitting her post, or failing in her duty under fire.

Activities

5. Study Source D. What is the purpose of this booklet? How does it get this message across?

Source E: From an advert for Hoover in 1944.

HOUSEWIFE 1944

The Hand that held the Hoover helps the Bombed!

When an "incident has occurred," nobody is more welcome to 'bombed out,' wardens, and demolition workers, than the W.V.S. with their mobile canteens. Now there is a bite to eat, and a cup of tea to hearten them. That's only one of the many jobs W.V.S. do, voluntarily, and without pay, and they nearly all have homes to run and families to look after as well. As a token of our very heartfelt admiration for this splendid Service we say —

Salute! FROM HOOVER

Hoover users know best what improvements they would like in the post-war Hoover. Suggestions are welcome.

BY APPOINTMENT TO H.M. KING GEORGE VI AND H.M. QUEEN MARY
HOOVER LIMITED, PERIVALE, GREENFORD, MIDDLESEX

Source F: A painting by an official war artist. It shows a woman working in an engineering factory.

WOMEN OF BRITAIN
COME INTO THE FACTORIE
ASK AT ANY EMPLOYMENT EXCHANGE FOR ADVICE AND FULL DE

Activities

6 What is the message of Source E? Use examples from the source in your answer.

7 Why was Source F produced? Use examples from the source in your answer.

Once again, as in the First World War, women worked in a variety of jobs. By September 1943 there were nearly 8 million women in paid work, 3 million more than when the war started. There were another million women working in voluntary services.

Factory work

By 1943 women occupied 57 per cent of the jobs in factories and, when they were in direct competition with men, often showed that they could do a better job. The Ministry of Information published details of women's achievements. A woman welder 'produced 120 pieces of equipment a day, compared to 100 by her male colleagues'.

Source G: A factory worker interviewed in 1942.

> Working in the factories is not fun. To be shut in for hours on end without even a window to see daylight is grim. The noise was terrific and at night when you shut your eyes to sleep all the noise would start again in your head. The work was often monotonous. I think boredom was our worst enemy.

Land Army

The Women's Land Army was revived in 1939, and 80,000 women volunteered for work. They had no choice where they worked and were often billeted in remote areas in very basic conditions. They proved themselves more than capable of coping with tough jobs and handled animals particularly well.

Source H: From an interview with Lily Halford who served in the Women's Land Army.

> I was called up in 1942. I did not mind being called up. I think all of us were eager to do some kind of war work. I chose the Land Army because I liked gardening and decided to apply for a job to do with the horticultural side of the Land Army.

Cross-referencing for support

How far do Sources G and H support the impression of women's work given in Source F?

Once again, the question above is asking you to cross-reference the sources and come to a conclusion about the extent of their support for a statement. Make a copy of the grid and use it to plan your answer.

	Support	Challenge	Extent of support
Contents			
Nature			

Voluntary services

Many women entered the voluntary services. By 1943 there were 180,000 in **civil defence** and a further 47,000 in the fire services. Approximately 130,000 women served as messengers and dispatch riders for the post office. Many others worked in medical centres, first aid posts, mobile canteens and rest centres.

7.4 Rationing

One key role of government in both wars was to control food supplies through **rationing** to prevent Britain from being starved out of the war.

First World War

One of the aims of DORA was to prevent food shortages. By 1917 the Germans were using their submarines to stop supply ships from getting through to Britain from America and the continent. In April 1917 Britain had only six weeks' worth of wheat stores left. Food was so scarce that prices rose sharply and queues to buy food grew. Coal was also in short supply and, in October 1917, it was rationed.

In 1917 the government was, at first, reluctant to bring in compulsory rationing. Instead, it asked people to voluntarily limit themselves each week to:

| Two and a half pounds of meat | Three-quarters of a pound of sugar | Four pounds of bread |

But voluntary rationing did not work; the food shortages continued and the queues for food grew longer. Moreover, the rich seemed to have access to as much food as they wanted through the black market and this caused widespread resentment. Therefore, in January 1918, the government introduced compulsory rationing. Everybody was issued with a ration card, and had to register with a local butcher and grocer. Every person could have the following ration each week:

| Fifteen ounces of meat | Five ounces of bacon | Four ounces of butter |

Rationing worked. Queueing more or less stopped, and the system was seen as fair. Indeed, many poorer people became healthier because they got a better share of healthy food.

Source A: A ration card of 1918.

HAMPDEN HOUSE, LTD.

Beer Ration Card.

Name _Leslie Curnow_   Room _409_

Week ending _March 23_ 1918

	LUNCHEON	DINNER
SUNDAY	½ Pint	½ Pint
MONDAY		
TUESDAY		
WEDNESDAY		
THURSDAY		
FRIDAY		
SATURDAY		
RATION.		

1 PINT per day.

Activities

1 What can you learn from Source A about rationing?
2 Give two reasons for compulsory rationing and two achievements of rationing.

Second World War

The government was much quicker to introduce compulsory rationing during the Second World War. In January 1940 the Ministry of Food under Lord Woolton worked out fair food rations. At first only butter, sugar and bacon were rationed. Eventually, almost all food except seasonal fruit and vegetables was rationed. Rationing soon went beyond food. Almost every other essential article could only be bought with coupons. In other words, even if you were rich, you could not legally get extra rations because you had the same number of coupons as everyone else. Even the Royal Family had ration books.

Source B: The average weekly ration for each adult each week.

meat	1 shilling to 2 shillings and a pennyworth
bacon	4 oz to 8 oz
cheese	1 oz to 8 oz
fat	1 oz to 8 oz
eggs	1 to 2
tea	2 oz to 4 oz
sugar	8 oz to 16 oz + 2 lb for jam making
sweets and chocolate	3 oz to 4 oz
dried milk	1 tin
dried eggs	one-eighth of a packet

Rationing was a success although there were some shortcomings.

Achievements
- It was a fair system that ensured that the poorer people were adequately fed with generally healthy food.
- It helped to unite people as they were all, rich and poor, sharing the same rations.
- The quality of rationed clothes was guaranteed by the government's utility mark.

Shortcomings
- The rich could buy extra rations on the black market.
- Very large families with several ration books were better off than small families with one or no children.
- Food supplies were more plentiful in certain areas. For example, vegetables were in greater supply in rural areas and pork and bacon were not rationed in Northern Ireland.

The government used other measures to control food supplies too:
- The 'Dig for Victory' campaign encouraged people to grow vegetables and keep chickens and pigs. Private gardens were turned into vegetable patches. Playing fields and railway embankments were ploughed up (see Source E).
- There were campaigns to avoid waste. For example, boy scouts and girl guides collected scraps for pigs.

Activities

3 Compare the message of Sources C and D. How similar are they?

4 What can you learn from Source E about the Dig for Victory campaign?

5 In what ways was food rationing better organised during the Second World War?

Source C: From a government leaflet of 1918.

I am a crust of bread. I am wasted once a day by 48,000,000 people of Britain. I am 'the bit left over'; the slice eaten absent-mindedly when really I wasn't needed. I am the waste crust. If you collected me and my companions for a whole week you would find that we amounted to 9,380 tons (9,530 tonnes) of good bread.

WASTED! Nine shiploads of good bread.

SAVE ME, AND I WILL SAVE YOU!

Source D: A Ministry of Food announcement, 1941.

Nearly half of our food comes across the sea. The U-boats attack our ships. Now, here is your part in the fight for Victory. When a particular food is not available, cheerfully accept something else – home-produced if possible. Keep loyally to the rationing regulations. Above all – whether you are shopping, cooking or eating – remember, 'FOOD IS A MUNITION OF WAR, DON'T WASTE IT'.

Source E: A British government poster of 1942.

DIG ON FOR VICTORY

7.5 Evacuation

Evacuation – the process of moving people from towns and cities into the countryside for safety – was brought in during the Second World War.

Reasons for evacuation

The British government believed that the Germans would bomb British towns and cities in order to destroy the morale of the people and force Britain to surrender. Therefore evacuation measures were put in place to protect civilians from bombings and gas attacks. Children were to be protected by being moved from the likeliest targets, the cities, to the countryside where it was thought they would be safe.

The organisation of evacuation

The first evacuation was announced on 31 August 1939, the day before Hitler invaded Poland. Many parents were reluctant to be separated from their children but accepted they would be safer in the country. Parents were told what the children needed to take with them and where they were to assemble for evacuation. The evacuation began on 1 September 1939. Many city schools were closed, and teachers went with the children to the countryside to carry on teaching them (see Source A).

Source A: From a government leaflet *Evacuation: Why and How?*, 1939.

> The government has made plans for the removal of schoolchildren from what are 'evacuable' areas to safer places. Householders have offered homes where the children will be most welcome. The schoolchildren will have their teachers and other helpers with them. The transport of 3 million children is an enormous undertaking. Of course it means heartache to be separated from your children, but you can be sure that they will be looked after.

At their destinations the evacuees gathered in village halls or schools where they were chosen by the foster family they were to live with. However, homesickness and the 'Phoney War', when little

fighting took place and there were no enemy bombing raids, meant that many children had drifted back to the cities by Christmas 1939.

When German bombers began blitzing London in 1940, a second evacuation from the cities took place. There was a further wave of evacuations in 1944 when the Germans used their V1 flying bombs and V2 missiles to bomb Britain.

Activities

1 What was the main reason for evacuation?
2 What can you learn from Source A about the organisation of evacuation?

Source B: A government poster of 1942.

Experiences of evacuees

The children had varied experiences of evacuation, some pleasant and some unpleasant, as the sources describe.

Source C: The memories of Rita Wright, written in 1989. She was evacuated at the age of nine from the East End of London.

> One really good thing about being evacuated to the countryside was the fact that my health improved so much. Although my parents had fed me well, I suffered from pneumonia every winter because of the crowded living conditions at home. From the time I was evacuated I never suffered from it again. The abundance of locally produced fruit and vegetables kept me very healthy.

Source D: An interview with the actor Michael Caine, who remembers life as an evacuee.

> The woman said, 'Here's your meal' and gave us a tin of pilchards between the two of us and some bread and water. Now we'd been in a rich woman's house before, so we said: 'Where's the butter?' And we got a sudden wallop round the head. What we later found out was that the woman hated kids and was doing it for the extra money. So the meals were the cheapest you could dish up.

Source E: Beryl Hewitson describes what happened to her when she was evacuated.

> We were told to sit quietly on the floor while villagers and farmers' wives came to choose which children they wanted. Eventually only my friend Nancy and myself were left. A large, happy-looking middle-aged woman rushed in asking: 'Is that all you have left?' A sad, slow nod of the head from our teacher. 'I'll take the poor bairns.' We were led out of the hall and taken to a farm where we spent two years.

Source F: Ted Cummings, who was evacuated from Manchester to Sandbach in 1939, remembers his experiences in the 1960s.

> We left feeling sad for our parents and afraid that they would be killed by bombs. When we arrived in Sandbach we were chosen for a variety of reasons. For the extra income they received for us, to help on the farm or with the housework. A very few were lucky because they lived with families who really cared for them. For those, life was like a holiday and they did not want to leave. I was upset because I was separated from my sister. I was glad when I returned home for Christmas.

Activities

3   What is the message of Source B? How does the poster get across this message?

4   In a group, study sources C–F. What do they suggest about the experiences of evacuees? Make a copy of the following grid and complete it. Give a brief explanation for each source.

Pleasant experience	Mixed	Unpleasant

Activities

5 Was evacuation a success?

- Evacuees were not used to rural life and there was a clash between city and country values.
- Evacuation saved many lives.
- The organisation was sometimes poor, especially the way in which the evacuees were chosen by their foster parents.
- Evacuees often found themselves in much wealthier homes and had to cope with different standards of behaviour.
- It meant that some children, from poor inner city areas, saw the countryside for the first time.
- Many evacuees stayed with better-off people and were given a better standard of living, for example, better food.

- Evacuation also showed better-off people in the countryside the social problems of families living in inner city areas and increased the demand for change.
- There is evidence that some people tried to avoid taking evacuees.

Working in pairs, make a copy of the scales and organise achievements on the left and shortcomings on the right. Include evidence from Sources C – E.

Overall, do you believe that evacuation was a success?

Cross-referencing for reliability

Historians frequently use cross-referencing and comparing sources to check that their descriptions are accurate and reliable. You may be asked to do this as part of the exam.

> **Do you think you can rely on the evidence of Source G? Explain your answer, using Sources G and H.**

There are two parts to answering this question.

1 evaluating the reliability of Source G
2 cross-referencing with H to test the reliability of G.

Follow these steps to answer it successfully.

- Have a clear idea of what it is you want to check in the first source (list the details you are checking).
- Check the second source to see what it says about each of those details. Are they confirmed?
- What attitude is shown in the first source. Is it positive or negative? Does it stress any particular aspect?
- Check the attitude of the second source. Is it similar or different?
- Weigh up the similarities and differences between the two sources.

- Are there any differences in the nature of the sources?
- Look at the differences. Are they small differences, e.g. in numbers, or big differences that might even contradict each other?

It is very rare to find a source that totally agrees with another, so you need to make a judgement about how far the second source backs up the first one, based on what you have found in this process of cross reference.

Set out around Sources G and H are some sub-questions to answer in order to help you to test its reliability. Now write an answer to the exam question: 'Do you think we can rely on the impression Sylvia Collier gives of evacuation?' Explain your answer using Sources G and H.

ResultsPlus
Watch out!

Many students assume that a secondary source is less reliable than a primary source because the historian was not there at the time. However, an account written by historians should actually be very reliable because they have investigated lots of sources and weighed them up in order to write full explanations.

What type of source is it?

What was the purpose of the source? How does that affect what Sylvia may have chosen to say?

In what ways do the contents of Source H corroborate the contents of Source G?

Source G: In 1995 Sylvia Collier wrote about her experiences for a local newspaper, which was commemorating the 50th anniversary of the end of the Second World War. She was evacuated from the East End of London to Wiltshire in 1939.

When was the source written?

Who wrote the source? It was written by an evacuee and should be reliable because she experienced evacuation.

Our school, near to Wormwood Scrubs, had forty classes so took most of the children in the area where we lived. On the morning of September 1st we assembled and made our way to East Acton Station to board the train for our unknown destination. My brother and I thought we were going for a fortnight, so unconcerned, waved goodbye to Mum as the train pulled away taking us to Wiltshire. All the children seemed happy enough about being evacuated.

In what ways do the contents of Source H not corroborate the contents of Source G?

Source H: A photograph of children being evacuated, September 1939

Summary

- The government had very far reaching-powers during the two world wars, with the Defence of the Realm Act and the Emergency Powers Act.
- They used these powers to introduce conscription. Those that opposed compulsory service were known as conscientious objectors and were often treated badly.
- Due to employment shortages the government recruited women into industry and transport. They also set up women's armed forces.
- Food shortages, due to the sinking of merchant ships by German submarines, led to rationing. Although at first voluntary, the government introduced compulsory rationing of food and other necessities.
- During the Second World War children, teachers and some mothers were evacuated to the countryside to protect them from the German bombing of cities.

8.1 The impact of war on society

Learning outcomes

By the end of this section you should be able to:

● describe the changing role of women during the First World War and the years after

● describe the part played by women in the Second World War

● explain the impact of the wars on society

● explain the value of sources.

Activity

1 Give two examples of:
   • when women seemed to make progress
   • when there was little or no progress
   • differences between the picture of the woman before the First World War (1) and the picture of the woman after the First World War (3) .

1 Before the First World War women were very much second-class citizens:
- They did not have the vote.
- They had few job opportunities.
- Jobs were generally low paid.
- They were expected to marry, have children and look after the home.

2 During the First World War:
- Many women played a key role on the home front.
- They worked in many new jobs especially heavy industry and transport.
- Some jobs, such as munitions, were very dangerous.
- Some joined the women's armed services.

3 In the years between the wars, 1918–1939:
- In 1918 women over 30 were given the vote, and ten years later this was changed to women over the age of 21.
- Some young women known as the flappers had a freer lifestyle. They wore shorter dresses, used make-up, cut their hair short, smoked and drank in public and went out unescorted.
- Most women during the wars had to give up their wartime jobs and go back to their original employment.

4 During the Second World War:
- Once again women played an important role on the home front.
- Many worked in heavy industry and transport.
- Others joined the women's armed forces.

5 In the years after the war, 1945–1950:
- The majority of women went back to their original employment.
- Married women were not expected to work but to stay at home and look after the family.
- Women were once again seen as the weaker sex.

8.2 The situation of women in 1914

Before the First World War a woman was seen as a second-class citizen whose main role was as a wife and mother.

Source A: A leading scientist, Thomas Huxley, writing in 1851.

> In every excellent characteristic, whether mental or physical, the average woman is inferior to the average man.

Employment

Most men and many women believed that a woman's place was in the home supporting her husband and bringing up their children. Married women were not expected to work (see Source A).

Source B: From the biography of Joseph Ashby, a farm worker.

> Their mother would teach them, by action and words, that girls and women find it best to submit to their husbands and brothers. Their duty was to feed them well, run their errands and bear all the burdens except the physical ones.

However, married working-class women often worked in order to supplement the family income. This was often in unskilled, low-paid jobs especially in the textile industry and the sweated trades, such as tailoring. Where women did the same job as men, they were almost always paid less.

For unmarried women, employment opportunities were limited to doing domestic work as maids or cooks in wealthy households, teaching girls and nursing. The better paid professions such as the law, medicine and accountancy were generally closed to women, who, in any case, usually lacked the necessary qualifications to enter these professions.

There was some progress in the field of medicine due to the example of Elizabeth Garrett Anderson who, in 1865, passed all the exams to qualify as a doctor. However, she had to overcome immense difficulties, first to get training and then to be allowed to practise as a doctor.

Source C: A statement made by students at a hospital in London in 1861.

> We consider that the mixture of sexes in the same class is likely to lead to results of an unpleasant character. Lecturers are likely to feel some restraint through the presence of females in giving explicit enunciation of some facts which is necessary. The presence of young females in the operating theatre is an outrage on our natural instincts and feelings and is calculated to destroy those sentiments of respect and admiration with which the sex is regarded by all right-thinking men.

Education

Girls were given an education to prepare them for their future domestic role. They were generally confined to reading, writing, some arithmetic and subjects such as needlework and cookery. There were few opportunities for higher education which limited their employment opportunities.

However, there was some progress before 1914. For example in 1872 the Girl's Public Day Trust was set up to raise money for girls' grammar schools. In 1886 St Hugh's and St Hilda's Colleges were founded at Oxford University, although women were still not able to take a degree.

Activities

1 What can you learn from Source B about the role of women before 1914?
2 How far do Sources A, B and C suggest that women were second-class citizens before 1914? Explain your answer using Sources A, B and C.

Socially

Single women were expected not to go out without an older escort or **chaperone**, and not to smoke or drink. They were expected to dress in a conservative way, wearing long dresses or skirts, and to have long hair, tied back. Make-up was frowned upon.

The campaign for the vote

Early in the 20th century there was one important right that women did not have: the right to vote and stand for Parliament. This was for several reasons:

- Many opposed votes for women. Queen Victoria called giving women the vote a 'mad, wicked folly'. Some men claimed that women were emotionally unsound and would be unable to vote sensibly.
- Others said that as women could not fight for their country, they should not be allowed to vote.

The campaign for the vote was stepped up in the years before 1914. There were two main groups of campaigners.

Source D: A march by the NUWSS in London, 1913.

The Suffragists

Suffragists believed that women should campaign peacefully. All they had to do was keep on the right side of the law, and do all they could to persuade the general public and Parliament that women ought to be given the vote. One such group was the National Union of Women's **Suffrage** Societies (NUWSS) led by Millicent Fawcett. This group organised marches (see Source D), posters and petitions. They tried to demonstrate that women were sensible enough for the vote.

The Suffragettes

In contrast, Suffragettes believed in using militant or extreme methods. They were prepared to break the law in order to get the vote as this would get them publicity and force the government to give way. They were led by Emmeline Pankhurst, who set up the Women's Social and Political Union (WSPU) in 1903. During the years 1906–1914 their methods became more militant. They began by interrupting the meetings of leading Liberals and moved on to going on hunger strike after being arrested, smashing windows, cutting telephone wires, setting fire to derelict buildings and assaulting leading Liberals.

Why did women not get the vote?

Despite all this activity, women did not have the vote by 1914. This was partly due to the militancy of the suffragettes which had convinced many people, including members of Parliament and the government, that women were not responsible enough to deserve the vote. Moreover, the two leading political parties, the Liberals and the Conservatives, were unable to decide which groups of women to give the vote to, since many men did not yet have the vote either.

Activities

3 What can you learn from Source D about the methods used by the Suffragists to campaign for the vote?

4 'Women were second-class citizens in Britain in 1914'. Discuss.

8.3 Changes for women 1914–1918

As explained in Section 7, the First World War saw women playing a crucial role on the **home front**, especially in employment and the women's armed forces. This did much to change some people's attitudes to votes for women and employment opportunities. However, in other respects, there was little change.

Munitions work

About 60 per cent of all workers in the munitions industry were women. They worked 12-hour shifts, seven days a week, packing explosives and cordite charges into bullets and shells (see Sources A and B). Sometimes they developed lead poisoning, or illnesses from the chemicals, which caused their hair to fall out and turned their skin yellow. This earned these women the nickname 'canaries'. Some workers were even killed when munitions factories blew up (see Source C). In 1917 a fire in Silvertown munitions works in East London caused an explosion that killed 69 people and injured 400.

Source A: An official war painting from 1917, of women at work in a munitions factory.

Source B: A photograph taken in a munitions factory.

Source C: Extract from the diary of a female munitions worker, May 1917.

I was doing some crochet work in my tea time when I heard the alarm. In my hurry to get to the fire I ran over an allotment and fell into a ditch. We had to push through a crowd of men who shouted at us not to go near. The exploding cartridges made a fearful noise. Most of us were struck by bullets but only bruised. There was not too much power in the hits.

Activities

1 What was the purpose of Source A?
2 Devise a suitable caption for this painting (Source A).
3 How far is the impression it gives supported by Source B?

 ResultsPlus
Build Better Answers

What can you learn from Source B about the work done by women in munitions factories? (4 marks)

■ **Basic, Level 1 (1–2 marks).**
Answer describes the picture or explains the work done by women during the war. It takes some detail and links it to a comment about women's work in munitions factories.

● **Good, Level 2 (3–4 marks).**
Answer takes several details from the picture and uses them to explain women's work in munitions factories.

Growing independence

The war brought other changes to women's lives, mainly as a result of the work they did. Women had to adapt to new ways of dressing for the work they were doing – having short hair or wearing trousers, for example. Some women appeared in uniform, in roles ranging from railway porters to ambulance drivers.

Women gained much greater freedom. With fewer men around, chaperones for wealthier girls became less common. Full wage packets meant that women had money to spend. They now smoked, drank in pubs, went to the cinema, on bicycle trips and on shopping trips in town unsupervised (read Source D). Some older people were scandalised, and troops returning home from France were amazed.

Source D: An article from the *Daily Mail*, September 1916.

> The wartime business girl is to be seen at night dining out in restaurants in London. Before, she would never have had her evening meal in town unless in the company of a man friend. But now, with money and without men, she is dining out more and more. The meal, of course, is accompanied by a cigarette.

Source E: A historian writing in 1965.

> Women became more independent. Women munitions workers paid for their round of drinks at the pub. Fashion changed for practical reasons. Never again did skirts sweep the ground. The petticoat disappeared. Women's hats became neater. A few women cut their hair. Not all the changes in work lasted after the war, but some did. The male clerk with his quill pen and copperplate handwriting was gone for good, replaced by the female shorthand typist.

Source F: An article called 'The New Woman' from *The Sphere*, May 1918.

> She has entered practically all the professions. She will get the vote next month. A postwoman brings you the letters and a girl brings you the milk for your morning tea. There are girls, uniformed or not, at the wheels of half the cars that pass. If you go by train, women will handle your luggage. If you choose a bus or tram, the conductress in her smart uniform has long become a familiar figure. You can even be shaved by a woman.

Activities

4 What can you learn from Source D about changes in the social life of some women?

5 How far does Source F support the evidence of Source E about the changes to women's lives as a result of the First World War?

Did the attitudes of men towards women change?

Source G: From M. Pugh, *Women's Suffrage, 1867–1928*, 1992.

> A very simplified view would see the vote as a reward for wartime service. However, careful study shows little change resulted from the war, not how much. In the newspaper reports of the time women received a warm welcome; but in farms, hospitals and factories they were greatly resented.

Source H: From a speech made in 1917 by Herbert Asquith, who was Prime Minister from 1908 to 1916.

> My opposition to women's rights is well known. However, for three years now the Suffragettes have not restarted that horrible campaign of violence. Not only that, they have contributed to every service during this war except of fighting. I therefore believe that some measure of women's suffrage should be given.

Source I: From a letter to the *Glasgow Herald* sent by a woman in 1916.

> To observe how men speak and write about women today is vastly amusing to us. We have not changed with the war. It is only in that some instances the scales have fallen from men's eyes. In the hour of Britain's need her sons have realised that if victory was to be won they could not afford to hem women in with the old restrictions.

Source J: A comparison of the quality of output by men and women. This was from a report by the National Employers' Federation (all men), 1918.

> Quality
>
> Sheet metal – Women's work better than men's output.
>
> Aircraft woodwork – Women equal to men in most areas.
>
> Cartridge production – Women equal to men.
>
> Shell production – Women's work poorer than men's.

Source K: A photograph taken in a munitions factory in 1917.

Activities

6 This is a group task. Make a copy of the following table. Decide which sources suggest a change in attitudes and which suggest no change. Give a brief explanation for each choice.

Change of attitudes		No change of attitudes	
Source	Brief explanation	Source	Brief explanation

7 How much change do you think there was in the attitude of men? Make a copy of the following line. Place your judgement somewhere on the line, with a brief explanation.

←——————————————————→

No change   Some change   Much change   Total change

8 'The First World War transformed the attitudes of men towards women.' Discuss.

8.4 Developments in the position of women 1918–1939

During the inter-war years, women did make some progress, especially in their political and social position. However, there was little or no change in employment opportunities.

Political position

There was some progress in the political position of women. The Representation of the People Act, which was passed in 1918 before the end of the war, gave women aged 30 and over the vote, together with men over the age of 21. This was due partly to the determination of the government to extend the vote to soldiers who had fought in the war.

Source A: From a speech by an MP in the Commons in 1917.

> Opinion is changing in favour of giving women the vote due to the excellent work they have done for us and the country during the war.

Source B: Written by an MP in 1922.

> The vote was won, not by burning churches, slashing pictures or damaging pillar boxes but by women's work during the war. It was not giving way to violence but a reward for patriotic service.

However, younger women, in their twenties, were disappointed with the age limit. They were considered too young and immature to cope in a responsible way with a vote. The real reason they were not included was that men feared that a female majority in voters, due to the death of so many men during the First World War, would elect a great number of female MPs.

In 1919 Nancy Astor became the first woman MP to take her seat in Parliament. In 1928, women aged 21 and over were given the vote. At last, they had equal voting rights to men.

Social position

There was some progress in women's social position. Labour-saving devices, such as washing machines and fridges, reduced the hours needed on housework and allowed women more leisure time. Better advice about contraception meant that women could choose when to have children and to have fewer of them.

Moreover, the war had given many women greater confidence and had changed their attitude to their appearance and social habits. Young women no longer had chaperones. They were able to go to the cinema or to dances with boyfriends without having to take an aunt or other female with them. Women's clothing became much simpler and less restrictive, and make-up became acceptable. Some women even dared to wear one-piece swimming costumes, instead of the pre-war costumes with sleeves and skirts. The **flapper** was the most extreme example of these social changes (see picture 3 on page 128). Flappers were young women, in their twenties, who challenged the old ideas about women's fashion. They wore revealing clothes, with short skirts, used a lot of make-up and had short hair. They drank and smoked in public and performed modern dances such as the Charleston.

Women also made progress in their legal rights. In 1923, they were given the same right as men to seek divorce on grounds of adultery. The Property Act of 1925 allowed married women to hold and dispose of property on the same terms as their husbands.

Activities

1 What can you learn from Source A about attitudes to votes for women?

2 How far do Sources A and B suggest that women were given the vote in 1918 because of their actions during the First World War? Explain your answer using Sources A and B.

3 What were flappers?

Employment position

In 1918, 3,000 women were asked: 'Do you wish to return to your former work or stay in the job you are doing now?' Of those women, 2,500 said: 'Stay in the work I'm doing now.' However, as soon as the war ended women were expected to give up their war work. Women who tried to hold onto their jobs were criticised by men and even, in some cases, physically attacked.

It was argued that women who stayed in these jobs were depriving men of jobs. Women returned to their traditional, unskilled, low-paid jobs or their roles as housewives. By the 1930s women's wages were only half those of men, even if they were doing the same job.

However, there was some progress. The Sex Disqualification Removal Act of 1919 meant that women could no longer be barred from any job because of their sex. In theory, they could now enter the professions, such as the law and architecture. However, the law still only applied to single women. Once married, a woman had to give up her job. In 1925 the Civil Service admitted women to government service for the first time.

Source C: From the *Southampton Times*, 1919.

> Women have still not brought themselves to realise that factory work, with the money paid for it, will not be possible again. Women who left domestic service to enter the factory are now required to return to their pots and pans.

Source D: From a report by the Chief Inspector of Factories, 1919.

> The first year after the end of the War has been a very important one for industry. It is remarkable how complete has been the changeover from war to peacetime production. The first step was the gradual and now almost complete withdrawal of women from the men's industries.

Source E: Graphs comparing women's employment in 1914 and 1931

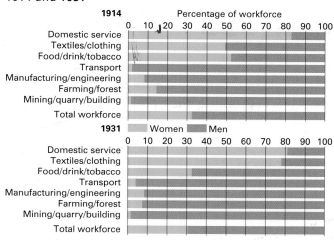

Activities

4 Study Sources C and D. How far do they agree about what happened to the employment of women once the war ended? Explain your answer using Sources C and D.

5 Does Source E suggest that the war brought changes in the employment of women? Explain your answer.

6 Work in pairs. Make a copy of the following scales.

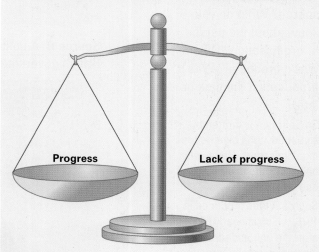

Make a list of progress or lack of progress in politics, social position and employment. Overall, do you think women made progress in the inter-war years? Explain your answer.

8.5 Source enquiry skills: evaluating sources

You should examine the nature, origin and purpose of a source when explaining its value or reliability. What do these words mean?

Nature
This means what type of source it is. It could be a diary, photograph, newspaper report, novel, speech, painting, cartoon. How will this affect its value or reliability?

For example, Source A is a letter, which should give the views of this woman.

What type of source is this?

Origins
Who produced the source? What do you know about the person or organisation? When was it produced? Was it produced at the time or later?

So Source A is written by somebody who experienced munitions work. However, it only gives the experience of one woman.

Source A was produced in 1976, which is nearly 60 years after the war ended. The woman may have forgotten some details of her work. On the other hand, she has had many years to reflect.

What comments can you make about the origins of Source B?

Source A: From a letter published in a local newspaper. It was written in 1976 by a female munitions worker describing her experiences of the First World War.

> I was in domestic service and hated every minute of it when the war broke out, earning £2 a month working 6.00 a.m. to 9.00 p.m. So when the need came for women 'war-workers' my chance came to 'out'. I started on hand-cutting shell fuses. We worked twelve hours a day, apart from the journey morning and night. As far as wages, I thought I was well off earning £5 a week.

Source B: A poster produced by the British government in 1916.

Purpose
Why was the source produced, written, drawn, etc?

- Is the source trying to get the audience (those reading or hearing the source) to support or oppose something?
- Is it propaganda?
- Is it trying to get the audience to do something?
- Does it want to sell a book or newspaper, to make money?

This letter could have been published to interest readers and widen the circulation of the newspaper. What difference will that make? For example, a lot of technical detail might be left out.

What was the purpose of this poster?

8.6 The impact of the Second World War on women

Once again, as was seen in the section on government organisation for the war, women played an important role on the home front during the Second World War, in industry, the armed forces and various voluntary bodies. This, in turn, influenced attitudes towards women's rights during and after the war although, once again, in many respects there was little change.

Pay

Women continued to be paid less than men for doing the same job, especially in factory work, where they usually received about 75 per cent of a man's wage (see Source A).

Source A: Average weekly wages for men and women in 1943.

Average weekly earnings, July 1943		
Men over 21 years	121s 4d	(£6.07)
Men under 21 years	47s 11d	(£2.40)
Women over 18 years	62s 11d	(£3.30)
Women part-time workers	29s 0d	(£1.45)
Women under 18 years	33s 11d	(£1.70)

From *M. Chandler, Britain in the Age of Total War, Heinemann 2002, page 21.*

Women complained because they did not receive enough money from the government while their husbands were serving in the armed forces. (The women were obviously not receiving their husbands' normal earnings because they were away fighting.) However, not all women believed they should be paid the same (see Source B).

The government set up the Equal Pay Commission in 1943, but it had no powers. By the end of the war women were no nearer equality with men in pay than they had been in 1939, unless they were on piece rates. That meant they were paid for every item that they produced, and not for the number of hours they worked.

Source B: An interview with a woman by the research organisation Mass Observation in 1942.

> I do feel that equal pay would upset the relations between the sexes. Personally, I like a man to have more money than me. It gives me twice as much pleasure to have a dress bought for me by a kindly man than to buy it myself, and this is because I am feminine.

Despite all this, many women were pleased to be involved in useful work that helped the war effort. Even if they were not as well paid as the men, they were still earning much more than they were used to getting before the war. Before the war the average woman's wage was about £2 a week. During the war some women doing dangerous munitions work were earning as much as £10 a week.

Activities

1 What can you learn from Source A about women's pay during the Second World War?

2 Study Source B. Write a response from a woman worker, possibly in a munitions factory worker, in favour of equal pay.

3 Give one example of a change and one of the lack of change in pay for women during the Second World War.

Attitudes of women

The war did change the attitudes of some women. War work gave them far more confidence and self-respect. They became far more confident about themselves and their abilities. Many enjoyed the independence and freedom the war had given them (see Sources C and D).

Source C: An interview with Mona Marshall in the 1960s. She worked in the steel industry during the war.

> To be quite honest, the war was the best thing that ever happened to us. I was green as grass and terrified if anyone spoke to me. I had been brought up not to argue. My generation of women had been taught to do as we were told. At work you did exactly as your boss told you and you went home to do exactly as your husband told you. The war changed all that. The war made me stand on my own two feet.

Source D: An interview with Pat Parker, in the 1980s, about her three and a half years in the Women's Land Army.

> Those years were absolutely fantastic. They were complete freedom, where I'd never known it before. I'd always had my father standing on the corner of the street saying, 'You should be indoors.' This was nine o'clock at night. And that went on until I was sixteen. Whereas, being away I could do as I liked. All of a sudden nobody was bothering me and my life was my own.

Attitudes of men

Many men, especially employers and politicians, were impressed with the work done by women.

Source E: Clement Attlee, the Deputy Prime Minister, writing in 1943 about the work done by women.

> This work the women are performing in munitions factories has to be seen to be believed. Precision engineering jobs which a few years ago would have made a skilled turner's hair stand on end are performed with deadly accuracy by girls who had no industrial experience.

The **trade unions** accepted women workers much more readily than they had done in the First World War. The Trades Union Congress (TUC) campaigned to make sure that women were treated the same as men. For example, the TUC successfully complained about the fact that women were paid 25 per cent less and received lower accident compensation than men in the Rolls-Royce armament factories.

Source F: A woman shop steward interviewed in 1941.

> We have no objections to working in the factories but we do object to the conditions we have to work in. Women in industry are called upon to bear burdens that are beyond imagination. Many are soldiers' wives who are obliged to go to work to keep their homes together as their allowances are so inadequate. We have to work up to ten hours a day but we still often only earn half the man's wages.

Moreover, the government even began to help women with childcare commitments. They provided nurseries and encouraged employers to allow women with children to job share. By 1944 there were 1,450 nurseries, compared to 104 before the war.

Nevertheless, there was not exactly a revolution in attitudes to women's role in society. The majority of men continued to believe that the traditional roles of women were as wives and mothers, and that once the war ended, they should return to the home.

Activities

4   What can you learn from Source C about the impact of the war on the attitudes of women?

5   Do you think you can rely on the evidence of Source C? Explain your answer, using Sources C and D.

6   Work in pairs. Make a copy of the following table, which compares the part played by women in the two world wars.

	Similarities	**Differences**
First World War		
Second World War		

7   Which war brought the greatest change in the position of women? Explain your answer.

8.7 Did the role of women really change 1945–1950?

Yes

- The war had given many women more confidence and self-respect. They had shown that not only could they do the same jobs as men but, in many cases they could do them better.
- The number of married women in paid work had increased by 1951 (see Source A).

Source A: Women in paid work (percentages) from N. DeMarco, *The Second World War*, Hodder 1997, page 54.

	Single women	Married women	All women
1911	69	10	35
1921	68	9	34
1931	72	10	34
1951	73	22	35

- There was some change in attitudes towards married women working. In the 1950s some women did find work when their children were growing up.

No

- Most women willingly left their wartime jobs because they wanted to return to the home. A government survey of 1947 revealed that 58 per cent of women believed that married women should not go out to work. Many had delayed having children during the war and now decided that they wanted to start families.
- Women's career opportunities weren't drastically improved by the war. For example, the new opportunities in areas such as metal manufacturing and engineering only lasted as long as the war. The shutting down of nurseries after the war meant the end of jobs for women with children.
- They continued to make only slow progress in professions such as medicine and law. As late as 1961 only 15 per cent of doctors and 3 per cent of lawyers were women.
- The Equal Pay Commission, set up in 1944, reported in 1946 that the average male manual worker's wage was £5.70 a week, while the wage for a woman was £3. The Commission did not recommend any changes, suggesting that women did different jobs from men, so equal pay was not an issue. The male was still seen as the main breadwinner.
- The media continued to portray women in their stereotyped domestic role (see Source B).

Source B: An advert for new cookers, 1947.

Handsome is and handsome does- that's the GAS idea!

The new gas cookers make you a better cook because they are so easy to use —and a prouder housewife because they are so attractive to look at.

BRITISH GAS COUNCIL · 1 GROSVENOR PLACE · LONDON · SW1

Source C: A woman remembers married life after the war.

> After a while we settled to some sort of married life but there were times when I thought it was hell on earth, I was living in. Many of us felt as though we were going back to prison.

Activities

1 Give two examples of the lack of change in the position of women.
2 What can you learn from Source A about changes in the employment of women?
3 What image of women is shown in Source B?
4 Does Source C agree with this image? Explain your answer.

8.8 Did the wars create a more equal society?

The mobilisation of the home front in both world wars did create greater national unity and stimulated demand for a more equal society. Indeed, the First World War accelerated the process leading to votes for women and for more men. However, it was more apparent during the Second World War because of the impact of rationing and evacuation. These experiences created a genuine desire to produce a new society in which people were protected from the problems of poverty and ill health. The election of a Labour government in 1945 was due very much to this desire for social change.

Rationing

Rationing was seen by the British public as both necessary and fair. Rich and poor alike were given the same rations. Moreover, many, especially the poor, had never had such a balanced diet (read Source A). This, in turn, encouraged many to insist that this standard of living should be maintained for all people once the conflict ended.

Source A: The writer George Orwell reported in 1943.

> Most people are better fed than they used to be. I can't help feeling that people in London look healthier than they used to. There are less fat people. For instance, with the adult milk ration of 3 pints a week, the amount of milk being drunk has actually increased since the war started.

Evacuation

The evacuation of children from poorer inner city areas to more affluent homes in the countryside also stimulated demand and support for a more equal society. Many foster parents realised, for the first time, the deprived conditions in which these children normally lived (read Source B).

Source B: From C. Bayne-Jardine, *World War Two*, published in 1968.

> The evacuation of children from danger spots in the towns showed the public that **slum** conditions still existed in Britain. The result of this was that the government was encouraged to provide better conditions. Cod liver oil, blackcurrant extracts and, later, concentrated orange juice from the United States, were given out free of charge.

Beveridge Report

This desire for change, for a better society, prompted the government to set up a Royal Commission in 1941 under Sir William Beveridge to consider how Britain could rebuild after the war. The Beveridge Report of 1942 recommended that the people of Britain should be protected from the Five Giant 'Evils': Squalor, Ignorance, Want, Idleness and Disease (look at Source C). It went on to explain how this could be done. Beveridge said that the government should take responsibility for the people of Britain 'from the cradle to the grave'. He recommended that a welfare state should be set up in Britain. Many of his recommendations were introduced by the Labour Government of 1945–1951.

The setting up of the Welfare State

The Labour Government of 1945–1951 brought in a series of reforms designed to remove the Five Giants identified by Beveridge. These reforms finally established a welfare state – that is, a system whereby the government took on the responsibility for helping those who could not help themselves.

The attack on want

Family allowances began in 1945 with a payment for each child after the first. National Insurance against illness and unemployment was made compulsory and extended to the whole workforce.

The attack on disease

In 1946 Aneurin Bevan, the Minister of Health, introduced the National Health Act. Under this act, everyone received free medical, dental, hospital and eye treatment. The scheme was launched in 1948.

The attack on ignorance

The 1944 Education Act, brought in by Churchill's wartime government, introduced 'secondary education for all'. Children had to be taught in separate primary schools and secondary schools to replace the previous all-age 'elementary' schools, and no one could leave school until the age of 15.

The attack on squalor

There were serious house shortages due to the effects of bombing and the lack of building during the Second World War. The Labour Government built a series of estates of council houses. In addition, the New Towns Act of 1946 provided government money for a series of new towns close to London and other cities. These reduced overcrowding in older urban centres.

The attack on idleness

By 1950 the Labour Government had managed to achieve virtually full employment. This was helped by assistance from the USA, known as Marshall Aid, which provided much needed finance and resources for new buildings.

Activities

1 In what ways did rationing and evacuation encourage demands for a better society?

2 How far do Sources A and B suggest the need for change? Explain your answer using Sources A and B.

3 What is the message of Source C? How does the cartoonist put across this message?

Source C: A cartoon from a British newspaper, 1942, showing Beveridge setting out to defeat the Five Giants.

8.9 Source enquiry skills: comparing the value of sources

Which of the Sources, A or B, is the most valuable to the historian who is enquiring into the working conditions for women in industry during the First World War? Explain your answer, using Sources A and B.

Information

Source A is of value because it suggests that working conditions for women were very unpleasant and harsh with little or no time for meal or drink breaks and that the health of many workers suffered. However, it is very generalised and does not name any specific industries.

Source B is of value because it suggests that women's health actually improved as a result of their work during the First World War. Moreover, it suggests that they found this work more interesting and challenging. However, it does not provide evidence of the dangerous and unpleasant work done by women in, for example, the munitions industry.

Source A: From a speech made in 1919 by the Suffragette leader, Sylvia Pankhurst.

Sometimes women wrote to me, broken down in health by overwork, complaining of long walks over sodden tracks, ankle deep in mud, to newly erected factories. Of night shifts spent without even the possibility of getting a drink. Of workers obliged to take their meals amidst the dust and fumes of the workshop.

Source B: From a report by the government's medical officers, 1919.

Most women enjoyed the more interesting, active and hard jobs, and in many cases their health improved rather than deteriorated. Women have with success undertaken work involving the lifting of weights, heavy machine work, and even forge and foundry work. This shows that light work is not by any means the most suitable for women. The conditions under which women worked before the war, long hours, low wages and poor diet, resulted in poor physical health.

Nature, origin and purpose of sources

Source A is of value because it is a speech made by a leading suffragette just after the First World War and she will have witnessed such harsh conditions. However, she is making a speech to win support for women's rights and may exaggerate the conditions.

Source B is of value because it was a report by medical officers employed by the government to investigate working conditions for women. It should be based on objective research findings because the government will not be trying to encourage female employment in these industries after the war, in 1919. In addition, the government may have wanted to justify the employment of women during the war.

In order to answer this question you have to compare the contribution the sources can make to this specific enquiry through assessing:

- the value and limitations of the information they provide for the enquiry, what the sources suggest, the contents of each source
- whether the nature, origins and purpose of the source adds to or reduces its value.

You then make a final judgement on which is more valuable.

Now make your final judgement. On the evidence presented, which source do you think would be the most valuable for this enquiry?

Source C: An interview with a land girl in 1941.

> In a large farm in Lincolnshire we worked for twelve hours a day at very hard and monotonous work and received no training. Wages were £1.40 a week, out of which we had to pay £1 for our lodgings. At a smaller farm in Huntingdon, where we expected to be trained in tractor driving, we were made to do odd jobs, including kitchen work for the farmer's wife. The farmer gave us no training and refused to pay us any wages.

Source D: An interview with a land girl, Jean Mundy, in 2005 for a website devoted to the work of women during the Second World War.

> We were then shown all the different parts of farming. It was a mixed farm, cows, pigs (300), and of course we had a big dairy. We worked in groups on a different section each week. When you were on pigs, which had to be cleaned out and fed before breakfast, no one would sit near you because of the smell. Before they let us loose on the dairy cows we had to train on a rubber udder, which was a laugh. We were taught how to record all the milk a cow gave and, of course, it went through several filters before it went into churns and off to the large dairy. We didn't get a lot of free time.

 ResultsPlus
Build Better Answers

Which of the Sources, C or D, is the most valuable to the historian who is enquiring about the work of the Women's Land Army during the Second World War?

Explain your answer, using Sources C and D.

 Basic, Level 1 (1–3 marks).
Will take some information from the sources (for example 'they show what work land girls did').

 Good, Level 2 (4–7 marks).
Will describe why information in the sources is useful in detail or explain why the nature and origin of the sources make one more useful than the other.

 Excellent, Level 3 (8–10 marks).
Will explain the usefulness of what we can learn from the content of the sources when we take into account their nature and origin. For example, Source C was an interview done at the time so it will be fresh in the mind of the girl, whereas Source D is an interview with a girl more than 60 years after the event so she may have forgotten details or alternatively the time difference may have given her more time to think carefully about it.

 ResultsPlus
Watch out!

Many students think that the usefulness of a source depends on how much information it contains – this does not have to be the case

Summary

- Before the First World War women were second-class citizens in education, job opportunities and politics.
- Women made an important contribution on the home front during the First World War, and females over the age of 30 were given the vote.
- There was some progress in women's rights between the wars, with women over the age of 21 given the vote. Most women, however, reverted to their traditional roles after the wars.
- Once again, women made an important contribution to the home front during the Second World War in industry, the armed forces, farming and the voluntary services.
- In the years after 1945 there was little progress as the majority of women reverted to their domestic role.

9.1 Factors influencing change

Learning outcomes

By the end of this section you should be able to:

● outline the role of government in the changes brought about by war

● explain the role of the media and entertainment in these changes

● explain the impact of changes in industry on the lives of civilians

● answer synthesis questions.

The two wars brought about many changes in British society, including changes in the position of women in employment and politics and the desire to create a more equal society. Which of the following factors played the most important role in these changes?

The role of government

The role of government greatly expanded during both world wars in order to organise the war effort. This new role included:

● recruitment and conscription for the armed forces

● recruitment and conscription for industry

● propaganda and censorship

● rationing and evacuation

● civil defence against air attack.

The use of the media

There was much greater use of propaganda and censorship in both world wars in order to ensure maximum support for the war effort and hatred for the enemy. Moreover, the range of media methods greatly expanded to include:

● the music hall

● the cinema

● the radio

● posters.

Entertainment became a key method of maintaining the morale of the civilians and the armed forces.

The impact of changes in industry

There were major changes in industry during both wars that, in turn, influenced the lives of civilians. These included:

● the employment of women in most heavy industries

● government control of industry to provide for the needs of war

● a greater role for trade unions who often negotiated improved working conditions

● the provision of crèche facilities for married mothers with children.

Source A: A 'Bevin Bar' in London in 1942. Ernest Bevin was the Minister of Labour. Female workers are getting their hands massaged and their fingernails painted.

Activities

1. State one change in:
   • the role of government
   • the media
   • industry.

2. Study Source A. Why do you think the government set up 'Bevin Bars'?

9.2 The government's role

The role of government greatly expanded during both world wars in order to organise the country for total war. This meant the central organisation of all industry and manpower towards the one aim of defeating the enemy, and it included control of:

- recruitment to the armed forces: during the early years of the First World War this was organised by the Minister of War, Lord Kitchener, in order to encourage volunteers for the armed forces;
- industry: central direction ensured that major resources and factories were diverted to the needs of warfare;
- food supplies: the government, reluctantly at first, introduced rationing and other measures to ensure that the country was not starved out of the war;
- propaganda and censorship: the central control of the media to control the flow and content of information maintained morale.

The change in the control exerted by the government:

- brought about the idea of total war, the whole country geared towards defeating the enemy through the mobilisation of manpower (and womanpower) and industry;
- showed the benefits of greater government central control of industry and society in general. Governments were able to make a difference. In peacetime, although less involved, the role of government was much greater than it had been at the beginning of the 20th century.

Key figures

Key figures in the government also played important roles in both wars.

David Lloyd George

Lloyd George transformed and greatly expanded the role of government during the First World War. In 1915 he became Minister of Munitions and found that the new government department had 'no staff, no tables and too many mirrors'. By the end of the war, as a result of his efforts, the ministry was employing a staff of 65,000 and had over 3 million workers under its direction. Lloyd George was the one who insisted on employing women in munitions factories. Moreover, as prime minister, 1916–1918, he ensured that government and the country were geared towards total war.

Winston Churchill

Churchill's role, as prime minister during the Second World War, was different again. He used his skills as a speaker to maintain the morale of the British people, especially after the Dunkirk evacuation and during the Blitz (read Source B).

Source A: A poster of 1940 featuring Churchill.

Source B: Churchill speaking to the House of Commons, June 1940.

> We shall defend our island. We shall fight on the beaches, we shall fight on the landing grounds, we shall fight in the streets, we shall fight in the hills. We shall never surrender.

Activities

1 Study Source A. How does the artist get his message across in the poster? Explain your answer, using Source A.

2 Study Sources A and B. Which of the Sources, A or B, is more valuable to the historian who is enquiring about the role of Churchill during the Second World War? Explain your answer, using Sources A and B.

9.3 The media and entertainment

The media and entertainment played an important role in influencing and even changing attitudes during both wars. Moreover, new forms of the media, most especially film and the radio, were used as methods of propaganda and entertainment.

Censorship

From the start of both wars all news, especially bad news, was strictly controlled. For example, despite the problems of the first few months on the Western Front in 1914, the British people were told only of great British victories or heroic resistance. It was not until November 1916 that the government allowed journalists to be at the war front. Their reports, however, focused on good news (see Source A). The true losses at Dunkirk in 1940 were also kept from the British public.

Newspapers that tried to give more balanced views of the war, or that were anti-war, were closed down. For example, during the First World War the newspaper *Tribunal* was shut.

Source A: The prime minister, Lloyd George, in a private conversation with the editor of the *Manchester Guardian*, December 1917.

> If the people really knew the truth about the war, the war would be stopped tomorrow. But of course they don't – and can't – know. The correspondents don't write, and the censors would not pass, the truth.

Source B: An article from *The Nation*, May 1916. This journal was later banned.

> It is a domestic tragedy of the war that the country which went out to defend liberty is losing its own liberties one by one, and that the government which began by relying on public opinion as a great help has now come to fear and curtail it.

The government was also concerned with stopping sensitive information from leaking out to the enemy. In 1916, the government press bureau and the intelligence services examined 38,000 articles, 25,000 photographs and 300,000 private telegrams. This continued during the Second World War, when the government also used posters to discourage people inadvertently giving information to potential spies. 'Careless talk costs lives' became the motto (see Source C).

Letters from soldiers at the front to loved ones in Britain were carefully censored. Nevertheless, during the Second World War, some servicemen and women devised coded messages to avoid censorship. For instance, the mention of 'yellow' meant North Africa and 'grey' meant Iceland and so on. A letter to a girlfriend suggesting that she painted the ceiling meant that her husband or boyfriend was coming home.

Source C: A Second World War poster with the title 'Careless talk costs lives'.

Although censorship was a severe curtailment of the normal liberties of the British people, there were few complaints during either conflict. The great majority of people accepted it as a necessity of wartime that would end once the enemy was defeated.

Source D: A British poster of September 1914.

HOW THE HUN HATES!

THE HUNS CAPTURED SOME OF OUR FISHERMEN IN THE NORTH SEA AND TOOK THEM TO SENNELAGER. THEY CHARGED THEM WITHOUT A SHRED OF EVIDENCE WITH BEING "MINE LAYERS." THEY ORDERED THEM TO BE PUNISHED WITHOUT A TRIAL.
THAT PUNISHMENT CONSISTED IN SHAVING ALL THE HAIR OFF ONE SIDE OF THE HEAD AND FACE.
THE HUNS THEN MARCHED THEIR VICTIMS THROUGH THE STREETS AND EXPOSED THEM TO THE JEERS OF THE GERMAN POPULACE.

BRITISH SAILORS! LOOK! READ! AND REMEMBER!

Activities

1 What can you learn from Sources A and B about censorship during the First World War?
2 Write a brief article from the government replying to Source B.
3 How does the cartoonist get across his message in Source C?

Propaganda

Propaganda was the other side of the coin. The government, in both wars, gradually developed more and more sophisticated methods of getting across key messages to the British public. Indeed, in the Second World War, they pioneered market research techniques to gauge public responses to various poster campaigns.

One way of convincing people that they were fighting for a just cause was to stir up hatred against the enemy. During the First World War, the government produced many posters that showed acts of brutality or atrocities supposedly carried out by the enemy. These were often exaggerations or outright lies.

In addition, government propagandists were responsible for spreading hostile rumours about the enemy (see Source D). For example, during the First World War British propagandists invented the rumour that the Germans sent corpses to a factory that then used the human fat to make candles and boot polish.

Activities

4 What rumours are being spread by Source D?
5 Give two reasons to explain why the government used rumours and even lies about the enemy in their propaganda.

Film

In 1914, the newest means of informing and influencing the masses was the cinema. By 1917, there were 4,500 cinemas in Britain. The British Topical Committee for War Films was a group of film companies who got together to make and sell films to the War Department. Their patriotic film *For the Empire* had reached an audience of 9 million by the end of 1916.

The committee made the most famous film of the First World War, *The Battle of the Somme*. It was a genuine propaganda triumph, showing real scenes from the battle, including real casualties as well as 'fake' scenes (see Source E). It was released in August 1916 and was a huge success. Many people had their first chance to see what it was really like on the Western Front (read Source G). By October 1916 it had been shown in 2,000 cinemas.

Source E: Three scenes from *The Battle of the Somme*.

Source F: Extract from *How I Filmed the War* by Geoffrey Malins, 1920.

The Somme film has caused a great sensation. I really thought that some of the dead scenes would offend the British public. And yet, why should they? They realised that it was their duty to see for themselves. They had been told by the press and by Parliament what was happening, but to no effect. They must be shown. They must see with their own eyes. Yes, the truth has at last dawned on the British public.

Source G: From the diary of Henry Rider Haggard, 27 September 1916.

Today I went to see the Somme War Film. It is not a cheerful sight, but it does give a wonderful idea about the fighting at the front, especially of shelling and its effects. Also, it shows the marvellous courage and cheerfulness of our soldiers in every emergency. As usual, all the pictures move too fast, even the wounded seem to fly along. The most impressive of them to my mind is that of a regiment scrambling out of a trench to charge and one man who slides back shot dead.

Activities

6 Study Source E. What was the purpose of the filmmaker in showing these scenes?

7 One scene is fake. Which one? Give a reason for your answer.

8 Do you think you can rely on Malins' account in Source F? Explain your answer using Sources F and G.

The cinema was popular during the Second World War too and, once again, a key method for government propaganda. The Ministry of Information set up the Crown Film Unit to make official propaganda films. It made short, ten-minute documentaries such as *Fires Were Started* and *Listen to Britain*. In addition, fictional films such as *In Which We Serve* were made, depicting generally heroic actions by British people. Between 25 million and 30 million seats were sold every week in Britain, with a large percentage of the audience going to the cinema to escape from the hardships and austerity of wartime life.

Radio

The BBC radio was a key method of government propaganda during the Second World War. At first only the Home Service was broadcast, but in February 1940, a second channel, the Forces Programme, was introduced. The news bulletins had massive audiences and had a reputation for truth, reporting reverses and victories alike. Nevertheless, it was subject to censorship. For example, reports about weather conditions were not allowed, nor were reports about the movements of Winston Churchill as these might prove useful to the enemy.

In addition, much of the information supplied to the BBC came from the headquarters of the armed forces, whose statements were either very cautious or wildly over-optimistic. For example, during the Battle of Britain in August 1940, the BBC reported that 144 enemy aircraft were destroyed. This figure was later reduced to 69.

Source H: From S. Womack, *The Home Front during World War II*, 1985.

> News presenters were required to read the news without showing any emotion. As a result, the news readers became among the best known men in the country and the voices of Alvar Lidell, Bruce Belfrage and Frank Phillips will forever conjure up vivid memories for those who lived through the war.

Entertainment

The government realised, in both conflicts, that entertainment would play a significant role in maintaining morale. The radio and cinema were not simply propaganda tools – they also provided escapism and humour. The largest percentage of cinema audiences was made up of young wage earners – especially females – who wanted to get away from the war and thoughts of absent loved ones. Hollywood movies were shown because they generally provided glamour and romance and an escape from the realities of war.

However, the most popular form of entertainment was the radio. In 1941, there were 21 dance programmes a week on the radio – with the most popular being Victor Sylvester's *Dancing Club*.

There was a host of programmes featuring British and American singing artists, with the national favourite being *Music While You Work*.

Humour was an important method of keeping up people's morale, especially humour that poked fun at the home front and government rules and regulations. *It's That Man Again* (ITMA) enjoyed a massive following. It starred Tommy Handley, who played the Minister at the Ministry of Aggravation and Mysteries. It enabled radio and listeners to poke fun at all the wartime **bureaucracy** (see Source I).

The government also encouraged live entertainment through organisations such as ENSA (Entertainments National Service Association), which provided entertainment not only to the armed forces but also to the civilian population, including people at work and families sheltering from the Blitz in the London Underground.

Source I: A selection of *ITMA* catchphrases.

> *Can I do you now, Sir?*
> Mrs Mopp (the office charwoman)
>
> *I don't mind if I do*
> Colonel Humphrey Chinstrap turning innocent remarks into the offer of a drink
>
> *This is Funf speaking*
> Funf, the German spy
>
> *It's being so cheerful as keeps me going*
> Mona Lott
>
> *Going down now sir*
> Diver

Activities

9 What can you learn from Source H about the importance of radio during the Second World War?

10 Study Source I. Why do you think humour was so important to British people during the Second World War?

11 'The cinema played the most important role in maintaining morale during the two world wars.' Discuss.

9.4 The impact of changes in industry

Changes in industry during both wars also had a significant impact on the lives of civilians.

Changes during the First World War

Lloyd George introduced 'War Socialism' in 1917. This meant that the government took control of the resources of the country:

- The railway network was taken over so that transport could be coordinated more effectively. In 1914 there had been 120 different railway companies. Lloyd George created a unified system.

- All coal mines were taken over, and production reached an all-time high of 262 million tonnes per year. At the same time the miners received a national minimum wage, and the safety record improved because of new checks.

- Shipyards were taken over to ensure that enough vessels were built to replace the many being sunk by German U-boats.

- Lloyd George encouraged the employment of more and more women in heavy industry, especially munitions. Their work did much to further the cause of female suffrage.

- The Ministry of Labour was set up to organise the nation's labour force. It introduced directed labour, which gave the government the power to force skilled workers to remain in occupations of national importance.

- Trade unions became far more important and powerful. Membership doubled, and the government was prepared to negotiate with union leaders especially in connection with directed labour and the employment of female workers. The increased influence of trade unions led to post-war strikes and clashes and was a long-term cause of the General Strike of 1926.

Changes during the Second World War

The government again took over control of most industry on the outbreak of the Second World War. Ernest Bevin, the Minister of Labour, worked closely with employers and with the trade unions to make Britain's wartime production as efficient as possible.

- Workers' freedom was severely restricted. Wages and hours of work were strictly controlled, and workers could be moved around. For example, when coal stocks fell dangerously low in 1940, some 30,000 miners had to leave the army and return to their old jobs.

- Coal supplies remained a problem throughout the war and from 1942 men could opt for the mines rather than the armed forces. Those that did were known as the 'Bevin Boys'. Men from wealthier backgrounds experienced, for the first time, the often unpleasant working conditions down the mines. Not surprisingly many preferred to join the armed forces.

- Women were, for the first time, conscripted into the labour force. The novelty of women doing men's jobs wore off much more quickly than it had in the First World War because women were taking on these jobs in such large numbers. Women workers were taken for granted. Eight times as many women took on war work in the Second World War as in the First World War. In both conflicts, the vast majority left these jobs once the war ended.

Source A: The memories of George Grainger, a Bevin Boy, written in 1985.

I worked on one of the worst shifts one could imagine, 6.30p.m. till 2.30a.m. Now just think about that if you would. We would be going to work when most people have finished, or going out for the evening. But someone had it to do and we were the unlucky ones. I had one nasty accident during my time at Chester-Moor. We were working tubbing stone at one of the (gates), that is a term used to describe a road way leading off the mainbye. Unknown to us some miners had pushed a tub into our gate, forgetting to tell us it was there and to make matters worse it was on a bit of an incline, chocked of course, but when me and my mate backed our full tub out, my rear behind touched this other tub and I'm afraid I wasn't quick enough to get my full body in between the pit props, and one of my hands got caught in two of the tub handles.

Source B: The front page of a *Boy's Own* comic, 1944.

Activities

1 What were meant by the following terms:
   - War Socialism
   - directed labour
   - the Bevin Boys.
2 'Source A is more useful than Source B to the historian enquiring about the experience of the Bevin Boys during the Second World War.' Discuss, using Sources A and B.

9.5 Source enquiry skills: reaching a judgement

'The media was the most important factor in influencing change during and after both world wars.'

How far do you agree with this statement? Use your own knowledge, Sources A, B and E below and any other sources you find helpful to explain your answer.

Source A: A poster advertising the first screening of the film *The Battle of the Somme*, August 1916.

A DUTY YOU OWE TO
THE IMPERIAL GOVERNMENT.

S E E
The Battle of the Somme.

COME AND SEE
The Battle of the Somme.

*The very punch of the Allies. Backed
by the hall-mark of*
THE IMPERIAL GOVERNMENT.

Source B: From S. Womack, *The Home Front during World War II,* 1985.

It's That Man Again gives a vivid impression of the variety of ways in which the life of the average Briton was changed by the war. The humour often reflected the increase in bureaucracy which affected everyone – an increase which would have been unacceptable during peacetime. It was set in ludicrous institutions such as the Ministry of Aggravation and Mysteries (a clear joke at the expense of the Ministry of Agriculture and Fisheries) and centred around its leading actor, Tommy Handley, who played the part of the minister.

Source C: A poster advertising the film *In Which We Serve*, 1942.

Source D: The Emergency Powers Act of 1939.

Such persons may be detained whose detention appears to the Secretary of State to be expedient in the interests of public safety or the defence of the realm. The Secretary of State for Labour has the authority to oblige any person in the United Kingdom to perform any service required in any place.

Source E: A postcard published by the government in 1915.

To answer the synthesis question, you have to give a balanced answer that:

- uses the sources
- draws upon your own knowledge
- examines the view expressed in the question
- examines the evidence against this view.

Here is a planning grid to help you with this question. It includes a few examples to get you started.

	Sources	Own knowledge
Supporting the view	Source A supports the view because it is a poster advertising the film 'In Which we Serve' Source B Source C	Films such as this not only encouraged support for the war but also provided a distraction from the home front
Opposing the view	Source E suggests that the government played a greater role in industry during the First World War, especially the provision of munitions	The government controlled industry during both wars; more especially, they employed women to work in many factories. This extended the role of government, and changed some attitudes to women

ResultsPlus
Watch out!

The final question in the exam will always tell you to use the sources and your own knowledge. Every year many students who produce an excellent answer lose marks because they only use the sources and do not add in comments from their own knowledge. There are also a number of excellent answers every year that lose marks because they do not refer to the sources in their answer.

Summary

- The role of the government greatly expanded during both wars in the areas of propaganda, censorship, control of industry and control of the labour force.

- The government used a range of media in censorship and propaganda, especially newspapers, posters, cinema and the radio.

- The media had a major impact on the lives of British people, especially the BBC and films during the Second World War.

- Industry was eventually controlled by the government in both wars. This changed working conditions, the status of trade unions and the position of women.

154

Introduction to the exam

This unit tests your understanding of the way that a historian uses sources. All of the questions will focus on source skills. Your knowledge of the impact of war will help you to evaluate and use the sources but you are not expected to have any other detailed knowledge of the topic. The final question will ask you to use the sources and your own knowledge in your answer. The mark scheme has a cut off point at 10 marks out of 16 if you do not use both the sources and your own knowledge.

In the exam you will have 1 hour and 15 minutes to answer five questions. You do not have any choice in the questions so make sure that you have covered all of the specification in your revision and you are prepared for the sorts of question that are likely to be asked.

Self-evaluation checklist

How well do you know and understand:

- the use of propaganda and censorship during the two world wars
- the impact of and attitudes to the Blitz during the Second World War
- the increased role of the government during both conflicts

- the impact of conscription during the First and Second World Wars
- reactions to rationing and evacuation
- the part played by women in both wars and its effects on women's rights
- the influence of the government, the media and industry in developments in the years 1914–1950?

1 Are the following statements true or false? If they are false, what is the correct statement?

	True	False
The Defence of the Realm Act was introduced during the First World War		
Zeppelins bombed Britain during the Second World War		
Women over the age of 30 were given the vote in 1918		
Lloyd George was Minister of Munitions 1915–1916		
The flappers were women who wanted greater freedom		
Rationing was only used in the Second World War		
Conscription was introduced for the first time in 1939		
Censorship was only used in the First World War		
The Blitz destroyed the morale of the British people		
The majority of women remained in their wartime jobs once both wars ended		
The Emergency Powers Act was introduced during the Second World War		

2 The following paragraph is not an accurate account.

   a) Find the errors.

   b) Write out the paragraph and correct the errors, replacing them with the correct answer.

> Before the First World War the suffragettes campaigned for the vote peacefully. Their campaign was supported by most men and women. Once the war broke out they called off their campaign. In 1915 Winston Churchill, the Minister of Munitions, decided to employ women due to labour shortages. Women earned less than they had done before the war. The government was not impressed with the work done by women. As a result, women over the age of 25 were given the vote in 1921.

Support activities

Making inferences
Source A: Extract from a letter by Humphrey Jennings to the local newspaper, during the Blitz of 1940–1941.

> What warmth – what courage! What determination! People singing in public shelters. WVS (Women's Voluntary Service) girls serving hot drinks to fire-fighters during raids. Everyone secretly delighted with the privilege of holding up Hitler. Certainly of beating him.

Read Source A.

   a) What can you learn from Source A about the effects of the Blitz?

   b) Which of the following statements are simple comprehension, inferences and/or supported inferences from the source?

Support activities

	Comprehension	Inference	Supported inference
The Blitz did not destroy the morale of people because they were singing in the shelters.			
The Blitz did not destroy the morale of people.			
The Blitz made people even more determined as they were confident Hitler would be defeated.			
People were singing in public shelters.			
Everyone was delighted with holding up Hitler.			

Support activities

Making comparisons

Working in groups, make a copy of and complete the following table comparing the impact of the two world wars. Use all the knowledge you have gained in this book.

	Similarities	Differences
Propaganda		
Censorship		
Recruitment		
Impact on women		
Role of government		
Rationing		
Impact of bombing		

Patterns of change, 1914–1950 activity

Below is an empty graph of Britain in the years 1910–1950 for you to use to show how the role of women in society (in red) and the role of government in society (in green) became greater and lesser at different times over this period.

Make a copy of the graph and complete it. Ensure you make entries at regular intervals; include 1910, 1915, 1920, 1939, 1945 and 1950.

What conclusions can you make from your graph about changes in:

• the role of women
• the role of government?

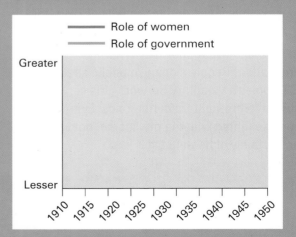

1: What can you learn from Sources A and B about reactions to women working during the First World War? (6 marks)

Source A: A government report written after the war, describing reactions to women working in industry in 1915.

> In every industrial district there was continuous opposition from men to the introduction of women. There were cases of refusal to instruct women, or attempts to restrict the scope of their work to discredit their efforts. In some cases this opposition was overt to the point of striking.

Source B: From the diary of the Reverend Clark, November 1915.

> Mr James Caldwell called. He had talked with a foreman, who said the women workers were doing splendidly. Lads were often selfishly thoughtless and larked about. The women worked thoughtfully and steadily.

Mark scheme

Level 1	Comprehension – selects details from source or sources.
Level 2	Makes inferences from the source or sources.
Level 3	Makes supported inferences from the source or sources.

Student answer	Examiner comments	Improved student answer
Men did not like women working in industry. Some would not work with women.	This is a valid inference about the attitudes of men towards women and would be awarded a low level 2. However, the answer does not provide support from the source.	Source A shows that some men did not like women working in industry. For example, men used extreme methods such as striking to show their dislike. Source B shows that not all men thought like this and that some employers thought that women were good workers, implying that they are better than their male workers..

Source C: A poster produced by the government in 1916.

Source analysis

2: Study Source C. Why do you think this poster was produced by the government? Explain your answer, using Source C.

Mark scheme

Level 1	Simple statements with no support from the source or description of the source
Level 2	Supported statement on message/purpose
Level 3	Explanation of message/purpose

Read the three answers on page 158. Which is Level 1, Level 2 and Level 3? Copy and complete the grid below.

Candidate	Level	Reason

Candidate A

This poster was produced by the government to put across the message that the work done by women in the munitions industry was of vital importance. This is shown by the message 'These women are doing their bit'. This is reinforced with the image of the soldier in the background. Moreover, the poster had a specific purpose, which was to encourage more women to work in the munitions industry. This is achieved through the slogan but also the rather glamorous image of the woman worker in the foreground.

Candidate B

The poster shows a woman at the front who is tying her hair back. She is putting on her work clothes. It has the message at the top 'These women are doing their bit' and at the bottom it is asking women to become munitions workers. In the background there is a soldier waving to the munitions worker. The poster was produced by the government in 1916 in order to show the important work done by women in the munitions industry.

Candidate C

The poster was produced by the government. It is to encourage more women to work in the munitions industry.

Source D: From a speech in 1916 by E. S. Montagu, the Minister of Munitions.

Women of every station have proved themselves able to undertake work that before the war was regarded solely the province of men. Where is a man now who would deny to women the civil rights which she has earned by her hard work?

Cross-referencing

3: How far do Sources A, B and D suggest that men supported the work of women during the First World War? Explain your answer using Sources A, B and D.

Mark scheme

Level 1	Generalised statements with no support from the sources.
Level 2	Supported answer that matches details of the content of the sources.
Level 3	Balanced judgement – cross-references the sources and makes a judgement on the extent of support.

Candidate's answer

Source A suggests that the work of women during the First World War was not supported by men. Men seemed to strongly resent the work done by women and refused to work with them and even went on strike. Unlike Sources A, Sources B and D seem to support the work of women. In Source B it seems that men and women work well together and that the women work better than the men. In Source D it says that women have proved themselves through their work in the munitions factories.

The candidate's answer above is a Level 2 answer. What does the candidate have to do to improve to Level 3? Look at page 116 to help you.

Utility

4: Which of the sources, A or E, is more valuable to the historian who is enquiring about reactions to the work of women during the First World War?

Mark scheme

Level 1	Simple statements that summarise sources, or make generalised comments on reliability.
Level 2	Judgement based on the usefulness of the information in each source OR the nature and purpose of each source.
Level 3	Judgement based on usefulness of information taking account of its nature and purpose.

Source E: From a speech by Asquith in Parliament in 1917.

How could we have carried on the war without women? Wherever we turn we see them doing work which three years ago we would have regarded as exclusively 'men's work'. But what I confess moves me still more in the matter is the problem of what to do when the war is over. The question will then arise about women's labour and women's functions in the new order of things. I would find it impossible to withhold from them the power and the right of making their voices directly heard.

Here are a series of extracts from answers.

a) Which are level 1?

b) Which are level 2 statements?

c) How could you make them into a level 3 answer? Looks at pages 142–143 to help you.

1 Source A is less useful because it was written after the war.

2 Source A is useful because it is a government report designed to give accurate information, but its use is limited because it only relates to 1915.

3 Source A is useful because it gives us more information than Source E.

4 Source A is useful because it gives information about reactions in every industrial district, and details of how men opposed women working.

5 Source A is useful because it is a report.

6 Source E is useful because it was said at the time.

7 Source E is not useful because it is only one man's view.

8 Source E is useful because it reflects the views of Asquith and show us how the work done by women during the First World War had changed the views of many about votes for women.

9 Source E gives the views of a leading politician – the Prime Minister. Because his attitudes were important in influencing other people, this is important evidence about reactions to women's work.

10 Asquith is speaking in parliament and he is also trying to persuade MPs so his speech may contain some exaggeration. However Source E should be reliable because he is only giving his own views.

Judgement

5: 'The First World War changed attitudes towards the role of women.' How far do you agree with this statement? Use your own knowledge, Sources A, E and F, and any other sources you find helpful to explain your answer.

Source F: Part of an account, written in 1919, of one woman's experiences during the First World War.

Over and over again the foreman gave me the wrong or incomplete directions and altered them in such a way as to create hours more work. I had no tools that I needed, and it was only on Saturdays that I could get to the shop. It was out of the question to borrow anything from the men. None of the men spoke to me for a long time, and would give me no help as to where to find things.

This is a group task. Prepare a plan to answer this question by copying and completing these planning grids.

	Changed attitudes	Not changed attitudes
Sources in question		
Other sources		
Own knowledge		

Introduction	Show you are focused on the question. For example, begin 'There is evidence for and against the statement…'
Supporting the view	Which source(s) supports the view? (Remember to take account of their nature, see page 140.) Own knowledge.
Opposing the view	Which source(s) opposes the view? Own knowledge.

Welcome to examzone

this part of the book we'll take you through the best way of revising for your exams, step by step, to ensure you get the best results possible.

Zone In!

Have you ever become so absorbed in a task that suddenly it feels entirely natural and easy to perform? This is a feeling familiar to many athletes and performers. They work hard to recreate it in competition in order to do their very best. It's a feeling of being 'in the zone', and if you can achieve that same feeling in an examination, the chances are you'll perform brilliantly.

The good news is that you can get 'in the zone' by taking some simple steps in advance of the exam. Here are our top tips.

UNDERSTAND IT

Make sure you understand the exam process and what revision you need to do. This will give you confidence and also help you to get things into proportion. These pages are a good place to find some starting pointers for performing well in exams.

FRIENDS AND FAMILY

Make sure that your friends and family know when you want to revise. Even share your revision plan with them. Learn to control your times with them, so you don't get distracted. This means you can have better quality time with them when you aren't revising, because you aren't worrying about what you ought to be doing.

DEAL WITH DISTRACTIONS

Think about the issues in your life that may interfere with revision. Write them all down. Then think about how you can deal with each so they don't affect your revision.

COMPARTMENTALISE

You might not be able to deal with all the issues that can distract you. For example, you may be worried about a friend who is ill, or just be afraid of the exam. In this case, there is still a useful technique you can use. Put all of these worries into an imagined box in your mind at the start of your revision (or in the exam) and mentally lock it. Only open it again at the end of your revision session (or exam).

DIET AND EXERCISE

Make sure you eat sensibly and exercise as well! If your body is not in the right state, how can your mind be? A substantial breakfast will set you up for the day, and a light evening meal will keep your energy levels high.

BUILD CONFIDENCE

Use your revision time not only to revise content, but also to build your confidence in readiness for tackling the examination. For example, try tackling a short sequence of easy tasks in record time.

The key to success in exams and revision often lies in good planning. Knowing **what** you need to do and **when** you need to do it is your best path to a stress-free experience. Here are some top tips in creating a great personal revision plan.

First of all, **know your strengths and weaknesses**.

Go through each topic making a list of how well you think you know the topic. Use your mock examination results and/or any other test results that are available as a check on your self-assessment. This will help you to plan your personal revision effectively, putting extra time into your weaker areas.

Next, *create your plan!*

Remember to make time for considering how topics interrelate.

For example, in History you will be expected to know not just the date when an event happened, but why it happened, how important it was, and how one event relates to another.

The specification quite clearly states when you are expected to be able to link one topic to another so plan this into your revision sessions.

You will be tested on this in the exam and you can gain valuable marks by showing your ability to do this.

Finally, *follow the plan!*

You can use the revision sections in the following pages to kick-start your revision.

MAY

SUNDAY	MONDAY	TUES
29	30	1

Be realistic about how much time you can devote to your revision, but also make sure you put in enough time. Give yourself regular breaks or different activities to give your life some variance. Revision need not be a prison sentence!

Find out your exam dates. Go to the Edexcel website to find all final exam dates, and check with your teacher.

Review Secti...
...complete t...
...ractice ex...
...question...

Chunk your revision in each subject down into smaller sections. This will make it more manageable and less daunting.

Draw up a list of all the dates from the start of your revision right through to your exams.

| 13 | | |

Review Sectio...
Complete three
practice exam
...ions

| 20 | 22 |

Review Sectio...
Try the Keywor...
Quiz again

Make sure you allow time for assessing your progress against your initial self-assessment. Measuring progress will allow you to see and be encouraged by your improvement. These little victories will build your confidence.

EXAM DAY!

| 27 | 28 | 29 |

Don't Panic Zone

162

As you get close to completing your revision, the Big Day will be getting nearer and nearer. Many students find this the most stressful time and tend to go into panic mode, either working long hours without really giving their brains a chance to absorb information or giving up and staring blankly at the wall.

Panicking simply makes your brain seize up and you find that information and thoughts simply cannot flow naturally. You become distracted and anxious, and things seem worse than they are. Many students build the exams up into more than they are. Remember: the exams are not trying to catch you out! If you have studied the course, there will be no surprises on the exam paper!

Student tip

I know how silly it is to panic, especially if you've done the work and know your stuff. I was asked by a teacher to produce a report on a project I'd done, and I panicked so much I spent the whole afternoon crying and worrying. I asked other people for help, but they were pan-icking too. In the end, I calmed down and looked at the task again. It turned out to be quite straightforward and, in the end, I got my report finished first and it was the best of them all!

In the exam you don't have much time, so you can't waste it by panicking. The best way to control panic is simply to do what you have to do. Think carefully for a few minutes, then start writing and as you do, the panic will drain away.

ExamZone

For the **Changing nature of warfare** paper, you will have an hour and a quarter for the exam, and in that time you have to answer four questions. You need to answer Questions 1 and 2. Then you must choose to answer one question from Questions 3 and 4, and then choose to answer one question from Questions 5 and 6.

For the **Impact of war on Britain c1914–c1950** paper, you will have an hour and a quarter and in that time you have to answer five questions. There are no choices for this exam.

Each question on each paper is worth a different number of marks and it is important that you use your time effectively. Don't waste precious time on a 4-mark question that might then leave you with too little time to spend on a question which is worth 16 marks!

Don't panic

Meet the exam paper

This diagram shows the front cover of the exam paper. These instructions, information and advice will always appear on the front of the paper. It is worth reading it carefully now. Check you understand it. Now is a good opportunity to ask your teacher about anything you are not sure of here.

Print your surname here, and your other names afterwards. This is an additional safeguard to ensure that the exam board awards the marks to the right candidate.

Here you fill in the school's exam number.

Ensure that you understand exactly how long the examination will last, and plan your time accordingly.

Note that the quality of your written communication will also be marked. Take particular care to present your thoughts and work at the highest standard you can, for maximum marks.

Here you fill in your personal exam number. Take care when writing it down because the number is important to the exam board when writing your score.

In this box, the examiner will write the total marks you have achieved in the exam paper.

Make sure that you understand exactly which questions from which sections you should attempt.

Don't feel that you have to fill the answer space provided. Everybody's handwriting varies, so a long answer from you may take up as much space a short answer from someone else.

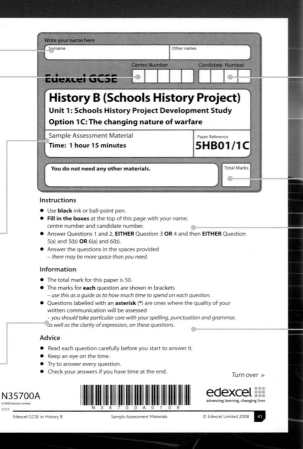

Understanding the language of the exam paper

Describe	The examiner is looking for a concise and organised account. Jot down three or four points in the margin that you want to include in your answer. Arrange them in the most logical order.
Explain how	The examiner is trying to discover whether you understand the key ideas about how and why developments happened in the history of warfare. The more detail you can give, the more marks you will receive.
Give reasons for your answer	You need to provide an explanation.
How far	The examiner is looking for points for and against the statement. Make sure you find some on both sides.
Do you agree?	You are free to agree or disagree. What makes a difference is how well you back up your case.

This section provides answers to the most common questions students have about what happens after they complete their exams. For more information, visit www.heinemann.co.uk/hotlinks (express code 4424P) and click on ExamZone.

About your grades

Whether you've done better than, worse than, or just as you expected, your grades are the final measure of your performance on your course and in the exams. On this page we explain some of the information that appears on your results slip and tell you what to do if you think something is wrong. We answer the most common questions about grades and look at some of the options facing you.

When will my results be published?

Results for summer examinations are issued on the **middle** two Thursdays in August, with GCE first and GCSE second. January exam results are issued in March.

Can I get my results online?

Visit www.heinemann.co.uk/hotlinks (express code 4424P) and click on Results Plus, where you will find detailed student results information including the 'Edexcel Gradeometer' which demonstrates how close you were to the nearest grade boundary. You will need a password to access this information, which can be retrieved from your school's exam secretary.

I haven't done as well as I expected. What can I do now?

First of all, talk to your subject teacher. After all the teaching that you have had, tests and internal examinations, he/she is the person who best knows what grade you are capable of achieving. Take your results slip to your subject teacher, and go through the information on it in detail. If you both think there is something wrong with the result, the school or college can apply to see your completed examination paper and then, if necessary, ask for a re-mark immediately. The original mark can be confirmed or lowered, as well as raised, as a result of a re-mark.

How do my grades compare with those of everybody else who sat this exam?

You can compare your results with those of others in the UK who have completed the same examination using the information on Edexcel website at www.heinemann.co.uk/hotlinks (express code 4424P) by clicking on Edexcel.

I achieved a higher mark for the same unit last time. Can I use that result?

Yes. The higher score is the one that goes towards your overall grade. The best result will be used automatically when the overall grade is calculated. You do not need to ask the exam board to take into account a previous result. This will be done automatically so you can be assured that all your best unit results have gone into calculating your overall grade.

What happens if I was ill over the period of my examinations?

If you become ill before or during the examination period you are eligible for special consideration. This also applies if you have been affected by an accident, bereavement or serious disturbance during an examination.

If my school has requested special consideration for me, is this shown on my Statement of Results?

If your school has requested special consideration for you, it is not shown on your results slip, but it will be shown on a subject mark report that is sent to your school or college. If you want to know whether special consideration was requested for you, you should ask your Examinations Officer.

Can I have a re-mark of my examination paper?

Yes, this is possible, but remember that only your school or college can apply for a re-mark, not you or your parents/carers. First of all, you should consider carefully whether or not to ask your school or college to make a request for a re-mark. It is worth knowing that very few re-marks result in a change to a grade – not because Edexcel is embarrassed that a change of marks has been made, but simply because a re-mark request has shown that the original marking was accurate. Check the closing date for re-marking requests with your Examinations Officer.

When I asked for a re-mark of my paper, my subject grade went down. What can I do?

There is no guarantee that your grades will go up if your papers are re-marked. They can also go down or stay the same. After a re-mark, the only way to improve your grade is to take the examination again. Your school or college Examinations Officer can tell you when you can do that.

How many times can I re-sit a unit?

You may re-sit a modular GCSE Science or Mathematics module test once, prior to taking your terminal examination and before obtaining your final overall grade. The highest score obtained on either the first attempt or the re-sit counts towards your final grade. If you enter a module in GCSE Mathematics at a different tier, this does not count as a re-sit. If you are on the modular History GCSE course, and sat the first unit last year, you may re-sit module 1 when you sit module 2 to maximise your full course grade.

For much more information, go to www.heinemann.co.uk/hotlinks (express code 4424P) and click on ExamZone.

Glossary

This Glossary contains all the key word definitions, plus some other terms used in the book that may be unfamiliar to you. When appropriate the definitions are particularly directed to the period being studied.

Alliance system – Two rival groups of powers in Europe in the years before 1914.

Anaesthetic – A substance that affects your nervous system so that you are less aware of sensation and don't feel pain.

Anderson shelter – A small shelter made from corrugated iron sheets that was half buried in the ground and covered with earth for protection from bomb blasts.

Aqueduct – A bridge that allows water to flow over or past obstacles.

Arquebus – An early type of gun supported on a forked rest or tripod.

Artillery – Large guns used in warfare on land; light artillery could be pulled around quickly by horses, while heavy artillery were much larger, stationary cannon for attacking castle walls, etc.

Assassination – Murder of a prominent person for political reasons.

Atomic bomb – An explosive device that gets its incredibly destructive force from a nuclear fission reaction.

Attrition – A process of steadily wearing down an enemy bit by bit over a period of time.

Auxiliary – Providing additional help or support.

Bastion – A projecting part of a fort's wall to increase the angle of fire.

Battering ram – A large wooden ram, the size of a tree trunk, often tipped with metal, which was swung from a harness against the gates of castles or fortified towns.

Bayonet – A long knife that could be attached to the end of the barrel of a musket or rifle, enabling soldiers to stab at the enemy in close combat.

Billet – Temporary accommodation for soldiers; before barracks, soldiers were often billeted in local homes or inns.

Blackout – A period of darkness imposed on citizens as protection against air raids; windows were blacked out with curtains or paint and all lights were turn off.

Blitzkrieg – Literally 'lightning war', consisting of rapid attacks, coordinating **artillery**, bombing, tanks, troops and dive bombers, such as the Blitz in 1940–1941.

Booty – The goods that soldiers took, during warfare, from prisoners, the bodies of the enemy or from captured villages or towns.

Bureaucracy – An organisation dominated by rules, restrictions and paperwork.

Caltrop – An iron ball with protruding spikes, thrown on to the floor in the path of cavalry to injure the horses and disrupt their charge.

Camaraderie – A spirit of trust and friendship among a group of people.

Campaigning season – The months in the year, usually late spring until late autumn, when fighting was possible before modern times.

Catholic Church – That part of the Christian Church owing loyalty to the Pope in Rome.

Cavalry – Soldiers mounted on horseback and fighting in groups.

Censorship – The control by a government of the spread of all information that might be useful to the enemy or that might upset the **morale** of the public.

Centenaur – The leader of a group of one hundred archers.

Centurion – A Roman soldier who was in charge of a unit of soldiers – confusingly not 100 but usually about 80.

Chain mail – Protective clothing made up of many small interlinked pieces of chain that could be worn alone or with plate armour for extra protection.

Chaperone – An older woman who accompanied a younger one on social occasions, to keep her safe and make sure she behaved properly.

Chivalry – A code of conduct, for example among medieval knights, which emphasised social graces, such as courtesy and courage, and Christian virtues, such as mercy and forgiveness.

Ciphers – A system for making and breaking secret codes; used by the British during the Second World War to interpret secret German messages.

Civil defence – The organisation of civilians to deal with enemy attacks.

Colonies – Territories or areas controlled by another country.

Conscientious objector – Someone who refuses to fight because of their moral or religious beliefs.

Conscription – The requirement that all men (and sometimes women) of a certain age group must join the armed forces.

Continuity – A period of continuity is when there is little change; things carry on much as they were before.

Depleted uranium – A very dense metal that can be used as armour to protect military vehicles, such as tanks, or for very hard points of **artillery** shells, which can pierce the armour on enemy vehicles.

Desertion – When a soldier leaves his post or leaves the army completely, without permission.

Dragoon – Lightly armed soldier who can fight on foot or on horseback; evolved in the 17th century to include those fighting with pistols.

Drill – Repeated training of soldiers in military exercises, so that they become second nature and to instil discipline.

Ducat – Gold coin accepted in most European countries from the 12th to 19th centuries.

Emetic – A substance given to people who were unwell, to make them vomit, which was believed to rid the body of bad substances.

Enlightenment – An 18th-century movement that rejected traditional social, religious and political ideas.

Entrepreneur – A person who takes financial risks to set up a business.

Evacuation – The process of moving people from towns and cities to the countryside for safety, to protect them from German bombing.

Feigned retreat – When an attacking force pretends to be forced back, hoping that the enemy will abandon their disciplined, defensive position and chase the attackers out into the open, where they can be confronted on better ground.

Firearm – A **gunpowder** weapon small enough to be carried by a soldier, for example a pistol or a rifle.

Flappers – Young women who challenged traditional ideas about women's fashion and social habits.

Foraging – Searching the countryside for food to purchase or, more usually, to take.

Freeman – Someone in medieval times who was given their own land in exchange for services – including military duties – for the king.

Friendly fire – The term recently used to describe incidents when troops are accidentally killed by other troops on their side; such accidents have probably always happened, but the term was only coined after the deaths of UK soldiers caused by US troops in the Gulf War of 1991.

Front line – In general terms, the front line is the area of fighting in which opposing troops are in direct conflict with each other; in trench warfare, the front line was the trench closest to enemy troops.

Fyrd – The main body of the Saxon army; they were infantry, called up from the Saxons with small landholdings. Originally poorly armed and organised, by the time of King Harold, in 1066, many were experienced, well-armed soldiers.

Gaiter – Protective covering for the lower leg.

Galling – Harassing the enemy, for example with arrows, **firearms** or **artillery** fire.

Gambeson – A protective jacket worn by infantrymen, usually made of quilted linen or wool and stuffed to provide extra protection, it could be worn alone or under **chain mail** or plate armour.

Gauntlets – Large, sometimes armoured, gloves that have long loose wrists.

Gladiator – Literally a 'swordsman', but in ancient Rome a slave or skilled professional fighter who fought other gladiators, criminals or animals for the entertainment of spectators.

Greek fire – A flaming liquid that could be hurled, in pots, by catapults and was very hard to put out, as it even burned on water. Ingredients could have included naphtha, quicklime and sulphur.

Guerrilla warfare – From the French 'guerre' (war), this refers to small independent groups using irregular means to attack larger, regular forces.

Gunpowder – An explosive mixture of sulphur, charcoal and saltpetre that burns rapidly and can be used to propel bullets, cannonballs or shells from guns.

Halberd – A pike with a sharpened axe-head added to the spike on the end, producing a weapon that could not just stab, but also slash, hook and pull.

Hauberk – A tunic or shirt for protection, quilted or made of leather or **chain mail**, worn by a soldier on the upper body.

Herald – A person who carried official messages.

Holy Lands – The lands around Jerusalem (now Israel, Syria and the Lebanon) where Jesus and the early Christians lived.

Home front – The support given and work performed by the civilian population during wartime.

Housecarls – The king's personal guard and most powerful troops of the Saxon army.

Howitzer – A cannon that fired at a very slow speed and steep angle to lob projectiles on to the enemy. Early versions used cannonballs; later versions used explosive shells.

Indenture – A contract under which a ruler would employ troops.

Inference – Identifying the underlying message or messages of a source rather than relying on what it says explicitly.

Intelligence – Useful information, usually about your enemy.

Ironsides – The name given to Oliver Cromwell's well-trained, well-disciplined **cavalry** regiment, from his nickname of 'Old Ironsides'.

Jingoism – Extreme patriotism, especially involving an aggressive attitude towards other countries.

Legion – The heavy infantry that was the main military unit of the Roman army; legions usually consisted of about 4,000 legionaries, or heavily armed soldiers, and several hundred other supporting troops.

Levée en masse – The French term for mass **conscription**.

Limited warfare – A term used to describe warfare before modern times, when it was conducted with restricted resources and for limited aims.

Mangonel – A wooden **siege** engine that used torsion in a twisted rope to catapult objects at the enemy.

Manoeuvre – To carefully move one's army into a position of advantage; manoeuvres are also large-scale military exercises.

Media – Methods of communicating information, including the press and radio.

Mercenary – A soldier who sells his services to any commander willing to pay him.

Militia – Part-time, volunteer soldiers, who act as a reserve or emergency military force.

Mobilisation – Preparing and organising people or resources for a particular task, especially war.

Morale – The confidence, enthusiasm and sense of purpose of a group of people at a particular time.

Mortar – A cannon that fired at a very slow speed, at an angle even steeper than **howitzers**, to lob projectiles on to the enemy. Early versions used cannonballs; later versions used explosive shells.

Munitions – Weapons, ammunition and shells.

New Model Army – A new army, set up by Parliament in 1645, during the English Civil War. It was an efficient, permanent, paid army recruited mostly from **Protestant** volunteers. See also **Ironsides**.

Nuclear warfare – War that involves the use of nuclear weapons – very powerful weapons that produce massive explosions caused by reactions in the nucleus of an atom.

Overpressure – This is caused when an explosion taking place overhead changes normal air pressure on the ground, causing terrible injuries.

Pillage (or **plunder**) – Stealing from the enemy or civilians.

Propaganda – One-sided information used to persuade people to support certain ideas or beliefs.

Protestant Church – That part of the Christian Church that became distinct from the **Catholic** and other churches, when their members 'protested' the centrality of the Bible and other beliefs.

Purging – Deliberately giving diarrhoea to people who were unwell, believed to rid the body of harmful substances and return a natural balance.

Quadrant – An instrument for measuring angles; gunners used one to calculate the angle of the cannon barrel needed to fire a given distance.

Radar – A name formed from radio detection and ranging to describe a system that sends out microwaves or radio waves and then picks up waves that are reflected back.

Ransom – Money demanded for the release of a captive.

Rationing – The setting of a fixed allowance of food and provisions to prevent shortages.

Recruitment – The way in which armies were raised; methods included feudal duty, paying **mercenaries**, volunteering, forced enlistment or **conscription**.

Regiment – A part of an army used as an organisational unit; because of their long history, regiments can vary in size from a few hundred to 5,000 soldiers.

Salvo – A group of cannon or other **artillery** all firing together.

Sapper – A soldier used for building or engineering work.

Scout – To send out small groups or individuals to gather information, usually about the enemy's position.

Scutage – A system, under the feudal system, in which rulers would accept payment from their subjects as a substitute for military service. They could then use the money to pay for troops.

Shield wall – A traditional form of defence, in which infantry interlock their shields to create a barrier against attack, through which the defenders can stab attackers with swords, spears, etc.

Siege – A blockade of a fortress or town, with the intent of starving it into surrender or using force to destroy its defences.

Siege tower – A large wooden tower, often on wheels, which was capable of carrying concealed soldiers and could be pushed up against a castle wall in a **siege**, to allow the soldiers to gain access to the top of the wall.

Skirmish – A brief fight between small groups of soldiers.

Slum – An overcrowded, dirty and unpleasant area in a city, such as London, where very poor people lived.

Standing army – A permanent army, employed during peacetime as well as during war; it is highly skilled and can form the core of fighting forces if the army is expanded in wartime.

Suffrage – The right to vote in political elections; Suffragettes were women who campaigned for the vote using more militant or illegal methods, while Suffragists used peaceful, law-abiding methods.

Telegraph – A system for sending messages from a distance by electrical means along a wire.

Tenants-in-chief – The most wealthy and senior supporters of a king or lord; they held their land in exchange for military service in their lord's army.

Total war – Unlimited warfare, fought with all possible or available resources, intended to destroy entirely all enemy resistance and affecting civilians as well as soldiers.

Trade union – An association of employees set up to improve their working conditions.

Trebuchet – A wooden **siege** machine, which used counterweights to sling objects at the enemy.

Tribunal – A type of court set up to judge certain types of cases, especially in the military.

Trunnions – The two projections on each side of the barrel of a cannon on which the barrel rests when it sits on the cannon carriage; they allowed the barrel to be raised or lowered to change the angle of the shot.

United Nations – An international body, made up of most nations of the world, which tries to promote international security, peace and human rights.

USSR – Union of Soviet Socialist Republics, sometimes called the Soviet Union, this was a collection of states in eastern Europe and northern Asia, dominated by Russia, which, between 1922 and 1991, acted as one, very powerful country.

Volley of fire – Pistol, musket or rifle fire in which, rather than firing separately, all the soldiers fire at the same time, to increase their killing power.

Index

Definitions of terms that are in **bold** type can be found in the Glossary on pages 166–9.

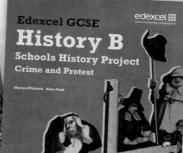

edexcel
advancing learning, changing l[...]

History B
Edexcel GCSE
Schools History Project
The American West
Rosemary Rees

History B
Edexcel GCSE
Schools History Project
Crime and Protest
Martyn Whittock   Allan Todd

History B
Edexcel GCSE
Schools History Project
Life in Germany
Steve Waugh
Series editor: Angela Leonard

History B
Edexcel GCSE
Schools History Project
Warfare and the Impact of War
John Child Steve Waugh

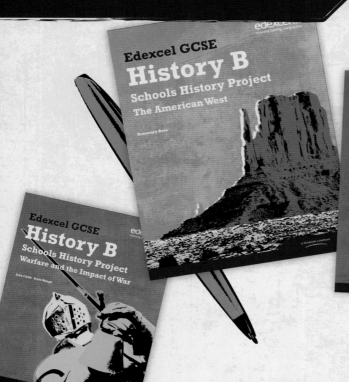

ResultsPlus Revision

History B
Edexcel GCSE
Schools History Project
The Transformation of
British Society
Rosemary Rees

History B
Edexcel GCSE
Schools History Project
Medicine and Surgery
Cathy Warren   Nigel Bushnell
Series editor: Angela Leonard

With our wealth of resources
for Edexcel GCSE SHP, you
can be confident that we've got
you completely covered! To find
out more about the series, visit
www.pearsonschools.co.uk/history

Controlled Assessment

A PEARSON COMPANY